Still in
the
Image

Still in the Image

Essays in Biblical Theology and Anthropology

Waldemar Janzen

Institute of Mennonite Studies Series Number 6

Faith and Life Press, Newton, Kansas
CMBC Publications, Winnipeg, Manitoba

Library of Congress Number 82-83886
International Standard Book Number 0-87303-076-1
Printed in the United States of America
Copyright © 1982 by Faith and Life Press, 718 Main Street, Newton, Kansas
CMBC Publications, 600 Shaftesbury Boulevard, Winnipeg, Manitoba

Biblical quotations are taken from the Revised Standard Version of the Bible, copyrighted 1946, 1952, © 1971, 1973 by the Division of Christian Education of the National Council of the Churches of Christ in the U.S.A. and used by permission. Exceptions are noted where they occur.

Design by Jim Friesen
Printing by Mennonite Press, Inc.

The Institute of Mennonite Studies is the research agency of Associated Mennonite Biblical Seminaries, 3003 Benham Avenue, Elkhart, Indiana. Other publications in the Institute of Mennonite Studies Series are:

John Howard Yoder, *The Christian and Capital Punishment*, 1961 (No. 1)
Paul Peachey, *The Church in the City*, 1963 (No. 2)
John Howard Yoder, *The Christian Witness to the State*, 1964 (No. 3)
Paul Peachey, *Who Is My Neighbor?*, 1964 (No. 4)
Gordon Kaufman, *Nonresistance and Responsibility*, 1979 (No. 5)

Foreword

This collection of essays on biblical themes represents a new subject area of contribution in the Institute of Mennonite Studies Series. Several factors have converged to make this a timely contribution.

The Mennonite church in various ways has asked for more help in biblical study. The Institute has responded to this need by giving biblical studies more priority in its agenda of work. Further, the author of this volume, Professor Waldemar Janzen, has distinguished himself as an able Bible teacher and careful scholar. Representing the fruit of Janzen's work in several significant thematic areas and prompted mostly by congregational, church-wide and classroom assignments, these essays on sexuality, land, war and peace promise to contribute widely to the biblical instructional needs of the church, both in its institutional and congregational settings.

With the satisfaction of facilitating this good and helpful endeavor, I commend to you this volume for both personal study and discussion of the issues with your brothers and sisters in the faith. The writer's point of view on these contemporary issues is not intended to be the final word, but to be an exegetical and expository gift that enables the community of faith to go forward in its task of discernment and pilgrimage in obedience.

Willard M. Swartley
Director, Institute of Mennonite Studies

to Martin, Hildi, and Edwin

Preface

The essays collected in this volume represent, for the most part, addresses delivered during the last decade. Their subjects were selected mostly by committees responsible for planning the various study conferences, colloquia, retreats, or other church-sponsored events. As such, they reflect the corporate needs of the church rather than my own solitary preoccupations. As a teacher of Bible in a church college, I have received many invitations to reflect on various issues from a biblical perspective. The preponderance of the Old Testament both in the choice of subjects and in their treatment betrays my own specialization.

In responding to these assignments I have been keenly aware of the fact that the church expects of its biblical scholars not only biblical data and insights, but also assistance in assimilating these into contemporary thought and life. I have therefore not stopped short at the borders of my academic specialization, leaving it to the systematic theologians to make biblical insights useful for the church in our time. Instead, I have taken the risk of tackling the hermeneutical task, knowing well that I am exposing myself to the danger of short-circuiting the theological process.

In doing so, I in no way wish to devaluate the more sophisticated hermeneutical methodology by which the systemic theologian translates biblical revelation into contemporary modes of thought, or to suggest that a simple leap from biblical data to modern relevance is all that is required. On the other hand, I believe that if one is a Christian as well as a biblical scholar, one must not shirk the responsibility of building bridges between the biblical past and the contemporary life of faith. As one builds such bridges, one will not so much venture out into the field of systematic theology, as engage in a different and alternative mode of hermeneutics. At the risk of considerable over-simplification, one could put it thus: The systematic theologian appropriates biblical content in its characteristic forms, styles, and images, and proceeds to rework it into contemporary thought forms and modes of expression, so as to allow modern readers or hearers to read or hear biblical truths in their own language and mentality. The biblical theologian, on the other hand, attempts to introduce modern readers or hearers to the biblical modes of thought, images, and forms of expression, giving them enough help to be able to appreciate these, to gain some empathy for them, and thereby to appropriate the biblical message for themselves.

Such an appropriation may well be rather personal and intuitive. It will need to be supplemented and clarified by the more vigorous philosophical and theological thought of the systematic theologian. As an example, Jesus' statement that he is the good shepherd may lead the systematic theologian to expound a theology of the rule of Christ in the church, while the biblical theologian may explain what shepherds did in ancient Palestinian economy, appealing to modern readers or hearers to appreciate and appropriate this image of Jesus Christ's leadership of his flock.

I must add a comment on the title and structure of this book. While the essays gathered in it were largely given as addresses upon invitation, the present volume as such does not represent a cross section, much less a complete collection, of all addresses delivered by me during the last decade. Instead, it offers several groupings of essays on subjects that attempt in one way or another to respond biblically to the question: What does it mean to live as a human being under God? The first group of essays addresses the question of divine — human communication: Bridging the Distance. The second group looks at human existence and limitation: Blessings and Boundaries. The third group considers our orientation in God's world: In Quest of Place. The fourth group responds to the problem of human destructiveness and destruction: The Burden of War.

For the reader versed in the field of Old Testament theology, I might point out that most of the essays, proceeding from contemporary quests as they do, are closer to the methodology of Walther Eichrodt than to that of Gerhard von Rad.[1] This is so not from scholarly partisanship, but from practical consideration. Each of these two methodologies, often considered mutually exclusive rivals in the field, seems to me to be better suited for certain ends. For proclaiming the message of the various biblical units, von Rad has shown us a model that is hard to surpass. For responding to questions shaped by the synthetic thinking of our time, Eichrodt provides the better way.

I am somewhat apologetic with respect to the use of the term "anthropology" in the subtitle of this volume. As J. W. Rogerson has pointed out, Old Testament scholarship is inconsistent here.[2] German scholarship in particular has tended to apply "anthropology" to the biblical view of the theological nature and being of humanity. Alternatively, the term has been employed to designate the (essentially non-theological) study of Israel's culture as it existed in biblical times. As I see it, these two perspectives must be kept in constant dialogue. The Bible conveys its theology through the concrete realities of history and culture. Thus these realities are never totally non-theological. It is through them — be they Israel's clan structure, her mode of land holding, or her practice of warfare — that God could, and did, communicate. On the other hand, biblical faith is never an attempt at harmonious integration of human beings into their (natural and historical-cultural) habitat, but rather a constant challenge to transcend it. Thus, what was in fact happening in ancient Israel and what the Bible proclaims to be God's will both overlap and stand in tension. Faith cannot simply shake off the shackles of culture, but culture cannot claim to express God's will fully. Thus my considered use of the term "anthropology" remains somewhere between the better defined positions advocated by Rogerson. In several essays I have tried to draw the complementarity of, as well as the need for distinction between, the descriptive and the prescriptive sides of the subject to the reader's attention. Precise relationships can be worked out only in the detailed interpretation of a topic or passage.

Considering the occasions where the addresses were delivered, as well as the publication data, the reader may well ask how **Mennonite** in perspectives this volume may be. I acknowledge unashamedly my Mennonite heritage and church context. The selection of certain subjects, such as war and peace, or modes of relating to the land, are undoubtedly influenced by my denominational roots. However, the biblical scholarship offered here is not narrowly denominational either in its perspectives or in the readership it addresses. It has been my aim to draw on the exegetical and theological heritage of the worldwide church and to address everyone who seeks to understand his or her human identity under God.

Waldemar Janzen
Winnipeg, Manitoba

Acknowledgements

Many of the essays in this book were presented in their original form as speeches in various church settings. I am grateful for this context to develop biblical and theological understandings. I acknowledge the following settings:

Chapter 1, "Where Are We?" was an address delivered as part of a Deeper Life Week series "From Experience to Faith," First Mennonite Church, Winnipeg, Manitoba, January, 1966.

Chapter 2, "Which Way to God?" was a lecture delivered in the "School for Ministers" series, Conrad Grebel College, Waterloo, Ontario, January 14-18, 1980. The general theme of the "school" was: "Religion in the 1980s: Biblical Faith for the New Decade."

Chapter 3, "Sign and Belief" was an article in *Call to Faithfulness,* edited by H. Poettcker and R. A. Regehr (Winnipeg: Canadian Mennonite Bible College, 1972), pp. 33-44. Reprinted by permission.

Chapter 4, "Modes of Appropriating the Bible" was presented at a workshop for Sunday school curriculum writers, held at the Associated Mennonite Biblical Seminaries, Elkhart, Indiana, in 1968. A fuller version of Part I of this paper is to appear in *Biblical Interpretation: Anabaptist and Mennonite Perspectives,* Willard Swartley, editor.

Chapter 5, "In the Beginning" was prepared for classroom use at the Canadian Mennonite Bible College in October, 1976.

Chapter 6, "Created in God's Image," was an address delivered at the Pastor's Workshop: The Pastor as Person, Professional, and Person of Prayer; Associated Mennonite Biblical Seminaries, Elkhart, Indiana, January 29-February 2, 1979.

Chapter 7, "Human Wholeness in Biblical Perspective" was an address delivered at the Ministers' and Deacons' Session of the

Conference of Mennonites in Canada, Vancouver, British Columbia, July 4, 1981. The session's theme was "Healing Ministries in Dialogue."

Chapter 8, "Sexuality in the Old Testament," was originally an address delivered at the Conference on Christianity and Sexuality held at the Associated Mennonite Biblical Seminaries, Elkhart, Indiana, August 5-9, 1968.

Chapter 9, "Male and Female Roles in the Old Testament: Outside of Genesis 1-3," was originally an address delivered at the Workshop on the "Roles of Men and Women in Theological Perspective" held at Camp Assiniboa, Manitoba, October 3-5, 1975.

Chapter 10, "Education in the Old Testament and in Early Judaism," was originally delivered as an address at the Seminar on Congregational Education held at the Associated Mennonite Biblical Seminaries, Elkhart, Indiana, March 23-25, 1982.

Chapter 11, "Biblical Perspectives on Youth," was an address delivered at the Summer Institute "Teaching Youth in Church and School," held at Canadian Mennonite Bible College, Winnipeg, Manitoba, August 5-12, 1981.

Chapter 12, "Quality of Life: A Biblical Study," was originally two addresses delivered to the 1979 session of the Western District Conference of the General Conference Mennonite Church, held at Hutchinson, Kansas, October 26-28, 1979.

Chapter 13, "Geography of Faith: A Christian Perspective on the Meaning of Places," was originally an address given at the Institute of Ecumenical and Cultural Research, Collegeville, Minnesota, in the spring of 1972. It was later published in *Studies in Religion/ Sciences Religieuses* 3:2 (1973), pp. 166-182.

Chapter 14, "The Biblical Basis for Stewardship of Land," was an address delivered at the MCC (Ontario) Consultation "Stewardship of Land," held at Conrad Grebel College, Waterloo, Ontario, March 15, 1980.

Chapter 15, "War in the Old Testament," was published earlier in the *Mennonite Quarterly Review* 46 (1972), 155-166. Reprinted by permission.

Chapter 16, "God as Warrior and Lord," was published earlier in the *Bulletin of the American Schools of Oriental Research* 220 (December, 1975), 73-75 (G. E. Wright Memorial Volume). Reprinted by permission.

Chapter 17, "Christian Perspectives on War and Peace in the Old Testament," was first delivered at the Peace Studies Colloquium, Conrad Grebel College, Waterloo, Ontario, November 23, 1979. It was later published in *Occasional Papers No. 1* of the Council of Mennonite Seminaries and Institute of Mennonite Studies (1981), pp. 3-18.

[1] For a comparative study of the two approaches see D. G. Spriggs, *Two Old Testament Theologies,* Studies in Biblical Theology, Second Series 30 (London: SCM Press, 1974).

[2] J. W. Rogerson, *Anthropology and the Old Testament* (Atlanta: John Knox Press, 1978), chapter I, esp. p. 9.

Contents

Part I
Bridging the Distance

Quest for Orientation

As little babies we are unconscious of our surroundings, of the space and the time in which we live.

Gradually we gain terms of reference: Certain toys evoke a smile of recognition, and so do moving objects which others call "Mamma" and "Papa." We, too, begin to call them that, and we learn or invent sounds for other items in our surroundings; we become oriented in a very small world.

Each relationship which we thus establish to a person, a toy, a room, a house, evokes a certain amount of satisfaction in us, a satisfaction that drives us on to identify further features of our surroundings. In other words, the meaning of our little life grows as we get better oriented to the world around us.

From the home, its inhabitants and its objects, our orientation broadens out in widening circles to include the neighbors, the street, certain features of the city or countryside in which we live, such as churches, stores, father's place of work, or the home of an aunt. Eventually we will identify ourselves as inhabitants of our city, town, or area. Such identification, by relating ourselves to families, towns, schools, churches, and the like, will mean an increasingly rich and meaningful existence. We will have pride and joy in identifying ourselves in such ways, and we will look down with slight pity on the younger set who have not yet established such identities.

Hand in hand with this orientation proceeds our orientation in time. Mealtimes and bedtimes break the even stream of life. Father's coming home from work is a significant occasion in the day. Eventually Sundays lift themselves off from the rest of the week, and holidays, sacred and secular, break the round of the year. These experiences then become correlated with clock and calendar. School term and summer break underscore this frame of reference. Consciousness of one's own birthday and age perhaps constitutes the first placing of oneself into the course of history.

And again, all of these advances in placing ourselves into widening frames of reference as to time make for greater satisfaction and meaning. We feel pride at each further step, and life becomes more significant. Eventually we will see ourselves in a time relationship to our ancestors and the history of the area or group to which we belong.

When we have reached a certain degree of orientation of ourselves to "our" surroundings and "our" time (by "naming," classifying them, as Gen. 2:20 suggests), our need for further orientation, for relating ourselves to people and countries further away or to ages of the more remote past, will decrease. We will have reached sufficient satisfaction in the space-time relationships achieved to live within them and devote little further attention to them unless events in our lives force us to look beyond.

Now we have only occasional experiences of disorientation in time and surroundings, freakish episodes which we shake off as soon as they are past and we feel secure again within our homey sphere. We may get lost in a blizzard, look frantically for some object of familiarity, and then regain our sense of direction. Or there may be moments of sitting in a train, or driving a car on a wet night when suddenly and for an instant we don't know whether we are moving, or something else about us is in motion, or whether a car before us is coming or going.

Our episodes of disorientation regarding time may be even rarer. Waking up from a narcosis after an operation is a modern experience that many of us have had; we don't know where we are and whether it is before or after the operation. The twilight between sleep and waking offers further momentary experiences of disorientation, moments where we do not know whether it is morning and breakfast time, or the end of an afternoon nap.

Such experiences are reminders that the orientation in space and time at which we worked so hard during and after childhood, and which we then came to take so much for granted, is a possession that makes us what we are, that gives our lives identity, security, and meaning, but one that is open to question or loss.

While our quest for orientation in space and time comes to rest after we have related ourselves to our time and surroundings with a certain amount of thoroughness and satisfaction, there are occasions and times when this halted quest strikes us again.

In times of war, or while filing papers for a visa to enter a foreign country, or upon encounter with someone from another continent or race we suddenly stand before the question: What does it mean if I leave Canada for the United States? What is my relationship to the British or the Chinese? or to other nations generally, or to the United Nations? We might, further, read of rocket shots to the moon or look at the starry sky and remember what our science texts said about movements of heavenly bodies, about distances of millions of light years, about distant galaxies of heavenly bodies, so huge and so hard to imagine that they shade over into the unreal for our limited minds.

If we pursue further that process of relating ourselves to our surroundings which was so enriching to life in our childhood and youth we find that the same process, carried further and further, becomes less and less satisfying, more and more threatening. We come to see ourselves as small specks whirling about on a little ball among innumerable other balls in an apparently endless, unimaginable vastness of space. We have completed a thought arc and are utterly disoriented in this universe again, without sense of direction and identification. However, now we consciously question our disorientation because we have had a taste of place, while the lack of it in our childhood was more unconscious and therefore less painful.

It is no different with time. We live with satisfaction within the framework offered by our clock and our calendar, our birth date, the awareness of our parents and grandparents, a stretch of our church's history, of national history, and of world history, and we feel secure. But there are times and occasions that lead us to pursue the question: What was before, and before that, and still earlier? And what will follow after, and after that, and still further? Can we imagine that these questions should ever be answered with sufficient finality to stop the further asking of, What beyond that? Time, which was so satisfactorily structured and gave our lives form and orientation, shades away into unimaginable remoteness and, as with space, we are left "hanging in midair" without clear points of reference. Again we are more disturbed by our ultimate lack of firm time foundations than we were in childhood because we have had an experience of what it means to be "on solid ground."

Physicists and astronomers tell us that one can, by abstract symbols, trace space and time even beyond the powers of one's imagination to the point where they merge into a space-time continuum. We take their word for it, and it makes our loss of orientation in the universe even more complete. Our minds reach out into nothingness and cannot grasp it.

Quest for Ultimate Meaning

If we were to hold a very exalted view of ourselves and our mental capacities, we might now be ready to say, "Such is reality, let us face it." But we should then be like people on a little boat in the ocean surveying the horizons. Not able to see anything but water, they might conclude that there is no reality to the world other than their little boat and water all around into infinity.

No, it would be better to think of the fading away of meaningful orientation as we move out further and further into space and time in thinking of the horizon of our vision. We know that reality does not stop at the horizon but rather that there is a limit to our vision. There may be many things to be seen beyond the horizon, and their existence or reality does not depend on our ability to see them.

In fact, we know something else: the way things at the horizon look to us is probably not their real appearance. The closer we come to the limits of our sense of vision, the more likely things will look distorted. To see what the world is like is a much more fruitful undertaking when we look at it from a distance that does not strain our eyes.

Applied to our orientation in space and time, this analogy may suggest the following: the mind can take in a limited segment of reality. Then it reaches its outer limits where it ceases to grasp clearly, where our language, and therefore our thinking, becomes inadequate. If the mind is at all capable of laying hold on reality, on something firm, on that which can be a foundation for our existence, this will hardly happen at the outskirts where the mind works at its strained and failing horizons; it will be most likely to happen where the mind is most adequate and competent. It is not that we should not scan the horizons—that is good for perspective—but adequate orientation of ourselves in our world will hardly be found there. Neither telescopes nor geological dating of the earth's strata hold the key to our place in the universe.

We said earlier that the child, in establishing more and more relationships to surroundings in time and space, feels an enrichment of life; life becomes more and more meaningful and significant. Let us return from the horizons of space and time to this process. Why should life be more meaningful and significant if we come to see ourselves as people of a particular place or a part of this or that historical movement or segment of events?

Our immediate answer may be that it is worthwhile living in Winnipeg and in Canada at this particular time because of some positive characteristics of the particular place and time: Winnipeg is a large and prosperous city, and to be a young person in the second half of the twentieth century in a country as advanced as Canada, is wonderful. Our more considered reactions immediately reject this answer. Winnipeg was a great and prosperous city when I came here years ago, but to be a "Winnipegger" was not very significant to me then. The significance that Winnipeg or the second half of the twentieth century holds is not grounded in Winnipeg or the twentieth century, but in me. Winnipeg is a pattern of physical, chemical, and biological objects standing in certain relationships to each other, and the time in which we live is a sequence of interrelated events. But such patterns are meaningless until they gain significance in someone's mind.

Let me illustrate: The tile floor of a certain room may be analyzed as to its color, pattern, and material and be described precisely. The floor in another building may meet exactly the same description. But if one should ask the question, "What is the meaning of this pattern?" an answer satisfactory to a human being would need to trace the pattern to the mind of another human being. In one instance the designer may say, "I like this color combination in relation to the rest of the colors of the room." In the case of the second building the builder may answer, "I looked for nonslippery tiles, and the only ones available are those you see." Each answer would carry the question as to the meaning of the pattern to a somewhat satisfactory conclusion, while the pattern as such, the same in each case, does not answer the question.

Applied to our orientation in space and time this analogy illustrates that it is not the patterns of our surroundings and our time which give meaning to our lives, but our lives which give meaning to these patterns. Meaning, or the sum total of our orientation to the world, resides in personality, both in our own and, indeed, in that of other people. At least this is how our limited minds experience it at the points where our hold on life is at its best, where life is most meaningful.

As the whole universe transcends its many parts, so a coherent meaning may unite and transcend all the little islands of meaning that we encounter in our moment-to-moment, place-to-place experiences. If the space-time universe as a whole, then, with all its space-time patterns, is to have meaning, we can visualize or grasp mentally such meaning only as relating to, or arising out of, a personality that transcends our little spheres of life. This would need to be a personality analogous to human personality, having such characteristics as consciousness, reason, will and direction, feeling, or whatever categories we might employ to subdivide human personality. Hence we speak of a personal God.

At this point someone might raise the question: Is this one of those old-fashioned attempts to prove the existence of God, one of those current in the Middle Ages, but long since disproved by Kant and other philosophers? The answer is no. This is a much humbler reasoning process, and one that does not at all try to do away with the need to accept God by faith. It is only a meditation on the path that might be taken in seeking for the meaning of life.

If there is to be meaning to life, some such way of moving from our daily experiences to universal and ultimate meaning is appropriate. Whether life *has* meaning, however, is a question that can be answered in faith only. If someone says that it is meaningless, these thought paths will hardly convince him or her otherwise.

The question of meaning is always before us. We read of a car accident in which someone was killed and we ask: Why? Two answers are open: (1) There is no sense to it; the world is a network of interacting objects or forces, and this is part of the pattern. (2) There is some significance or meaning to this, even if I cannot say in detail what it is. Such meaning can only proceed from a mind, which we call God. Both answers are based on personal faith; they cannot be substantiated in a compelling way to the one who does not want to accept them. But the one answer leads to despair or to superficiality, while the other leads to a life of purpose and hope.

In our next two essays we will consider how we can perceive this God who alone can give meaning to the universe and to human life.

If the "new religions"[1] express a hunger for authentic religious experience, for an encounter with the holy, we need to realize first of all that such a hunger is an age-old (perhaps universal?) phenomenon of humanity, of *homo religiosus.* All religions seek, and in turn promise, access to divine reality. We must remind ourselves further of the comparatively reticent response of the Bible to this widespread human longing. While the religions of the Ancient Near East saw humankind as being surrounded by a plethora of gods, demons, and spirits permeating all of nature, biblical faith required humanity to abandon all of these in favor of one God. It is difficult for us to perceive the degree of spiritual-emotional self-denial which must often have been involved for the believer. While young Christians today may feel that the church requires them to believe so much in terms of invisible reality, the biblical people of old must often have wondered why they should believe and practice so little. We recall that even in the Roman Empire Christians were accused of atheism, for their limited and restrained worship of one invisible God seemed to the adherents of ancient religions like nothing at all.

But we must go even further. Not only were the biblical believers required to reduce their perception of divine reality from a world saturated with deities to one single God; they were further expected to accept great restraint in their interaction with God. Even this one God was not immanent in the surrounding world, but transcendent instead. The phenomena of the world were God's works, but in themselves they were not divine at all. They were capable of revealing their Maker and Sustainer in a limited way, as a piece of craftsmanship reveals the craftsman, but in another way they constituted the veil that concealed God.

Furthermore, these believers of biblical times were expressly forbidden to resort to several of the widespread means of bringing the divine powers near. First, they were forbidden to make any image or likeness of God, according to the Decalogue (Exod. 20:4). Such images were the hallmarks of religion in the Ancient Near East. The image shares in the reality it represents. The gods, represented by their images, dwelt in temples, literally their "houses" among men, where they could be approached, worshiped, implored, and—to some extent—controlled. Israel was denied this form of communion.

For a second restriction, Israel was forbidden to practice magic, i.e., the exertion of sacred expertise to manipulate the powers to do one's bidding. The commandment against images undoubtedly relates to this, as does the one against using the name of the Lord in vain. But the application extended much further. While Ancient Near Eastern worship was largely founded on magic, biblical worship was based squarely on obedience to a completely autonomous and nonmanipulable God. Just one instance must suffice to illustrate this: blood was always considered a potent substance for magical manipulation. The Old Testament shares with other religions the use of blood in various rituals. But here it is not the inherent potency of the blood that stands in the center, but the obedience to the divine command. This becomes patently clear when we read that a poor man could substitute a cereal offering for an animal offering (Lev. 5:11-13). Israel was to refrain from any attempt to manipulate God.

A third stricture had to do with places of worship. The battle of biblical monotheism against idolizing a multitude of things in heaven above, and on the earth beneath, and in the waters under the earth expressed itself forcefully in the Deuteronomic restriction of worship to one central sanctuary, the place where the Lord would choose to make his name to dwell (Deut. 12:5). This was in no way a parochializing of God; his sovereign authority over the whole world fills the pages of the Bible. It was, instead, a safeguard against idolizing the phenomena of the world by regarding all kinds of mountains, springs, rivers, towns, and so forth, as holy places. It was also an expression of the gracious sovereignty of the one God who would himself choose the place of special access to him (Deut. 10:14-15; 1 Kings 8:27-30). In all this we need to remember that biblical religion does not teach people the way of access to, and manipulation of, God; instead, it proclaims the good news of the coming of the otherwise transcendent and inaccessible God to humanity, and that on his own sovereign but gracious terms.

Having emphasized the great restraint which biblical teaching imposes on the believer's longing to experience the reality of God, we can now affirm also with the Bible that God is indeed to be found. In spite of what has been said so far, God is present both in nature and in history, though transcending both. Neither of these realms is divine, but in both of them divine reality can break through to humanity. The Bible calls such breakthroughs "signs and wonders," or sometimes "mighty acts" (*dunameis*). Everyday life is interrupted by a great manifestation of power which makes one stop short and marvel or wonder and then recognize that a sign, a pointer to the reality and the will of God, has been given.[2] How does one know that this is actually so? No criteria can be given; such a sign-experience carries its own power to convince in itself. It results in a "subjective certainty" on the part of the one experiencing God. Such an experience is always subjective. It becomes a sign *to someone;* it is never universally evident as a sign for *everyone*. But one whose life is touched by it is never the same again. He or she is thrown out of the daily routine and into the service of God, for a sign is never given for personal spiritual enjoyment but always to draw its recipient into God's service. Thus Moses and Amos left their flocks, and Peter and Andrew their nets, to follow an urgent calling not anticipated by them before.

Much of this follows the general typology of religious experience as worked out by Rudolf Otto[3] and others. The distinctiveness of biblical faith expresses itself more in its content than in its dynamics of revelation. But the dynamics show distinctive accents as well. The first of these has already been implied, namely the reticence and economy with which the Bible speaks of God's presence. Signs, or encounters with the holy, are both more exceptional and more momentous than they were in the religions of immanence. Further, human life and human togetherness have a primacy over nonhuman nature as the arena of biblical humanity's experience of God. Thus historical experiences, like the exodus from Egypt, and exceptional divine direction of human beings, such as the judges and the prophets, represent the focal points of Israel's contact with God. In the New Testament, the focus of revelation is, of course, the person of Jesus Christ. We must add, however, that natural phenomena can also convey a sign, as is illustrated by the Book of Job where the mystery of creation makes Job see his suffering in a new, God-given perspective.

The Bible testifies to a rich heritage of experience with God through many centuries. However, if we consider the reported revelatory events in proportion to the length of history covered, we must conclude that they were few and far between. The ordinary believer did not move from one lofty revelation to another but by the witness of those chosen and by faith or trust that the God who had shown himself forcefully at focal points in history was also present and acting—though in a more hidden manner—in the rest of life. To use an image, the high points of revelation were like the pillars of a long bridge, spaced at intervals and bearing up the bridge's span. To realize this is important when we consider the hunger for revelation in our own time and when we assess the availability of direct revelation to us.

Before we do that, however, we must draw an important distinction. We have said that a sign is always subjective and personal, not given generally, but given *to* someone. Those who experience it constitute an "in-group" in possession of something not shared by outsiders. Outsiders can only receive the in-group's witness to the experience; the experience itself cannot be handed on. However, if a larger community, like Old Testament Israel or the Apostolic Church, recognizes in the testimonies from many persons and times certain common truths, a revelatory tradition that supports and authenticates itself, and defines these and commits itself to them, the process can be called *canonization*. The result is a "canon," or a body of publicly confirmed and authenticated data.

Beyond these, many believers in Israel and in the church have experienced privately what they felt to be signs to them. Anyone who hears the life stories of many believing Christians will hear of dreams, visions, healings, apparent unusual coincidences, sudden opportunities, and seemingly impossible accomplishments, which the reporter in each case interpreted as God's "speaking" with a direct message that shares in the character of the revelatory signs received by prophets and apostles. Who could or would want to deny the personal and subjective validity of these? How impoverished would be our religious life without them? How much strength, initiative, labor of love and service has been generated through them?

Only one thing must be stressed with firmness: the recipients of such private revelation must not make the claims of canonized revelation for their experiences. When person X tells me that God gave him a dream to reveal this or that to him, I will listen to his testimony with respect and appreciation. He has subjective certainty in the matter. But if he claims that I should see his dream in the same way, he is abusing it. If it was authentic revelation, it was for him alone. Let him act on it. I will evaluate his subsequent actions on their own merit, without any need to let his claim to revelation influence my judgment. It is at this point that the adherents of the charismatic movement, for example, err so often when they wish to impose their private, noncanonical spiritual experiences upon others and demand public revelatory status for them.

Having made the distinction between canonical revelation and private revelation, we can return to our original question: How do we respond to the hunger of so many in our time, and especially the new religions, for authentic encounter with divine reality?

First, this hunger in the new religions, as well as in phenomena in the church such as the charismatic movement, demonstrates that modern people are not satisfied with the "secular Christianity" of Bonhoeffer, Cox, and others. Modern humanity, just as humanity at all times, seeks to break out of the realm of the common, the secular, and to encounter the holy or sacred.

Secondly, this hunger teaches us that another form of secularization, subtly present in the church, will not satisfy in the end. Psychological experience cannot replace religious experience. To meet human beings, even on a profound level of personal encounter, cannot substitute adequately for meeting God. Encounter with the other is not yet encounter with the Wholly Other. The new religions challenge us to seek religious reality, and not to stop short with psychological reality.

On the other hand, we should not allow the general hunger for religious experience to lead us back into the ancient heathen (or in some aspects Eastern) divinization of the world. The fact that people wish to be able to commune with God face to face on a daily basis does not mean that God will become available on call. Here the biblical reticence must speak to us. God grants signs, but in his own time and place. Those who would summon God at their pleasure will end up mistaking idols for God. Above all, God is not automatically found in other people, and least of all in the seeker's own self. From a biblical perspective, the search for God through self-awareness equated with God-awareness is nothing other than idolatry of the worst kind.

Where then do we meet God? In spite of our own and other people's hunger for seeing God face to face (cf. Moses, Exod. 33:17-

23), our regular daily encounter with God must remain more indirect. God has revealed himself significantly through signs. We have the witness to these signs in the Bible, and in the people who live out its truth. They testify to God. As we accept their testimony and live by it, we will experience the power of that tradition to live new lives. Perhaps God will grant us what we have called "private signs" that impress upon us God's reality and guidance. We must not, however, make these the center of our life of faith. Luke (11:27, 28) tells of a woman who apparently envied Mary for her special experience of bearing the Messiah. She called to Jesus: " 'Blessed is the womb that bore you, and the breasts that you sucked!' But he said, 'Blessed rather are those who hear the word of God and keep it!' "

And at the end of the parable of the rich man and Lazarus (Luke 16:19-31), where the rich man asks God to give his brothers on earth a special sign by sending them a messenger raised from the dead, God said to him: "If they do not hear Moses and the prophets, neither will they be convinced if some one should rise from the dead" (v. 31).

In other words, the way of living with God is to hear the Scriptures, and not to clamor for special revelations. The latter are given by God, in God's own time and place, to those whom God chooses.

Notes

[1] I am following my colleague, Dr. Rodney Sawatsky, in using the term *new religions* for such contemporary religious movements as the Unification Church ("Moonies"), the Church of Scientology, the Apostles of Infinite Love, and the Krishna Consciousness movement.

[2] For a fuller treatment of "sign" see my article "Sign and Belief" in this volume, pp. 15-26.

[3] Rudolf Otto, *The Idea of the Holy,* trans. John W. Harvey (New York: Oxford University Press, 1958). First German edition 1917.

Sign and Belief

Why Signs

A sign is a visible or otherwise perceivable clue to something hidden, something out of sight. The sign tells us that something exists and, perhaps, in part, what it is like. A road sign pointing toward a town makes sense only where the town itself is not yet in view, or not identified as to its name, population, and the like. The sign indicates that the town lies ahead, and it shows also how it can be reached. Let us illustrate by another example. Imagine a child storming into the house and seeing mother standing in front of the closed bedroom door with serious face and a finger held over her mouth. Mother is giving a sign. She tells the child about something in the room. The child does not know what is happening in that room. Is someone sick? Has a guest arrived and is resting now after traveling through the night? Or could there be a thief? The child cannot tell, but it is certain that there is something unusual in that room, for mother has given a sign. The child knows also at least one fact about that something behind the door: it is important enough that one must take special note of it, and the right way to take note of it is to keep silent.

When the Bible speaks of signs that point to God and his purposes with us, it treats God as if he were hidden, figuratively speaking, as if he were beyond that hill, like the town in our first illustration, or behind the closed door, as in our second example. It speaks of God as "transcendent" in the technical language of theologians. We see and know of God only as much as he reveals or "unveils," about himself.[1] This never happens so fully that mystery no longer surrounds God. We find out only certain things about God according to the clues or signs that he grants us. These signs do not describe God; who would have the words for that? They indicate to us, instead, his existence and reality, and they tell us how to respond to that reality. In this they are quite like the sign of the mother to the child in front of the closed door.

Apart from such signs, God is hidden from us. The observable world, the sky, mountains, trees, animals, and even people do not express what God is like. This does not mean that God is not at work in the whole universe; it merely asserts that his ways do not become understandable and meaningful to us except through signs. The various features of the universe are like a veil; they both reveal and conceal God. A veil may allow certain features to show through, but not enough to let us recognize the person or determine, for example, whether the person is friendly or angry. [2] Another illustration might be helpful. Imagine a man standing in a large factory hall, surrounded by complicated machinery, with wheels turning, pistons pushing, lights flashing, and so on. The whole thing is awe inspiring, perhaps impressive, but meaningless. He may not even know— assuming that he had never seen anything similar—whether he is surrounded by one purposeful process, or by a chaos of unrelated activity. But suddenly he is struck by the recognition that a certain wheel at one end of the hall starts to turn whenever a green light goes on at the other. This becomes to him a sign that there is connection between the various things he sees. He generalizes that, if these two features are related, all the rest may work together in some fashion also. There is a purpose here! In fact, he hesitates now to touch a lever here or stop a wheel there, for that might interfere with the whole, a whole which still remains mysterious, but about which something has been revealed to him now through the green light and the wheel. These two, in their togetherness, have become for him a sign.

To understand the whole, this man would have to study engineering for several years. From his present short stay in the factory hall he could never comprehend it. Too many factors for its understanding lie outside the hall. The Bible sees humanity's situation in the universe in similar fashion. It opposes those religions and philosophies which say that humans can study the universe, or experience it intuitively, and arrive at insight into the nature of the whole. Our standpoint is too limited and our life too short to "read off" God's purposes from the visible phenomena around us. Only through signs, through certain features that will suddenly light up with meaning for us, can we sense the hidden realities as being there and are we able to know how to respond to them.

Here biblical faith has a much more profound understanding of God and his world than those religions and philosophies that consider the universe as a more or less decipherable blueprint. In their search for God, truth, reality, being, ancient people as well as modern have always attempted to arrive at an understanding of these by observing the visible world. Thus the ancient nature worshipers of the Near East, as well as those of Greece and Rome, experienced the powers operative in nature—storm and lightning, sunshine and fertility, mountains, rivers, and the sea—and worhiped them as gods. These ancients observed, further, certain relationships, such as those between rain, sunshine, and the growth of vegetation on the earth. They expressed these relationships in story form. Such a story might tell, for example, how the sun god kept the rain god in captivity for some time, but how the latter was freed eventually, married the goddess of fertility, and produced offspring. Such stories are called *myths*. A myth is a story that relates the deified phenomena of nature to each other. [3]

While the gods of the Canaanites, Egyptians, Mesopotamians, and other ancient nature religions are no longer worshiped today, it is still equally tempting to seek ultimate truth through a study of the visible world. The visible world should be studied, of course; that is the legitimate domain of the natural and social sciences. But if the insights arrived at in such study are considered as ultimate, that is, as having the possibility of unlocking the meaning and mystery of the universe and of human life, science has become Scientism, a faith which can be considered the counterpart of ancient Baalism. How such Scientism affects us might be illustrated from the way people try to deduce right and wrong from "what is natural." Is it right or wrong to go to war? Well, observe the animals, or primitive societies; do we not always find a struggle for survival? Therefore it is natural to fight, and what is natural—so Scientism assumes—is right. But biblical faith holds that the matter of moral right or wrong is more complicated. Through Jesus Christ, who has given us a sign of the presence of God's reign or kingdom in the world, we have come to see that what is ultimately the will of God often transcends nature. It is natural—in nature which shares in humanity's fallen state—to fight, but God's intention for humanity is to attain to love and peace. There is a mystery to the fullness of God, a mystery which is not "immanent" in the visible world in such a way that it can be deciphered, but "transcends" it, so that it becomes accessible to us through signs.

Signs in the Bible

The Old Testament speaks of "sign" (*'ôth*) close to eighty times. The corresponding term (*semeion*) appears some seventy-three times in the New Testament. The usage varies somewhat between the Testaments and within each Testament, but certain main lines seem clear.[4] These words are not reserved for specifically religious contents. The kiss of Judas, for example, was a sign pointing out Jesus to the soldiers (Matt. 26:48; cf. also Num. 2:2; Ps. 74:4). On the whole, however, both Testaments associate signs with those acts of God that make him known to people.

Even so, however, signs are not necessarily miracles, in the sense of unusual and normally impossible happenings. Circumcision is a sign (Gen. 17:10ff.), and so are the twelve stones from the bed of the Jordan (Josh. 4:6ff.), as well as the fact that the infant Jesus had a manger as his bed (Luke 2:12). On the other hand, the miracles in the Bible fulfill the function of signs, in particular the miracles associated with the exodus from Egypt (cf. Exod. 7:3; Deut. 11:3; 29:3; Josh. 24:17; Jer. 32:21; Ps. 105:27) and the miracles of Jesus.[5] That the latter are called signs only in the Johannine writings (John 2:11; 2:23; 3:2; 4:54; 6:2; 11:47; 20:30), while the synoptic Gospels characteristically refer to them as "mighty works" (*dynameis;* Matt. 11:20; 13:54; Mark 6:2; Luke 19:37), has to do with the particular vantage points of the writers. John intends to demonstrate that Jesus is the Christ (John 20:30f.) and sees his acts (often interpreted by longer speeches) as signs or pointers to that fact. Matthew, Mark, and Luke see these acts, first of all, as manifestations of the divine rule or kingdom which is showing its power in Jesus. From the recipient's vantage point the manifestation of God's power becomes a sign.

The term *sign* describes an act or happening or object as to its function, not its content. The most varied events—some "natural," in our contemporary terminology (Gen. 17:11; Isa. 20:3; Luke 2:12), and some "miraculous" (2 Kings 20:8-11; John 2:11)—can be called signs as long as they perform the function of pointing up the power and leading of God *for some who perceive them.* The last phrase is important. It is not quite right to say that a certain event "is a sign"; it "becomes a sign to" some individual or group. In the Old Testament we find such formulations as "This is/will be a sign to/between . . ." (Gen. 9:12; Exod. 3:12; 12:13; Num. 16:38; 1 Sam. 2:34).

Furthermore, a sign is never "there" externally, waiting to be discovered by human intellect or intuition. It proceeds from God's initiative and is given, as promise or judgment, to a group or a person. The "raw facts" of nature and history are mute; they need interpretation. [6] Even the observable aspects of a miracle do not yet constitute a sign, but become so only as they are understood in their pointing capacity by a receiver. The interpretive sermons that accompany them frequently in the Gospel of John (e.g. chapter 6) make this clear, though the understanding that makes the facts light up as a sign may consist also of a completely inward awareness (e.g. John 2:11; 4:54f.). [7]

The "raw facts" may be interpreted differently by different observers, and are therefore inconclusive in themselves (John 9:16; 11:37; cf. Exod. 7:11; Matt. 12:24). To those for whom some event or fact has become a sign pointing to a divine reality, however, alternative interpretations are no longer open. The sign-character of an event imposes itself inescapably when it breaks in on someone and evokes in that person a *subjective* certainty, even though he or she knows intellectually that others may see it differently. [8] When the Bible says—as it does frequently in both Testaments (cf. Exod. 7:13; Num. 14:11; Amos 4:6-13; Matt. 11:20-24; 12:37; etc.)—that signs have been rejected or missed because of unbelief, it refers most probably to the absence of that stance of faith generally which needs to precede the reception of a sign, rather than to faith evoked by the sign; disbelief in a sign appropriated as a sign would be a contradiction in terms.

The relationship between signs and belief is well illustrated in John 4:46-54. The official from Capernaum whose son is ill requests healing from Jesus. Jesus rebukes him, "Unless you see signs and wonders you will not believe" (v. 48). Then he reassures the man that his son will live, and "The man believed the word that Jesus spoke to him and went his way," even before he had seen the healing. When he hears that his son has recovered, we read again "and he himself believed, and all his household" (v. 53). Faith, then, precedes the sign and makes receptive for it but is in turn supported by the sign. Where faith does not prepare the ground, a sign is not likely to be given (Matt. 13:58). We note also the interpenetration of sign and word. Signs are part and parcel of the proclamation of God's word (Exod. 4:28, 30; Mark 16:20; Heb. 2:1-4). Word and sign mark the ministry of Moses, the prophets, Jesus, and his followers. Signs separated from the context of a biblical confession in words and life are to be discounted (Deut. 13:1-2; Matt. 7:21-23). [9]

Once received, the sign brings a new and powerful dimension into the life of its recipient, a dimension that makes him see life in a different focus. The signs which Israel perceived in its history led it to a self-understanding not shared by any other nation. The sign-character, not only of the individual signs of Jesus but of their totality which made up his life (Luke 2:34), changed their perspective on their existence for the disciples. This change of perspective does not remain intellectual, although a sign certainly leads to new insight and understanding; it becomes a claim upon the life of the person or group that experiences it. Thus it not only interprets life, but calls to new forms of life, to responsible action based on a new commitment.

Even this is not its final effect. Beyond the action which it calls forth, it becomes an impetus to praise. For what shines through in every particular sign—different as one is from the other in its specific content and in the insight and action if evokes—is ultimately the glory of God (Exod. 10:1; Num. 14:22; Isa. 66:12f.; John 1:14), and a taste of the glory and majesty of God issues in praise. [10]

Praise of this kind—praise evoked by recognizing certain acts or events as showing forth with special clarity God's will and activity, results in festive celebration (Exod. 13:9) when expressed communally. The great festivals of Israel are the praises of a people for the manifestations of God in its past. Here the sign takes on the character of a memorial recalling and affirming the relationship to God and the covenant (Gen. 9:12; 17:10ff.; Isa. 55:13). In the Old Testament even a commemorative item can be called a sign (Deut. 6:8; Josh. 4:6ff.). As a succession of festivals was called forth, there arose an awareness of the ongoing presence and leading of God, that is, of a *"Heilsgeschichte,"* a salvation history. [11]

Such a response to signs, a response consisting of the intellectual, ethical, and emotional subjection to the impact of the taste of a new reality, is faith in the biblical sense. But while God's people celebrate the sign-events experienced in the past, one should say that a sign is extended to humanity from the future into the present. The city that lies ahead is not yet visible, but the road sign which the traveler has seen some stretch back has transformed his journey from groping and uncertain wanderings to a purposeful pursuit, even though the road seems externally the same and the means of travel may not have changed. A sign, then, sets up a promise which draws the traveler ahead to its fulfillment. It defines him in relation to a destination and it leads him on. Even when the sign lies far behind the wanderer, it keeps its effectiveness, though a further sign along the road may reinforce and confirm it.

Signs Today

After we have considered the significance of the sign in the Bible, we must turn to the question of its significance for us. This question has two aspects. First, we ask what the biblical signs mean for us. Secondly, we ask whether we can expect signs in our time and experience.

In the Bible the sign has a double impact. There is, first, its content. God calls, leads, forgives, restores to life. Secondly, it evokes certainty concerning God. The healed man or woman for example, comes to see that it was God at work to heal him or her. While this latter function is the sign-function proper, it is only the former, the content, which can be handed on to later generations or even to contemporaries. That Jesus healed the official's son (John 4:46-54) became to the official a sign that evoked belief. For us today it does not have that power to convince, at least not at first and automatically. Its report merges with the rest of biblical proclamation to say something about God: when God's power is at work, it is a healing power. The official's faith, on the other hand, is not immediately transferable to the reader of his story.

While we get the content of the biblical proclamation from such biblical accounts, that which gave certainty to the believers in the Bible cannot be our source of certainty. [12] Only as divine reality breaks through *my* observable world—only as a new sign is given to me—will I be gripped with that certainty which, though subjective, is nevertheless sure. To say this is to say that each time derives its certainties from its own signs.

To illustrate, we might consider the discovery of electricity. Certain experiments convinced Edison of the existence and the properties of this phenomenon. The content of his discovery comes down from him—elaborated and perfected—to our time. Our certainty concerning electricity, its existence and its properties, does not derive for us from Edison's experiments, however, but from that which happens every time we throw a switch.

Now, that "something" which may become a sign for us may be a biblical word. God speaks again, to us, through the words of Scripture, including those that tell of signs. But it need not be so. Many things that gave assurance of God's acts to Israel and to the early church are read with detachment by modern readers, including Christians, and do not grip them in the same powerful way, even though these modern readers may derive instruction about God's ways from such reading. The effect of sign-stories on the modern reader may be parallel to that of parables, which also teach divine truths without having the character of signs. [13]

With these observations we have already entered upon our second question: Can we expect signs in our own time? To my mind it is clear that we not only can, but that we must, if there is to be faith at all. To say this does not mean that each Christian can expect an equal ration of signs. Some lives may be blessed with abundance, while others may live a life of faith by giving the benefit of the doubt to the testimonies of those in the past and present whose lives have won their confidence. And further, the important question is not whether we can and ought to be sign doers, but whether God will grant us to be sign receivers. Will God's Word and world light up for us here and there in such a way as to grip us with reality and draw us into his service? [14] That is the question.

On the basis of biblical teaching and of Christian experience we can confidently answer in the affirmative. Signs are God's continuing way of pointing to himself and evoking certainty. There have been and will be differences in signs. Some are more frequent, others rarer. Some take on a more unusual form, others remain ordinary and yet shape lives and give certainty. Some will have more private character, while others may produce a wider impact. Some such signs may be miracles, in the sense of unusual, unexpected and unexplainable phenomena: healings, instances of protection, of guidance. To believe this does not mean that one ought to jump on the bandwagon of movements that glory in the irrational; it simply means that one does not limit God in his possibilities.

Some signs will appear more common and modest. A little incident of reconciliation may so irresistibly impress itself on someone in its ultimate rightness that it may call forth in him or her belief in the biblical peace teaching, for that teaching's truth, its ontological truth, to speak with the philosopher, has been tasted in sample form. Thus lives of people may become translucent for us, showing the will of God concerning right and wrong. All illustrations run the risk of seeming trivial to persons for whom the event in question has not become sign. Nor can its significance as a pointer to God ever be demonstrated, though its unusual features, if such are present, may be pointed out. [15]

While each age derives its certainty of faith from its own signs, these signs are not unrelated to the biblical message, just as the signs reported in the Bible are intimately related to the Word. For the Christian it is this divine Word, handed on through the centuries, which defines the content of that faith for which a sign can evoke certainty. In other words, a measure of faith comes first, but is supported and strengthened by the sign. For the people of Jesus' time the preparation for receiving his signs was provided by their Old Testament faith. Such preparatory, or communal and historical, faith—whether the community be Israel or the church—affects us doubly: it prepares for the appropriation of new signs, and it provides criteria for them. [16] The latter means that there can be no contradiction between signs which claim to point to the same God.

When we say that each generation needs its own signs, we do not mean, therefore, that God reveals himself in a discontinuous way, showing sporadic signs intermittently. Signs are embedded in an ongoing tradition of faith, a tradition which prepares new times for new signs and which, in turn, is authenticated by these. There is discontinuity of *certainty,* however, from generation to generation. Each young Christian builds on the witness of others, tests and doubts this secondhand faith, and struggles for personal certainty. [17] And yet the *content* of his or her faith is not discontinuous, but comes from the tradition within which he or she stands.

More than that, there is some continuity in the signs themselves. As persons and groups have witnessed to the events that became signs to them, certain themes emerged. Signs tended to be acts of leading, of sustaining life, of healing, of deliverance from external and inner enslavements. Though there have been terrifying signs, signs of warning and of punishment to come, the balance weighed heavy on the side of favor, grace, salvation, and that with a consistency which, in itself, became a revelation of the ways of God. The Bible calls it God's faithfulness. [18]

With such observations we have left the discussion of the sign, in its more specific definition, and have crossed over into the more comprehensive topic of revelation. [19] The individual sign, taken by itself, does not reveal such creedal content as God's grace or faithfulness; instead, it testifies to the truth or rightness of love, justice, peace, and forgiveness. But as the cumulative witness of the ages shows forth certain themes, the chain of signs becomes God's revelation of himself, supported by the signs, and in turn providing criteria for evaluating signs and preparing for the possibility of new signs.

Notes

[1] To speak thus may raise the question whether we are not extending the meaning of *sign* to become synonymous with *revelation.* While these concepts belong to the same divine self-manifestation, so that statements made about the one will often be true of the other also, they are nevertheless distinct, and that in three ways. First, the term *sign* derives from common life and retains its nontheological usage, both in the

biblical languages and in English, besides its specialized theological usage. *Revelation,* on the other hand, is basically a theological term, though it has spilled over into common talk. Secondly, *revelation* has the totality of God's self-manifestation in view while *sign,* when employed theologically, designates a specific instance of revelation. Signs are revelation in dissembled form, one might say. Therefore *revelation* is most properly used in the singular, while *signs,* in the plural, is appropriate and customary. This is so in spite of such plural formations as *revelatory events* on the one hand, or the singular use of *sign* to refer to the whole life and ministry of Jesus (Luke 2:34). Thirdly, *revelation* concerns itself with the content of God's self-disclosure, while *sign* focuses on the certainty evoked in the recipient. *Revelation* is the more comprehensive concept, but the *sign* is revelation at the point of most intense impact on humanity. For a helpful discussion of revelation, see Gordon D. Kaufman. "The Concept of Revelation," *Systematic Theology: A Historicist Perspective* (New York: Charles Scribner's Sons, 1968), pp. 13-40.

[2] Theologians have long debated the existence of "natural revelation," i.e., true knowledge of God available to everyone through reason, feeling, and conscience. The proponents of natural revelation believe that people can discover certain insights pertaining to God, while those opposing it, notable among them Karl Barth, assert that nothing about God can be known unless God initiates such knowledge specifically. My formulation in the text is not meant as a rejection of all natural revelation; but even where the Christian accepts the possibility of such, it must be understood as revelation, *i.e.,* as a *selective* manifestation of truth, rather than as truth spread out before humanity like an open book in all phenomena of nature and history.

[3] An excellent exposition of mythical thinking in the ancient Near East is given in H. Frankfort, et al, *Before Philosophy* (Pelican Books A198); first published as *The Intellectual Adventure of Ancient Man* (Chicago: The University of Chicago Press, 1946).

[4] For a detailed and thorough word study of the Greek term *semeion, sign,* in the New Testament, as well as its Old Testament antecedent, *'ôth,* see K. H. Rengstorff's article in *Theologisches Wörterbuch zum Neuen Testament,* VII, 199-261. A collection of scholarly studies on miracles has been edited by C. F. D. Moule, *Miracles* (London: A. R. Mowbray, 1965). *Cf.* also Quell, Gottfried, "Das Phänomen des Wunders in Alten Testament," in *Verbannung und Heimkehr,* Arnulf Kuschke, Herausgeber (Tübingen, J. C. B. Mohr [Paul Siebeck], 1961).

[5] The association of "signs and wonders" in both Testaments highlights this proximity of sign and miracle. *Cf.* S. Vernon McCasland, "Signs and Wonders," *Journal of Biblical Literature* 76 (1957), pp. 149-52.

[6] The relationship between act and word has been debated by both theologians and philosophers. Some say that reality is basically nonverbal, but is interpreted secondarily by words. Others argue, that reality is basically linguistic, and that humanity appropriates it in language symbols, or not at all. For our purpose it suffices to say that a sign can take the form of a word, as well as of a less overtly verbal act, but neither words nor acts are signs in themselves; they may light up with illuminating significance here or there, a significance that goes beyond their inherent natural meaning.

[7] The same is true of the relationship of the so-called symbolic acts of the prophets (e.g. Isa. 20; Jer. 13; Ezek. 5; etc.) and their verbal message. The acts are often interpreted, but they need no special interpretation, as they carry their message within themselves, for those for whom they become a sign. *Cf.* G. Fohrer, "Die Gattung der Berichte über symbolische Handlungen der Propheten," *Zeitschrift für die alttestamentliche Wissenschaft* 64 (1952), pp. 101-20; also the same author, "Prophetie und Magie," *Zeitschrift für die alttestamentliche Wissenschaft* 78 (1966),

pp. 25-47; and G. von Rad, *Old Testament Theology,* II (New York: Harper & Row, 1965), pp. 95-98.

[8] This statement pertains to the relationship between sign and certainty; to the extent that something is a sign, it creates certainty. It does not mean that a specific person need be certain that something is a sign. If our earlier characterization of the sign as "revelation at the point of most intense impact on humanity" (above, note 1) is correct, one can think of a continuum of increasing impact, from that revelation which is relatively unfocused and general to that which is appropriated fully as being a sign. But to the extent that something is appropriated as a sign, to that extent it evokes certainty.

[9] L. Monden, S. J. in *Signs and Wonders* (New York: Desclee Company, 1966; first Flemish edition 1960), says that a miracle, to be acceptable to the Christian, must be free from qualities that contradict the salvation-oriented intent of divine revelation, on the negative side. Positively, the authenticity of a miracle requires three preconditions: 1. The person performing it must be himself one transformed by the Christian revelation. 2. The context must be fitting, which means that it must be above all, prayerful. 3. Its specific features, or content, must be in keeping with the symbolism of salvation (pp. 58-79). Some such context is expected for the sign also, though not every sign is a miracle. (In spite of many good insights, Monden's book cannot be recommended here, as it is overtly tendentious. The Protestant reader is shocked to hear that genuine miracles, while abundant in Catholicism, are almost by definition absent from non-Catholic Christianity!)

[10] Some passages speak of the terrifying signs, particularly of the end time, performed by the anti-godly powers (Rev. 12:1; 13:13; 16:14; 19:20; etc.). This is not surprising, as these signs point to a reality of evil that is much more "diabolical" than the sum total of what we perceive as "evils" here and there in the world. In a different sense, every manifestation of God has something terrifying, awe-inspiring about it, so that those who see his holiness or glory break through may express their fear (e.g. Isa. 6:5; Luke 2:9) or even ask Jesus to depart (Luke 5:8; Matt. 8:34). And yet one is attracted to this awe-inspiring God. *Cf.* Rudolf Otto, *The Idea of the Holy,* tr. by John W. Harvey, (New York: Galaxy, 1958).

[11] *Cf.* G. von Rad, *Old Testament Theology, II, op. cit.,* pp. 99ff.

[12] This is a strong statement, to make a much neglected point clear. In its details, the matter is more complex. Signs and miracles cannot be lumped together here, nor are either of them all of one kind. With respect to miracles, G. F. Woods, in a cautious and sober study, arrives at his own tentative conclusion that some biblical miracles can perhaps make certain truths of the Christian faith more probable to us today ("The Evidential Value of the Biblical Miracles," *Miracles,* ed. Moule, *op. cit.,* pp. 21-32. C. S. Lewis's chapter "On Probability" in *Miracles* (New York: Macmillan, 1947), pp. 121-30, points in the same direction, though the author is more optimistic.

[13] *Cf.* John R. W. Stott, "Christ's Dramatized Claims," *Basic Christianity* (London: Inter-Varsity Fellowship, 1965), pp. 30-32.

[14] A most helpful and clarifying discussion of the possibility and the significance of miracles is the book of C. S. Lewis, just cited (see above, note 12). The real problem does not lie in this or that phenomenon and its evaluation, but in the total world view within which one approaches life. The concept of transcendence, of a reality beyond that which is accessible to the methodology of the natural and social scientist—no matter whether understood in Newtonian or Einsteinian terms—presents the basic problem to many in our time, for whom the historian of science Mary Hesse may be representative when she says: "The offence of particularity is still with us, whether these special acts violate or conform with the laws of nature. The fundamental problem is not about miracle, but about transcendence." ("Miracles and the Laws of Nature," *Miracles,* ed. Moule, *op. cit.,* p. 42.) For a

defence of transcendence, and the subsequent need for revelation through the particular, see G. D. Kaufman, *Systematic Theology, op. cit.,* pp. 94-116, and throughout. An analysis of more recent tensions between transcendence and immanence within theology can be found in E. Farley, *The Transcendence of God* (Philadelphia: Westminster, 1958).

[15] It is their person-directed quality that makes the recounting of signs seem as trivial as the sincerely meant—and thus received—love declarations of a young couple. Nevertheless, signs are not altogether private, but impress themselves at times upon a group, either as a group experience or as a number of sufficiently similar individual experiences to create a sense of communal unity among the individuals involved. The Mennonite migrations from the Soviet Union to America contain some moments—such as the unexpected possibility of certain groups encamped at the gates of Moscow in the 1920s to leave Russia, or the unexpected escape of some thousand Mennonites from Berlin to West Germany in 1945— which were experienced by many as significant beyond the ordinary when interpreted in faith. While our time is reticent—and rightly so—to boldly affirm the sign character of such experience for their participants, these are nevertheless recounted with awe as significant for faith. For the descendants of the participants, as well as for detached observers, they become no more than stories, such as Barbara Smucker's children's novel *Henry's Red Sea* (Scottdale: Herald Press, 1955), based on the Berlin escape referred to. We can assume that, due to the reticence of our age in this respect, more sign experiences are treasured by individuals and groups than receive publicity.

[16] G. Kaufman's analysis of the interrelation on the personal-individual level and revelation on the cultural-historical level applies, *mutatis mutandis,* to the sign also (*Op.cit.,* pp. 23-32). If tradition would not provide criteria for individual experience, the sign would become a phenomenon limited to personal and mystical piety, but that is patently not the case.

[17] When we speak of such faith as "secondhand," we do not at all mean that it is ungenuine, but rather, that it is based on trust in the authority of others. In a sense, most of our knowledge comes to us first as someone else's claim, and only a certain amount of it is eventually validated through personal experience. What is not so validated, need not be false; few of us validate through astronomical observation and calculation what we hold concerning the movement of heavenly bodies.

[18] C. S. Lewis (*op. cit.,* pp. 159ff.) makes the further claim that there is consistency between miracles and the nature of the world: "I contend that in these [biblical] miracles alike the incarnate God does suddenly and locally something that God has done or will do in general" (p. 162). And: "Christ's isolation [as one doing unusual acts] is not that of a prodigy but of a pioneer" (p. 163). Used by permission of Wm. Collin Son & Company Ltd.

[19] See above, note 1.

Modes of Appropriating the Bible

LEARNING FROM HISTORY

Every Christian who witnesses to the faith is confronted with the need to bridge a gap between the Bible and modern life. Only if this gap can be closed does Bible teaching gain that much-needed quality which we have become accustomed to call—though by way of a cliché—"relevance."

Air Routes

1. The history of Bible interpretation offers a variety of avenues through which the Bible might become meaningful to later generations. One of the earliest and most influential of these was that followed by rabbinic Judaism of New Testament times and later. The rabbis understood the Old Testament as a guide for life, valid in detailed application to subsequent ages. [1] The words spoken to the Israelites at Moses' or Jeremiah's time were to be heard by Jews living centuries later as if spoken to them. As this resulted in obvious incongruities of situation, the science of adapting the biblical statements to later needs had to be developed, the result of which can be seen in the Mishnah, the Talmud, and other rabbinic literature.

The criticism to be leveled against the rabbis cannot be aimed at their desire to make Scripture relevant; it must be directed at the fragmentation of Scripture in the process. The complex and profound revelation of God's grace during the exodus from Egypt and the resultant relationship between God and Israel, the covenant, could no longer be appreciated in their coherence and in their significant order of God's grace followed by man's response of

27

obedience. Instead, small segments were asked to yield self-contained meanings to be carried over to limited areas of later life. Out of the Law came laws.

In the history of the church this approach has appeared again and again, always at those points where great reverence for the words of the biblical text led to a preoccupation with short excerpts of Scripture, to the neglect of its comprehensive themes.

The post-Reformation concern with the Word placed the Bible into the center of Protestant church life, but this very attempt to make it food for every day led to its fragmented distribution and consumption: detailed exegesis of a short sermon text; meditation on a brief devotional passage; concentration on one story during the Sunday school hour, a story carrying its message within its short self. Unless the preacher or teacher is very skillful in placing the story into its broader context by preserving the main themes from Sunday to Sunday, each short unit will become a hero-villain story leaving the hearer with the command to do as "good" Abraham, and not as "bad" Lot; as "good" David, and not as "bad" Saul. In other words, a "do-don't" application, a legalism or moralism is the result.

2. A different avenue toward relevance had its origin in Judaism but became prominent in the church during its first several centuries and dominated Bible interpretation during the Middle Ages. [2] When Philo and others found it necessary to interpret Judaism to the Greek world, they attempted to present it to the philosophical Greek mind as a different though legitimate philosophy.

As the Bible consists of very tangible and concrete stories very dissimilar to philosophical abstractions, this could only be done by attributing to the biblical stories hidden "spiritual" meanings. Job's camels and sheep now became his good and evil thoughts. This is called "allegorizing" and the product, an "allegory," is a story that appears to say one thing, but really means another.

It is important to note here that the "truth" contained in a biblical text is detached from the concrete details of the text. In Protestant liberalism at the end of the nineteenth century and the early decades of the twentieth century, but also in the existentialism of Bultmann, we find this same manifestation. Protestant liberals were ready to detach "truths" from the Bible, truths such as the fatherhood of God, the brotherhood of man, and infinite value and immortality of the soul, or to arrive at "the mind of Jesus" as over against the details of what he said and did. They were less willing to accept as relevant for faith the concrete words and details of Scripture, much as they were interested in these from a purely scholarly perspective.

In a different frame of mind, yet similar in his desire to detach—by "demythologizing"—universal truths from time-bound specifics, Rudolf Bultmann seeks to make the Bible applicable to modern man by confronting him "existentially" with the biblical truth, so as to lead him to "authentic existence."[3]

If rabbinic Judaism and its legalistic-moralistic successors treasured the biblical detail but lost sight of the wider perspective, the "detachable truth" approach, from Philo to Bultmann, cannot be criticized on this score. Its strength is its striving for wholeness. Its vulnerability arises from the fact that it needs to depart from the biblical medium. It abandons the confessional recital of the acts of God in the history of Israel, of Jesus Christ, and of the church, in favor of philosophically formulated truths, though supposedly distilled from biblical history. To the extent that the medium is the message, the loss of the medium must represent a loss of message. But even if we admit that the message can be translated to some extent from one medium to another, the danger that the orientation of the translator enters into the process unduly, is very real. This variety of the search for relevance has, therefore, been an open gate for the prevailing philosophies, whether they were Neo-Platonism, Idealism, or Existentialism.

Ground Routes

The avenues to relevance outlined so far could be compared to sweeping arcs that span, in grand manner, the distance between the Bible and the present. They largely ignore, or attribute little significance to, the intervening ages. Mosaic law becomes law for today; biblical stories yield "truths" to be accepted today. We now turn to those approaches that move "by ground route" from biblical history through church history to the present.

1. A first thrust in this direction begins in the period of enlightenment and—significantly, as we shall see—grows on the fringes of mainline Christianity. The thinkers of that period were concerned with history, though they took a rather detached and critical stance toward it. They were concerned to preserve distance between bygone benighted ages and their own enlightened present in which universal reason had come to a fruition not known before and had advanced far toward freeing itself from the shackles of the particulars of history.

Gotthold Ephraim Lessing, a great German man of letters, was typical of his time.[4] The thought that God, conceived as universal Reason, should have manifested himself through the time-bound and often repulsive events told in the Old Testament, was quite unacceptable to him. Nevertheless, he could not shake off the problem of religion, bitter as his attacks on Christianity became at times, until he found a way of accommodation. In his *Erziehung des Menschengeschlechts* (1780), he developed the view that God condescended to manifest himself in crude ways, appropriate to the "childhood of the race," in order to educate humanity to ever greater heights, leaving behind the lower stages and moving toward an increasingly universal and rational religion.

Even greater has been the impact of Hegel's view of history on the understanding of the significance of biblical history for modern man. Like Lessing, he saw the past, including the biblical past, linked to the present through a continuous process of historical movement, a movement in the course of which the absolute Spirit shed more and more of the clods of historical specifics, so as to emerge from the time-bound situations of history to ever greater universality. As Lessing, Hegel also accorded biblical history a place of special prominence in this process.

The effect of such schematic views of history on the church's understanding of the relationship of the Old Testament, the New Testament, and the Christian church to each other and to the present can hardly be overemphasized. In the field of Old Testament studies, Wilhelm Vatke[5] and Julius Wellhausen[6] made historical development the dominant answer to the question of the meaning of the Bible, but many others could also be named.

While historical development, or history understood as an educative process, seems to have run its course and to hold little appeal in the forms described, it is still with us in various new shapes. At the risk of premature categorization, one is tempted to see Bonhoeffer's[7] view of humanity's coming of age and Harvey Cox's[8] analysis of humanity's movement from tribal society to town culture to secular city in a grand movement of secularization in the same light.

In contrast to the "air route" approaches outlined earlier, such a "ground route" connection between Bible and present ties biblical history and the history within which we stand into one coherent movement, thus making us a part of the process proclaimed in the Bible. The problem created for us, however, lies in the fact that biblical history is swallowed up into world history as the lines between biblical history, ancient world history, church history and modern history fade in favor of one grand movement of history. It is not accidental that these approaches often grew on the fringes of mainline Christianity and that Christians among their advocates had to strain their understanding of "Christian" to the limits. Nevertheless, these attempts raise the extremely acute question of the relation between sacred history and universal history, a question to which we must return below.

2. A second "ground route" approach is associated with the term *Heilsgeschichte,* "salvation history," and is generally traced to the German Lutheran theologian Johann Christian Konrad von Hofmann and the so-called "Erlangen School" of the nineteenth century.[9] Hofmann distinguishes between world history on the one hand and the history of Israel and the church on the other. The latter is a "sacred history," a special strand of history through which God manifests himself to a select group, though for the purpose of showing the way of salvation to the whole world.

The *Heilsgeschichte*-approach has undergone numerous alterations and modifications up to the present. According to Oscar Cullmann,[10] a red thread of special divine events runs through history from creation to the coming of the kingdom. This special history is the revelation of God, calling the world to participation in salvation and bringing judgment on the world by its very presence as a standard. This special history, figuratively represented as a line, has Jesus Christ as its midpoint from which that which precedes and that which follows takes its bearings.

In contrast to the developmental philosophies of history held by Hegel and others, *Heilsgeschichte* gives due attention to the special nature of biblical history. The unsatisfactory aspect of it is its division of God's action with humankind into two kinds: a general government of the world and a special leading of the elect.

Concerns

1. This survey of the history of application of the Bible to later times, technically called *hermeneutics,* has brought us up to the present. It is impossible, of course, to see the main lines of any most recent development with the same clarity that the greater distance to the past allows. Names and emphases have not found their place in a clearly recognizable network of interaction. Nevertheless, certain very recent concerns have come to the fore rather persistently and point to directions for hermeneutics that seem promising and must not be ignored.

These concerns cluster around two pivotal concepts: language and history. Old as the words are in their general and common meaning, they have acquired a new significance in the modern understanding of humanity and the world, and this, we should note, both within and without the church. In a sense they are philosophical, rather than theological concepts, but as philosophy has tended to be the way to theology from the early church to the Middle Ages and to modern times, we cannot avoid these philosophical concerns.

The fact is, that both the time-honored medieval metaphysical understanding of the universe and the mechanistic-materialistic understanding which, though much older, was in the ascendancy since the Renaissance have lost their power to convince. To put it more simply: to speak of God "up there" in an invisible, "transcendent" upper story, reaching "down" from time to time to interfere in human affairs, can be said today only metaphorically by way of an image. While this realization seems to have come to Bishop John A. T. Robinson (*Honest to God,* 1963) as a new and revolutionary insight, many thoughtful Christians have assumed this long before the bishop's sensation-making book. As an image this language still has some usefulness, but even this is receding. It is equally inappropriate, however, to speak of "laws of nature" as new absolutes. Since the church has not done that in any case, little revision is necessary here.

The question that confronts our time anew, then, is the question of a new "ontology," in philosophical terms or, more simply, a new answer to the question: "What is really, really real? If reality is not lodged in a metaphysical upper story or in irreducible smallest particles of matter governed by unalterable law, where, we ask, is reality?" Or in theological terms: "If we do not look for God 'above' or 'beyond,' neither identify him with powers 'within' the universe, that is with the laws of nature, where do we look for him?"

The new answer that is beginning to emerge is: "In language! in history!" Are these two answers, or one? The two are certainly inextricably interrelated. Perhaps we could speak of one answer with a dual emphasis. The complex philosophical situation cannot be treated here; we must turn immediately to some manifestations in and consequences for theology.

2. Among those theologians who work at a new hermeneutic with the accent on language as a basis of reality, Ernst Fuchs and Gerhard Ebeling are prominent. [11] For them the biblical message is a "language event" (*Sprachgeschehen*). All language is, by definition, a claim (*Anspruch*) on us, a claim or challenge that confronts us with

reality. This is the avenue in which Jesus, as Word, confronts us with reality, the reality of the words of the New Testament texts. This is both a claim (*Anspruch*) on us and a hold or solid assurance (*Halt*) for us, and it demands our life as a response (*Antwort*).

In the terminology of this paper, we are dealing with another "air route" between the Bible and modern humanity. Bible, now understood in its "wordness," in its character as reality-bearing language speaks directly to modern man, gives him a world of (linguistic) reality within which to find his orientation (*Halt*) and claims his life's answer as a response. The indebtedness of this hermeneutic to existentialism and to Bultmann is evident, though the differences should not be minimized.

3. Among those theologians who place the accent on history as the bearer of reality, Wolfhart Pannenberg[12] is most prominent, though others, like Jürgen Moltmann,[13] could be named. Without denying the importance of language as carrier of reality, Pannenberg insists on a closer tie between language and that which must be its content and substance, the concrete events of life which, when carried forward and interpreted by language, become history.

Pannenberg refuses to take the "air route" from Bible to modern humanity; he moves by "ground route" through history. That which bridges the gap between the Bible and us is the fact that a movement of history connects us. But history does not become meaningful until it reaches its goal, or on short range, it does not gain its limited meanings until it reaches its limited subgoals. Since the ultimate goal, God's kingdom, lies in the future, history would be meaningless had God not brought this "end of history" into the middle of history by revealing his kingdom in an anticipatory way in biblical history leading up to its fullest manifestation in Jesus Christ.

A somewhat crude illustration may help us. The work of a carpenter on a table would be meaningless to an observer not knowing anything about carpentry or tables until the last step in assembling the pieces had been completed and the table stood before him. The process of the making, in other words, would become meaningful only when seen in reverse, from the achieved goal back. But if the carpenter would show the onlooker a small model of a table halfway through the process, telling him that this was in a limited sense what he was aiming to make, the process of making the table would acquire significance for the onlooker even before the table was finished. In a similar way God has, in the historical events of the Bible, given humankind that which tells what history, though still open toward the future, is all about.

It is evident that Pannenberg's approach to the significance of the Bible for today is related to both "ground routes" described earlier. He operates with a philosophy or theology of history, like Lessing, Hegel, and others. He states that the failure of Hegelian philosophy of history must not make us reject new attempts at a more adequate comprehensive view of history. Unlike Lessing, Hegel, and others, however, Pannenberg does not see history as a vehicle to or for a "higher reality" toward which it educates humankind or which it reveals more and more fully by allowing its own particular and time-bound events to recede in favor of pure spirit: for Pannenberg history itself is the reality.

We also recognize Pannenberg's connections to *Heilsgeschichte*. Biblical history is the medium of revelation of God. But he seeks to avoid any separation of history into two strands, sacred history and world history. History is one, yet the events of biblical history—and that includes "events" of a literary nature, like the origin, transmission and impact of literary texts—give meaning and direction to universal history.

FROM THEORY TO APPLICATION

We have reached the point where application of theory to actual Bible interpretation should be discussed.

Assessing the Alternatives

1. We note that all the approaches outlined deal with the Bible in its totality or in its main thrust. None of them is a sure guide to the interpretation of an individual passage. There is a difference between saying that the Bible is essentially law or allegory and saying that some passages of the Bible are laws or allegories and affect us correspondingly. And again, no one will deny that many a biblical passage has confronted many people with the reality of God and the need for decision in an existential way, but that is not the same as the claim that the chief significance of the Bible as such is to be an existential call to persons toward authentic existence.

The individual passage will confront the interpreter with the need to inquire into its very own concerns and possibilities and to work out its modern relevance in their light. Both the nature of the passage and the modern context to which it is to be applied will allow much room for variety. Even when one path to modern relevance has been chosen, overtones of other possibilities will be present and will assert themselves.

2. The important function of one's view of the relevance of the

Bible as such for our time is that of establishing priorities of significance, however. Let me illustrate: Genesis 13 tells of the quarrel between the shepherds of Abraham and of Lot and the solution of it through Abraham's willingness to let Lot choose one section of the land and to be satisfied with the remainder. No doubt Abraham acts admirably, and modern people should be exhorted to be as unselfish as Abraham. If my view of the Bible were a legalistic-moralistic one, I would see this story as being primarily an exhortation saying: Do not be selfish! Furthermore, I would be quite satisfied to take up the story as a unit and to find its modern meaning within this one chapter.

If, however, my view of the Bible is that it tells *Heilsgeschichte,* the accents fall differently. I cannot now be satisfied to see the story in isolation and to draw the moral of selflessness from it as chief gain. The story is a part of God's election of a family line and a people to carry on his purposes. This choosing on God's part often takes unexpected turns. It is not the advantageous and rich land of Sodom and Gomorrah and its inhabitant, Lot, whom God chooses, but, against all likelihood, it is the sparse hill country and its occupant, Abraham, who become significant in God's plan. For me today this furnishes an example of God's direction of history by putting up one segment or paradigm for close-range examination. But more than that, it traces one segment of a history that does not stop with Abraham, but extends through Israel and the church down to me, and thus is my own history, within which my life belongs and from which I take my bearings.

A different hermeneutic, then, has led to a basically different modern application, though the other application, the call to selflessness, is also there and, as a subordinate theme, legitimate.

Updating the Ground Route

It will have become evident that I prefer the "ground route" to the "air route" approaches. They are more appropriate to the biblical medium, the recital of the acts of God in history. They are comprehensive in their application of the Bible to modern life, while the "air routes" seem to have an affinity for spot-application, with a much greater haphazardness of result.

Of the "ground routes," the educative-evolutionary schemes explain some features of biblical teaching and offer some connection to the present, but on the whole they presuppose an optimistic faith in humanity and its progress that seems neither biblical nor realistic.

I am left, then, with *Heilsgeschichte* in its older and newer versions. The Bible is not so much a source of law or of abstract truth for humanity, as a story that gives orientation and meaning. The teaching of the Bible should not carry bits of law or of truth to me but show me how the story of Israel, Jesus Christ, and the early church still goes on and takes me up into itself.

The Bible teacher need not be worried that he or she must teach a "lesson" in terms of a detachable gain each time. Instead, the teacher should strive to make clear how each story picks up certain themes and concerns from previous stories, how it "fulfills" them and how it, by doing so, itself points to the future.

Take the story of blind Bartimaeus in Mark 10:46-52. He called, "Jesus, Son of David, have mercy on me!" Jesus gave him sight and said, "Go your way; your faith has made you well." A moralistic approach would say: "Do good to blind people and others in need!" An allegorizing approach would say: "As Jesus healed that blind man, he 'opens our eyes,' spiritually, to become discerning of sin." An existential approach might say: "This was the great moment for Bartimaeus; as Jesus passed him, he, in a bold decision, confronted the Wholly Other and received a new existence. How about you?"

These applications are not to be rejected lightly, and yet they are not the main points of the story's relevance. The story has its roots in the Old Testament expectation of a new David, a perfect ruler, who would restore humanity to that state where God's will would rule unhindered, where his kingdom would have come. In that kingdom there would be no injustice, no suffering, no wrong. Bartimaeus, in faith, expects such of Jesus, and Jesus, who has come to reveal the ways of the kingdom in an anticipating way, recognizes that his mission has here been understood, and therefore he shows a manifestation of the kingdom. Such "signs" of the kingdom, together with the other signs done by Jesus, as well as those continuing in his body, the church, illumine the goal of history and create a new community within which we can live.

We should note also that this approach does not isolate Jesus but makes him the fulfillment of the Old Testament, the bringer of the future, and the midpoint of history. Old Testament students find the individualistic Jesus-piety perpetrated in so many churches hard to understand. For the early church, Jesus was the fulfillment of the Old Testament and was interpreted by it.

We should note further that this approach avoids psychological interpretation. We are not concerned with what went on inside of Bartimaeus, nor do we see Jesus as the tenderhearted man who cannot pass by a sufferer. These aspects may be there, but they do not constitute the significance of the story in the light of the whole Bible. Certain Bible passages, such as the story of Abraham's journey to offer up Isaac (Gen. 22) and the story of Tamar and Amnon (2 Sam. 13) certainly have a psychological content, but generally speaking, we are misled if we exegete the Bible psychologically.

If we Christians find orientation in life through receiving a place in the ongoing story of God's people, the question of the relationship between that story and the rest of world history remains to be treated. In past generations many Christians could live long lives and never leave an essentially Christian context. For them the straightforward Bible story gave orientation; they did not look to the right or to the left. Our world is rapidly becoming different, and more like that of the Bible, where faith always found itself set against the counterclaims of other faiths, be they Baalism for the Old Testament, or Pharisaism and Greek religions and philosophies for the New Testament.

In other words, we must write and teach comparatively. We must teach the Bible in its interaction with the Ancient Near East, and we must arrive at its significance for today in the light of world history and world religions. God was interested in the whole world then, not only in his elect, and God is interested in the whole world today. Then as now God chose special instruments to achieve his purposes with the world. An instrument, however, gains meaning only as it is used toward its destined end. How does God's elect community relate to the rest of the world? Some fruitful attempts to answer this have been made, such as Pannenberg's, but even to keep the question in mind constantly is in itself a gain.

Notes

[1] To characterize rabbinic interpretation as a system of prescriptions for every situation of life is a simplification. A fuller discussion would need to point out that rabbinic Judaism at its best is an ongoing dialogue between the Bible and later times. Valid cautions against popular caricatures of it can be found in two authoritative treatments of the subject: Hermann L. Strack, *Introduction to Talmud and Midrash* (Meridian Books and Jewish Publication Society of America, 1959). First German Edition 1887; W. D. Davies, *Introduction to Pharisaism,* Facet Books, Biblical Series 16 (Philadelphia: Fortress, 1967).

[2] A convenient survey of the history of Bible interpretation has been presented by Robert M. Grant, John T. McNeill and Samuel Terrien in "History of the Interpretation of the Bible," *The Interpreter's Bible,* Volume I (New York: Abingdon Press, 1952). See also Robert M. Grant, *A Short History of the Interpretation of the Bible,* Revised Edition (New York: Macmillan, 1963).

[3] See Bultmann's leading essay "The New Testament and Mythology" in

Kerygma and Myth, edited by Hans Werner Bartsch (Harper Torchbooks, The Cloister Library. New York: Harper & Row, 1961), pp. 1-44. First German edition 1948.

[4] The significance of Lessing in this connection is well presented by Hans-Joachim Kraus, "Das Geschichtsverstaendnis Lessings und Herders," *Geschichte der historisch-kritischen Erforschung des Alten Testaments.* (Neukirchen: Verlag der Buchhandlung des Erziehungsvereins Neukirchen, 1956), pp. 111-16.

[5] See Kraus, *ibid.,* pp. 179-182.

[6] Julius Wellhausen, *Prolegomena to the History of Ancient Israel* (New York: Meridian Books, 1957). German Edition 1883. See also Kraus, "Julius Wellhausens 'Prolegomena zur Geschichte Israels,' " *op. cit.,* pp. 240-49, and Herbert F. Hahn, *The Old Testament in Modern Research,* second expanded edition (Philadelphia: Fortress Press, 1966), chapter I.

[7] Dietrich Bonhoeffer, *Ethics* (New York: Macmillan, 1959), and the same author, *Letters and Papers from Prison* (New York: Macmillan, 1963).

[8] Harvey Cox, *The Secular City* (New York: Macmillan, 1965).

[9] Von Hofmann's main works are *Weissagung und Erfüllung* (1841-44); *Der Schriftbeweis* (1852-56); and *Biblische Hermeneutik* (1880). For a discussion see Kraus, "Johann Christian Konrad von Hofmann," *op. cit.,* pp. 207-210, and Otto W. Heick, "Erlangen Theology," *A History of Christian Thought* (Philadelphia: Fortress Press, 1966). Vol. II, pp. 203-16.

[10] Oscar Cullmann, *Christ and Time,* revised edition (London: SCM Press, 1965). First German edition 1946.

[11] A summary is given by Robert W. Funk, "Language as Event: Fuchs and Ebeling," *Language, Hermeneutic, and Word of God* (New York: Harper & Row, 1966), pp. 47-71. Also easily accessible to the English reader: Gerhard Ebeling, *God and Word* (Philadelphia: Fortress Press, 1967). German edition 1966.

[12] Some basic writings of Pannenberg are: Wolfhart Pannenberg, *et al.,* *Revelation as History,* trans. David Granskou (London: Collier-Macmillan, 1968); *What Is Man?,* trans. Duane A. Priebe (Philadelphia: Fortress, 1970); *Jesus—God and Man,* trans. Lewis L. Wilkins and Duane A. Priebe (Philadelphia: Westminster, 1968). "Hermeneutics and Universal History" in *History and Hermeneutic,* edited by Robert W. Funk; *Journal for Theology and Church* 4 (New York: Harper and Row, 1967), pp. 122-52.

[13] See especially Jürgen Moltmann, *Theology of Hope,* trans. James W. Leitch (London: SCM, 1967).

Part II
Blessings and Boundaries

5

In the Beginning

The biblical treatment of the beginnings (Greek: Genesis; Hebrew: Be-reshith), comes to us in two separate stories—the Priestly Account (Gen. 1:1-2:4a) and the Yahwist Account (Gen. 2:4b-3:24, and beyond). These accounts have been placed side by side and form a continuous story now, yet their distinctive character is clearly recognizable. They are in harmony with each other as to their theology (their teachings concerning the world and humankind in relation to God), but they express that theology in different ways, (just as the four Gospels use different styles and lift out different aspects when treating the same Jesus). Because of these differences, it is better for exegesis (detailed interpretation) to consider each account separately, rather than to treat Genesis 1 to 3 as a unit. They should not be left in isolation, however, but should be compared in order to discover their common teaching.

The Priestly Account (Gen. 1:1-2:4a)

This account is hymnic in tone, praising the one sovereign God who, by his powerful command, systematically and progressively forges primeval chaos into life-sustaining order. Chaos, which was held to be a threatening divine power (represented as the sea monster Tiamat) in Babylonian mythology, merely figures as God's raw material. It cannot assert itself against God. The sovereignty of God to achieve his purposes is further expressed by the formulation of his creative work in terms of the craftsman's six-day week, followed by the sabbath. This stands in contrast again to the Babylonian "creation" myth where life-sustaining order is wrested from the evil chaos powers in a fierce battle.

Within the six days of creation, a certain progression is evident. Most noteworthy is the fact that humanity (both male and female) appears as the goal and pinnacle of God's creative activity. Certain features of the sequence of creation seem puzzling at first, but gain meaning when compared with widely held Ancient Near Eastern mythical views. One of these is the creation of light long before the creation of the heavenly bodies. We must see here a deliberate demotion of the heavenly bodies, often regarded to be gods in the Ancient Near East, from primary significance to a secondary and subordinate function, namely to be the celestial clockwork.

A similar demotion happens to "the great sea monsters" (Gen. 1:21). Being the symbols of (divine) chaos in the Ancient Near East, as I have mentioned above, they are now placed side by side with the fish and the birds. In other words, whatever powers of chaos there be, they are not to be feared as rivals of God, but are subject to him just like the rest of his creatures. (This will be illustrated later in Genesis when God makes use of the chaos waters, in the flood story, as his instruments, being in total control of them, however.) Lest we miss this point, attention is drawn to the sea monsters through the use of the verb "to create" (Hebrew: *bārā'*),which is reserved for the unique creative activity of God and appears elsewhere in this story only in connection with heaven and earth (1:1; 2:4a) and humanity (1:27).

Humanity stands last among the works of creation. This is a position of honor. Humanity thus constitutes the pinnacle of God's creation activity. As previously mentioned, the special verb "to create" is employed for humankind, a further mark of significance. We must note, however, that human beings remain a work of God, created in the same process with the rest of the universe. Humanity is not above or outside the works of God, but among them. All theories of divinity or semi-divinity, so common in ancient religions, are categorically rejected here. What makes humans so special is not any divine or semi-divine nature, but a special commission.

Humanity is to be God's image and likeness. [1] These two terms are synonyms. Elsewhere in the Old Testament they often refer to the images (idols) which the heathen people made of their gods. Such images were to bring the gods near and make them accessible. According to biblical teaching, such image making is forbidden (Exod. 20:4-6). The fullest representation of God available on earth is to be the human being. (Jesus Christ, as the perfect human in God's sight, is God's Son; cf. Col. 1:14; 2 Cor. 4:6.)

As representative of God, humanity is to have dominion over

the rest of creation. Sharing with the animals the blessing, "Be fruitful and multiply and fill the waters/earth . . ." (1:22, 28), humanity's special assignment goes beyond procreation; it is to "subdue" the earth and "have dominion" over it and its creatures. They, in turn, are to serve humanity, though we note here that only the plants are given as food (1:29f). (Meat eating will be granted later, as a concession, in the context of God's covenant with Noah, 9:30.) It is important to note here that human sexuality is not marginal to a biblical understanding of human nature, but constitutes a vital aspect of the image of God (1:27).

With the creation of humanity and the definition of its role in the universe, God's creation activity is completed. After the repeated earlier statement "And God saw that it was good," the final verdict can now be spoken: "And God saw everything that he had made, and behold, it was very good" (1:31). In contrast to Babylonian mythology, where everything is created out of the bodies of evil chaos gods, thus inherently predisposing the world to evil, and where humanity was made to be the slave of the gods to do their menial work, our creation account proclaims a positive purpose in God's creative activity.

A human-centered view of creation would stop right here. Our story, however, goes on to a seventh day, a sabbath rest. In this way it completes the image of God as the skillful craftsman who works up to the day when he can rest, satisfied. The aim of God's work is not merely the product, but the sense of satisfaction it brings. Rest means more here than cessation of work; it is a goal reached, a purpose accomplished. While the penultimate goal of God's creativity is humanity, the ultimate goal is the accomplishment of God's own purposes, which are hidden from us. However, humanity is to be God's image, God's reflection, in this respect also. As humanity shares in God's governing activity, so also humanity shares in God's accomplished purpose by keeping the sabbath (Exod. 20:8-11). While no reference to covenant is found here, the sabbath is elsewhere called a "sign" of the God-human relationship (Exod. 31:12ff), just as the rainbow, circumcision, and the keeping of the law are "signs" of the covenants of Noah, Abraham, and Moses, respectively.

The concluding formula, "These are the generations of the heavens and the earth . . ." (2:4a) is a clear demarcation of this literary unit. Similar expressions open several other segments of Genesis. Here it closes a section, perhaps to allow the majestic "In the beginning God created . . ." to open the account.

Humanity's Creation and Fall (Gen. 2:4b-3:24)

In this account the focus is on humanity. Brief reference is made to God as the creator of heaven and earth (2:4b) and to their unfinished state (2:5-6). We move quickly, however, to God's first and foremost work namely, the creation of the first human. As to substance, he is dust of the ground (Hebrew: *'ădāmāh*), as his name, Adam (*'ādām*) also signifies. Life, the ability to breathe, is a special gift of God to him. Through this gift, he becomes a living being (*nephesh ḥajjāh*). God further provides a habitat for him by planting a garden in Eden (probably meaning "delight," i.e., given for human enjoyment; "Paradise" is a Greek word meaning "garden").

While up to this point, Adam is God's primary work and the object of his caring concern, nothing so far distinguishes him from the rest of creation. Trees (2:9) and animals (2:19) are also made "out of the ground." While no reference is made to God's breathing the breath of life into their nostrils, the fact that the animals also become living beings (*nephesh ḥajjāh* 2:19; the use of different terms for this by the RSV in Gen. 1:30, 2:7, and 2:19 is confusing) presupposes their reception of the breath of life as well. This is explicity said in Gen. 6:17 and 7:15. What is meant is animate biological life. (The KJV's rendering of *nephesh ḥajjāh* as *living soul* can easily mislead the reader to think of a Platonic division of body and soul, a concept totally foreign to this passage and to the Old Testament generally.) Thus the human becomes the brother to plants and animals, an affirmation which the priestly creation story expressed by including human beings among the works of the six days.

At this point (2:9-17) a description of the garden is introduced, which forms the setting for Adam and Eve's temptation and fall later in the story. We will return to it below. For now we merely note that the garden is God's gracious and bountiful provision, and that the human is to "till it and keep it." Work and supervision belong to his special assignment which places him above the rest of creation. (Gen. 1 referred to the image of God in this connection, and to humanity's assignment to subdue" it and to "have dominion" over it.)

Something incomplete remains: the man is alone—one of a kind. The animals, with whom he shares his biological being, fail the test of companionship. Adam's proper function toward them is again that of being in charge, expressed here in the activity of naming. (To "name" is to characterize and classify, i.e., to bring, in a sense, order into chaos. Thus the human shows himself as God's co-worker and representative.)

God meets the man's need again, as he has met his biological needs earlier. God creates woman out of man. We should not over-interpret the sleep and the rib. The sleep which fell upon the man probably means that the origins of sexuality are shrouded in mystery. One can marvel at the fact that he or she is confronted by another who is equally human and yet so different, but one cannot explain it. That woman is made from man's rib stands in contrast to the creation of animals out of the ground. Man and woman are made from the same clump of ground. They belong together more closely than humans and animals do. Upon awakening, the man immediately recognizes this belonging together and rejoices in it. (The Hebrew words for man and woman, *'ish* and *'ishshāh,* respectively, underscore this closeness.)

It is noteworthy that the basis of human sexuality, as given here, is not procreation, though that is a consequence ("they become one flesh," v. 24), but rather the function of being a helper and companion. The reference to the man's leaving of father and mother foreshadows the fact that the union of man and woman in companionship, mutual support, and procreation, will be the basis of the human future. [2]

The creation of humanity is now finished. (The last verse of the chapter introduces the theme of nakedness, shame, and clothes, which will become important in the story of the Fall.) Nothing more can be added to mankind to make it fully human. In the Babylonian Epic of Gilgamesh the association of man and woman is superseded by yet a further step: the companionship of man with man in a comradeship based on mutual respect for the other's strength and ability. The Bible does not allow for the introduction of added criteria to the basic biological definition of a human being. No special qualification raises some persons to full human status, leaving others to be semihuman. Every creature born of human parents is fully human and represents the end product of God's creation of humanity.

We must comment, further, on the order of the creation of the sexes. While Genesis 1:27 says tersely, "male and female he created them," our account seems to give man priority over woman and has been exploited in that direction. If one wanted to ascribe significance to the order, however, one would have to consider man (if wrongly understood as "male") to be God's incomplete work, in need of woman to bring him to full and complete human status. Probably we should not toy with the order at all. The point is that man (understood as "human being"), short of his bisexual existence, would not be fully human in God's plan. There is no basis of sex discrimination here. It is a firm affirmation of the divine intent of sexuality and the dignity of both sexes.

The Account of the Fall (Gen. 2:25-3:24)

Humanity is now complete and has been endowed with the significant commission to administer the garden of nature. This is to be done as God's stewards, though, and not as autonomous masters. Humanity's limits are represented by two special trees in the midst of the garden, the tree of life and the tree of the knowledge of good and evil (2.9). The former is not mentioned again in the story until 3:22-24. We will return to it below.

The tree of the knowledge of good and evil, later simply called the "tree which is in the midst of the garden" (3:3), becomes the test as to whether human beings will be willing to accept the role assigned to them, or whether they will strive to overstep it. To attempt the latter would mean punishment by death (2:17; 3:3). The thrust of the temptation is clear; it is to seek to be "like God" (3:3). Whatever else "knowing good and evil" and being "wise" may mean, they represent a grasping for something that properly belongs to God and not to humans.

"Good and evil" is best understood as a bracket enclosing all knowledge, from one end of the spectrum to the other, (just as expressions like "young and old," "rich and poor," etc., embrace the whole range in each case). Humanity is simply tempted to grasp for the whole of knowledge, not acknowledging its own limitations and the mysterious and greater wisdom of God. We need not assume, however that humanity was originally meant to live in "blissful ignorance," as modern romantic thinking has sometimes done. Humanity may strive for insight and understanding, as the naming of animals (2:19-20) suggests, as long as its limitations over against God are acknowledged.

Who is the tempter? To regard the snake or serpent as Satan would be overinterpreting the story. There is no developed doctrine of Satan, as a prince of all evil, here or elsewhere in the Old Testament. The serpent is one of God's creatures (3:1). Its choice for the tempter-role, as compared to another creature, may be due simply to its slippery agility and to the revulsion which most people feel for it. The Babylonian Epic of Gilgamesh, where a serpent snatches the shrub of life from Gilgamesh, may also have influenced the choice. It is best not to assign too much significance to the serpent, but instead to regard it as a minor character in the drama, which performs its function in order to facilitate the major developments to take place. It becomes evident later that the man cannot escape the guilt of his disobedience by blaming it on the serpent. The origin of evil is not explained here.

Much has been made of the fact that it is the woman who is tempted. Older interpreters tended to draw conclusions regarding woman's supposedly greater disposition towards sin, which was then linked to the greater centrality of sex and procreation in her life. However, one could also argue that woman is the more responsible moral agent here, who has to make a choice and at first resists temptation, while man simply follows her lead. Neither approach is justified on the basis of the text. It is the togetherness of male and female which is central. That companionship which had been provided by God and had brought his creation of humanity to its completion now also becomes a solidarity in disobedience. To be sure, the man attempts later to lay the blame on the woman (theologians have done so ever since!), but God does not accept the excuse. The punishment of man and woman is parallel in gravity, confirming that their guilt is equal.

The first consequence of transgressing the God-given boundary is the recognition of shame over nakedness (3:7), in contrast to an earlier unconcern (2:25). Whoever wants to be like God, receives a heightened sense of his exposedness. While awareness of sexuality and shame over it cannot be dissociated from the story, it would be quite wrong to see the Fall as a move from childlike sexual innocence to adult sexual awareness. After all, the recognition of the partner of opposite sex for what he or she is has been described earlier as part of God's design (2:23, 24).

Furthermore, the only explicit description of this new sense of exposure associates it with fear of God. Human beings, who want to move from a creaturely dependence on God to an autonomous equality with God, discover that this God is now indeed no longer close to them, but confronts them as a stranger, from whom they need to shield themselves. In a sense, human beings have become like God (cf. 3:22), making their own decisions. But it is a pitiful autonomy which they have achieved, and they feel immediately how little they are able to stand up to God. They want to flee and hide, but not even that is possible. The sequel to this situation follows later (3:21), when God, instead of exploiting their helpless exposure, makes clothes for them, thus graciously adapting his care for humanity to the new situation.

First, however, God pronounces the verdict of punishment, having brushed aside the feeble human attempt at self-justification. A surprise awaits us here: while a death sentence is expected (2:17; 3:3), the curse (deliberately) misses man and woman and hits the serpent and the ground instead. Man and woman are granted grace to live, albeit in a changed habitat. They will work a barren ground and be surrounded by hostile fellow creatures snapping at their heels.

Earlier interpreters, who were freer than we to read allegorical (spiritualizing) meanings into biblical passages, saw a reference to Christ's victory over Satan in verse 15. As an image, that may be fitting. As exact exegesis it cannot be upheld, firstly, because the very general wording hardly suggests so specific a conclusion, and secondly, because that verse forms a part of the punishing curse. It is the staying of the anticipated execution and the making of clothes that are the expressions of God's grace in this story.

Life in a cursed habitat is not all that is decreed, however. Woman and man are to feel their changed state in their own bodies. Central and characteristic elements are selected from the life of each to express the vitiation of what was originally meant as a blessing. Woman's blessed role as wife and childbearer is transformed into subordination and dependence, leading to the pains of childbirth. Man's commission to till the garden and keep it turns into a struggle with the cursed ground to wrest the daily bread from it. This is life as we all know it, life under the shadow of sin.

Even this life, however, does not belong to human beings forever. They are reminded of their origin and their end: "You are dust, and to dust you shall return" (3:19). Of course, humans were dust before the Fall, but just as their originally positive tasks of childbearing and working the ground have become permeated by pain and drudgery, so their end will now be perceived as a fearsome threat.

In connection with death, our story takes up the theme of the tree of life (3:22-24) briefly introduced earlier (2:9). Much discussion has surrounded the question of the two trees. Why does only one tree play a role throughout the story, yet under a name ("the tree which is in the midst of the garden," 3:3) which seems to describe the other tree? (Cf. 2:9, where it is the tree of life that is described as standing "in the midst of the garden.")

A few things seem clear: both trees are expressive of limits which God has set for humanity. That is evident already from their close association and the alternating description of each as the tree in the midst of the garden. But 3:22 states it explicity. The wording of that verse can only be understood to mean that eating of the tree of life, just as eating of the tree of the knowledge refers to a first and only eating. This has not yet happened, but the precedent of human's reaching for the fruit of the tree of knowledge makes it likely now that they will also reach for the fruit of the tree of life. This is prevented by God.

The assumption is not, however, that human beings, had they not eaten of the tree of knowledge, would have been free to eat of the tree of life. Instead, had they refrained from the tree of knowledge, the tree of life would also have been safe; since creatures which would have had regard for God-set limits as to knowledge, would also not have wished to transcend the boundaries to become like God as to immortality. The fact that eating from the tree of life is not forbidden explicity in 2:17 is due to the circumstance that we are there already concerned with humanity's attitude to the one tree, the other having been left aside for the time being.

Were man and woman, then, mortal even in the garden of Eden? One line of thought would be to think of them as biologically so, but without the fear and anguish that now surrounds death and that this fear is the reward of sin (Rom. 5:12; 6:23). That situation would be the counterpart to the eternal life available through redemption from sin through Jesus Christ, which also does not remove biological death, but transforms it into a going home to the Father. On the other hand, the question may have been wrongly put, for it presupposes that our story wants to have us think of a golden age for some chronological extent before the Fall. Yet the story's concern seems to be the characterization of humanity as inherently rebellious. An age of sinless humanity is not presented here.

Added Reflections

I have tried to interpret the biblical accounts concerning the beginnings of the universe and of humanity. My guiding question has been: What did they say to their Old Testament hearers or readers? To ascertain this, I have used for comparison viewpoints and myths widespread in the Ancient Near East. For we must assume that the first hearers or readers did not approach these accounts with an empty mind, but brought to them the common views of their day. Only if compared with those views does that which is unique in the proclamation of Genesis 1 to 3 emerge.

I might also mention that the positions taken are, of course, not my private views. They represent in each instance widely held insights and results of Old Testament interpreters. Of course, there is no clear unanimity on many points. In such cases I had to choose the position most convincing to me.

In the course of this interpretation I have left unmentioned many questions which you may have associated with these chapters. That is partly due to limitations of time and space. (Westermann's commentary on Genesis 1-11 contains 800 printed pages!) In part, however, many themes and questions have accumulated around the early chapters of Genesis which are quite foreign to the intent of the writer(s) or the early hearers or readers.

Thus the interpreter who wishes to let the Bible speak must not only be attentive to what it says; but must also clear away much interpretation that has accumulated around the biblical word. One such matter concerns evolution. Can Creation be integrated with post-Darwinian theories of evolution? There is certainly some awareness, in the order of God's created works in Genesis 1, that life develops in stages from lower to higher forms. People knew this long before Darwin. However, a precise integration of the six days with modern evolutionary theories becomes an artificial product. Just as Genesis 1 speaks in the pre-Copernican terms of a flat earth, it also speaks in terms of the scientific understanding of the ancient world. The Bible intends to teach theology, not natural science. This does not mean that we must not try to understand certain physical aspects of the universe in terms of modern scientific theories. Few today would want to argue for the flatness of the earth. God speaks to each generation in a language that it can understand. We obscure a proper understanding of God's word, expressed in ancient terminology, if we attempt to twist that terminology to fit modern expectations. God, however, is the same, and the theology of Genesis 1 to 3 is as valid today as when it was first expressed.

Notes

[1] For a more detailed treatment of this topic see my paper "Created in God's Image" in this volume, pp. 51-60.

[2] For a more detailed treatment of sexuality see my paper "Sexuality in the Old Testament" in this volume, pp. 68-83.

6
Created in God's Image

My treatment of this biblical affirmation consists of two parts. The first constitutes an exegesis of Genesis 1:26-30, with special reference to the meaning of the terms *image* and *likeness*. The second tries to identify some salient exegetical insights for our time.

Exegesis of Genesis 1:26-30

The passage opens with a divine monologue:
"Let us make man in our image,
after our likeness;
and let them have dominion
over the fish of the sea
and over the birds of the air,
and over the cattle,
and over all the earth,
and over every creeping thing
that creeps upon the earth." (v. 26)
The plural "Let us . . ." has invited Christian piety, to read the persons of the Trinity into this passage.[1] Others have preferred to see the plural of majesty here. Precise grammatical interpretation makes it more likely that we are dealing with a "plural of deliberation." When someone reaches a decision, it is as if the several selves within him agree upon a common course of action in an internal consensus.[2] This highlights the deliberate decision on God's part to proceed to an important and new phase in the creative activity. The use of the verb "to create" (*bārā*) in verse 27, a verb reserved for crucial points in the creation account (Gen. 1:1, 21, 27; 2:4), underscores the momentous nature of the next step, the

creation of humanity.

The words *image* and *likeness* are central, of course, to our understanding of this passage. What do they mean? The attempts to interpret them have become almost innumerable. Often these words have been, and still are, considered to be a summary of biblical anthropology. Their understanding within God's dynamic creative activity has tended to give way to their more static application as a description of humanity's being: humanity labeled as the "image of God," the *imago dei*.

Claus Westermann has surveyed the various trends of interpretation.[3] We can only sketch a few salient points. (1) Throughout church history there has been a tendency to distinguish between a natural and a supernatural dimension of the image of God in humanity. Often this has been linked to the two nouns respectively. This has generally been abandoned today, however. (2) The most pervasive interpretation of the image has probably been its association with humanity's mental superiority, seen in such capacities as reason, conscious personality, will, freedom of decision, but also with spiritual superiority and particularly the immortal soul. (3) Older interpreters rarely referred the image to humanity's external appearance, but in recent times this view has found several prominent advocates.

(4) All these views have one common weakness; they divide human personality into several component parts, asking which of these may constitute the divine image. Th. C. Vriezen has argued convincingly that such a fragmentation is unbiblical, and that the image can only refer to our total being.[4] But how does a human, in his total being, function as God's image?

(5) According to Karl Barth, one does so by standing in an I-Thou relationship to God, that is, by partnership in the Divine-human encounter (*als Gottes Gegenüber*).[5] Though not new, this understanding has received new prominence through Karl Barth, especially in conjunction with Vriezen's holistic approach.

(6) A new and different impetus proceeded from the study of the meaning of image in the Ancient Near East. J. Hehn (1915) pointed out that the images could represent the god in Babylonia. The same was true in Egypt. By analogy, humanity as the image of God should be seen as God's representative on earth. G. von Rad, E. Jacob, and others developed this interpretation.[6] It received a new turn when H. Wildberger[7] and W. H. Schmidt[8] associated humanity's image function with the frequent Ancient Near Eastern characterization of the king as the image of the god, being the god's representative on

earth. In this light, Genesis 1:26 to 30 would assign to humanity a royal, representative role on earth. The commission to "rule" and to "subdue" in verse 28 would support this, as would the vice-regal position accorded humanity in the related Psalm 8. According to Wildberger:

> There is but *one* legitimate image by which God makes himself manifest in the world, namely *man*. It is of immeasurable import that Israel . . . in a most daring reinterpretation of the image-ideology of its surroundings, proclaimed man as that figure in which God himself is present. [9]

(7) Westermann advances three arguments against this proposal. [10] a. The royal parallel is suitable for a king as an individual, with reference to the rest of society. But over whom would *Adam* (humanity) rule as king? b. The Priestly writer of Genesis 1:26 to 30 stresses God's holiness and separateness throughout. It is impossible to assume that he saw God as present in each human being everywhere and always. c. The royal parallels from the Ancient Near East do not come from creation stories and are therefore literarily unsuited for comparison with Genesis 1:26f. Instead, Westermann argues, Genesis 1:26f must be interpreted in the context of God's creative activity. It is not so much meant to characterize humanity's being as God's action. God is a God who decides to create a being according to his own model, that is, a being that has a relationship to God. This moves along the lines of Barth's interpretation though it places the accent differently.

To evaluate these positions and to arrive at our own conclusions, we must turn back to our text and especially to the two crucial words, *image* (*selem*) and *likeness* (*demût*). While the two nouns show a slight variation in meaning in their remaining Old Testament occurrences, exegetes agree today that they are used here in synonymous parallelism and must not be interpreted as carrying separate significance. [11]

Elsewhere in the Old Testament, *image* (*selem*) is used to describe a son's resemblance to his father (Gen. 5:3, "likeness"), a pictorial portrayal on a wall (Ezek. 23:14, "likeness"), man's shadow (Ps. 39:7, "nothing, breath"), a sculpture or model of something (1 Sam. 6:5, 11), or a dream (Ps. 73:30). Most prominent, however, is the use of "image" with reference to images employed in heathen worship, that is, to idols (Amos 5:26; Num. 33:52; 2 Kings 11:18; Ezek. 7:20; 16:7) although it did not become the technical term for "graven image" (*pesel*). *Likeness b)demut)* can also refer to resemblance (Gen. 5:3), to pictures on the wall (Ezek. 23:15), to sculptures or models (2

Kings 16:10; 2 Chron. 4:3). In the majority of instances, however, it is used to note the resemblance of something appearing in a vision to something known from real life (Ezek. 1:10, 13, etc.; 8:2; 10:1, 10, etc.; Dan. 10:16). Thus both nouns throughout their occurrences denote a common character shared actually or supposedly by two entities (father-son; person-shadow; reality-dream; gods-idols), yet they stop short of expressing total identity. Nevertheless, it is the common dimension and not the remaining disparity which is accented in each case.

When we return these nouns expressive of similarity (though not identity) to their context in Genesis 1:26f, where they describe the object of God's new and deliberate creative act, they most certainly express the great affinity of the Creator and this particular one of his creatures. In line with Barth and Westermann, man is characterized here as God's partner, (*Gottes Gegenüber*). One must ask immediately, however, whether such a partnership is not misunderstood if it is visualized in existential fashion as an I-Thou relationship, where face turns toward face and eye meets eye. Contrary to expectation, God does not embrace the man here in jubilation over the fitting partner who has finally been found, as Adam does towards Eve (2:23). Nor does Adam fall down in worshipful recognition of the Wholly Other who is nevertheless the Thou turned toward him. Instead the words that follow are words that equip human beings for a task and dispatch them to it (v. 28). But what is that task?

Before we attempt an answer, we must stop for a moment to consider the phrase "male and female he created them." It is not our task today to develop a theology of sexuality. Suffice it to say that the image and likeness pertains to humanity in its bisexual mode of existence. Any male (or female) claims to precedence before God tamper with humanity's god-likeness. Similarly, any attempt to obliterate sexual distinctiveness by relegating it to a few almost accidental biological externals, tampers with the divine image. Both male and female, in their sexual distinctiveness which permeates the whole being, *together* constitute the result of God's decision to create a being in his own image. On the other hand, Karl Barth goes too far when he sees the Trinity reflected in humanity's bisexuality. [12] If one considers the Old Teatament's adamant confession of one God in a world of fertility religions with their male and female deities, it is totally inconceivable to think that any sexual plurality in the Godhead could be as much as adumbrated in the phrase under discussion.

We return now to the question: What is the task implied in being God's image? Humanity shares the blessing to be fruitful and multiply and fill the earth (v. 28a), with the animals (1:22). Together with the other living creatures, humanity is to be sustained by the fruits of the earth (vv. 29, 30). As these creatures are not created in God's image, these aspects of being human are not distinctive to that image. What remains is the command

> . . . and subdue (*kābash*) it [the earth]; and have dominion (*rādāh*) over the fish of the sea and over the birds of the air and over every living thing that moves upon the earth (v. 28b).

Subdue (*kābash*) implies the assertion of full, sometimes even cruel control. It can refer to "the subjection of a country through war (Num. 32:22, 29), the subjugation of peoples (2 Sam. 8:1) and of slaves particularly (Neh. 5:5); but it can also be used for the raping of women (Esther 7:8). It always means an action in which someone reduces something to his use through the application of force (Josh. 18:1)."[13] *Rule* (*rādāh*) often means royal rule (Ps. 72:8; 110:2; Isa. 14:6; Ezek. 34:4). Psalm 8, a hymnic praise of humanity's exalted position (yet "little less than God"! v. 5) in God's creation, also characterizes humanity's function as royal rule over God's works:

> Thou hast given him dominion over
>
> the works of thy hands;
>
> thou hast put all things under his feet.
>
> (v. 6)

In view of this, the analogy drawn from the Babylonian and Egyptian references to the king as the image of the god, by Wildberger and Schmidt, becomes very appealing in spite of Westermann's protestations. It is not necessary to assume a simple and complete carryover that would say: in Genesis 1:26f. humankind is to God as the king in Egypt or Babylon is to his god (subtler nuancing would do much to mitigate Westermann's reservations).[14] It seems appropriate to hold, however, that humanity's creation in God's image indeed claims for humanity the status of God's royal regent over the rest of creation.

We must hasten to note what is neither said nor implied, namely that some persons should subdue and rule others. The earth itself is to be subdued. H. W. Wolff points out that this is the inversion of ancient nature religion.[15] In the Ancient Near Eastern mythological views of the world, nature with her powers was divine, and humanity lived in fear of the forces and destinies embedded in the earth and the stars. In a demythologized world there is only one supreme power, God, who has given to humanity, as a royal representative, the power and authority to make the earth subservient. We are dealing here with humanity's charter to live fearlessly in this world and to establish a mode of life that transcends subservience to the elements and accommodation to the animal ways. In other words, it is humanity's commission to establish human culture under God.[16] Parenthetically we may note that two forms of preversion of this task lead again to humanity's subjection to, and fear of, nature: pollution and mechanization.

Humanity's rule is to extend over the animals. Humankind's long struggle against the other creatures on this planet has led to the increasing assertion of human control, although this is by no means complete if we include the modern struggle against bacteria and viruses here. Wolff remarks perceptively that killing the animals may not yet be meant in Genesis 1, as there is a conscious limitation of food to vegetation (vv. 29f.), as compared to the concession of meat-eating after the Fall (Gen. 9:13). It is clear that a ruthless and unaccountable killing of animals is not intended, for even in the covenant with Noah, which accentuates the harshness of humanity's rule over the animals, their blood is not to be eaten (Gen. 9:1-4), undoubtedly because the life which it represents (Lev. 17:14) belongs to God, a fact acknowledged by pouring the blood to the ground.

If God's image in humankind, then, represents humanity's closeness to God and its vice-regal commission to rule over God's creation, it is remarkable that all this is expressed by a noun which can readily be applied to idols, as we have seen. Must not an Israelite of Old Testament times have heard Genesis 1:26f. as a commission for humanity to be God's idol or statue on the earth, in analogy to the images set up by the idol-worshiping heathen? Even though *image* (*ṣelem*) is different from *idol* (*pesel*), such a conclusion seems unavoidable. But what should be its purpose?

While Wildberger alludes to this,[17] not enough attention has been given to the Decalogue's prohibition of images in Israel (Exod. 20:4-6; Deut. 5:8-10). There the words are *graven image* (*pesel*) and *likeness* (*témûnāh*), rather than *ṣelem* and *démût*. However, the substantive contact with Genesis 1:26-30 seems clear. In the Decalogue the way in which the heathen subject themselves to the phenomena of nature, represented by "graven images" and worshiped as divine, is described. Thereupon the Israelite is forbidden to do the same. Genesis 1:26f. provides the positive supplement to this prohibition: the function performed for the heathen by their images, namely to bring the gods near, is to be performed by humanity alone; for only humanity is God's legitimate image and represents God's presence. Instead of the rule over humanity of divinized nature, as represented by the "graven images," humanity, as royal representative of the only God, is to exert its rule over demythologized nature.

If we assume further that the present priestly text of Genesis 1:26f. postdates the Decalogue versions, it is not hard to understand why the priestly writer avoided the standard terms for "idols." He intended to point out humanity's image-function without carrying over to humanity all the negative associations of the standard words for idols.

The New Testament has appropriated the image terminology somewhat freely and applied it to Jesus Christ. [18] While Genesis 9:6f. implies that God's image and blessing still characterize fallen humanity, [19] it is assumed in Colossians that Christ is the image of the invisible God (Col. 1:15) and that the Christian, having lost the image wholly or partly in the Fall, is now "being renewed in knowledge after the image of the creator" (3:10; cf. Eph. 4:24). From a similar perspective 2 Corinthians 4:4 states that the gospel of Christ, "who is the likeness of God," is obscured for unbelievers by the god of this world (cf. also 2 Cor. 3:15-18). Colossians 1:15 does underscore, however, that the image-function is that of bringing near and making real the otherwise more elusive presence of God. The command that follows humanity's creation in God's image in Genesis 1:26ff., namely to subdue and rule the world, is transformed in Matthew 28:18f. into a new commission to go out with authority and subdue all nations into discipleship when Jesus says, "All authority in heaven and on earth has been given to me. Go therefore and make disciples of all nations." [20]

Relevance for Today

What is the relevance of all this for us today and especially for "The Pastor as a Person"?

(1) The image of God, tying humanity to God the creator and sending humanity out to represent that God on earth by administering it with power and authority, is imprinted on all human beings. No one, not even the pastor, has prerogatives of closeness to God and special authority to rule over others. The pastor is "image of God" only together with all other people. In the Old Testament sense, at least, the pastor shares the image-character with all fallen humanity. He or she is human being among human beings. That is important for pastors to know.

(2) Over against all pride in specific human capacities, like reason, feeling, or immortal soul, the word concerning the image of God highlights a task: Subdue and rule the earth! We need to ask what that means today. Where are the dangers today that the world, given to us as our habitat, will assert itself against us, claim control over us, or become our master, in rivalry to the only Master whom we shall serve? Is it the pollution brought about by the mismanagement of our vice-regal powers? Is it the technology which our God-given powers have created but not subjected to God? Is it the fascinating culture and the life of ease which subduing the earth seems to have brought us, lulling us asleep to the fact that the material earth has subtly reaffirmed its control of our lives? We must ask these questions so that we may fulfill our stewardship in the image of God.

(3) Genesis 1:26 to 30, with its image-teaching, is not a complete definition of human nature in the light of the Bible. [21] Studying this passage and concept can provide one perspective in our search for a biblical anthropology. It remains silent, however, on two topics of great concern, namely on the relationship of person to person (ethics) and on the matter of sin and redemption.

(4) Genesis 1:26 to 30 is a polemic against a view of humanity which pervaded the whole Ancient Near East. Humankind was captive to the powers of nature, seen as divine. People adored them, feared them, brought them near through sculptured images, and worshiped them. The Old Testament forbids all this and enthrones humanity, freed from the fear and veneration of nature, as God's royal representative to rule a demythologized world.

We in our time are also surrounded by theories of personality which must be challenged by this biblical view of humanity. Many pastors today are influenced heavily by the psychological and social sciences and thus easily slip into certain social science perspectives that are contrary to a biblical doctrine of human nature. Will we, consciously or unconsciously, allow Freudian psychology to shape our image of humanity as driven about by libido, held captive by the grip of the id, and in need of salvation through a pastoral version of psychoanalysis? Or will we let Carl Rogers tell us that humanity is basically good and competent to resolve its own problems, that the pastor (shepherd), contrary to the meaning of the title, should not assume responsibility for the sheep of the flock, but should merely reflect back to them nondirectively their own saving feelings and insights? Will we let certain clinical counselors tell us that conflict is the basis of life, that a marriage without fights must be sick or dull, and that salvation comes through conflict resolution as hostilities are voiced and compromises reached with little scope for one-sided agape-love, for covenant faithfulness (*ḥesed*), for forgiveness, and for strength to bear suffering and injustice?[22]

I know I am simplifying, and perhaps unfairly. But I know also how tempted pastors are to eat from the fruit of the psychological and sociological tree. And if a biblical perspective on humanity as the image of God should merely become an act of homage to the Bible before we turn away to the apparently more relevant truths of the social sciences, or if all our exegesis of Genesis 1:26 to 30 should simply serve to bolster our assumption of a humanistically understood "dignity of man," we should be honest and confess our biblical shortcomings.

Notes

[1] This view still stands behind Karl Barth's formulation of the matter; cf. *The Doctrine of Creation*, trans. J. W. Edwards, *et. al.*, *Church Dogmatics* III/1 (Edinburg: T. & T. Clark, 1958), pp. 182f., 196-99.

[2] Claus Westermann, *Genesis, Biblischer Kommentar* I/1; (Neukirchen-Vluyn: Neukirchener Verlag, 1974), p. 200; cf. Gesenius-Kautzsch-Cowley, *Hebrew Grammar*, 2nd English Edition, 1910; (Oxford: Carendon; 1960), par. 124g, n. 2. Barth fittingly speaks of "inter-divine unanimity" *op.cit.*, pp. 182f. This should not be read in a Trinitarian sense, however, at least not in its Old Testament context.

[3] Westermann, *Genesis*, pp. 205-14.

[4] Th. C. Vriezen, *Oudtestamentische Studien II* "La création de l' homme d' apprès l'immage de Dieu," (1943): pp. 87-105; referred to by Westermann, *Genesis*, p. 207.

[5] Barth, *op.cit.*, p. 184. See also Friedrich Horst, "Face to Face: The Biblical Doctrine of the Image of God," trans. John Bright, *Interpretation* IV (July 1950), pp. 259-70.

[6] Gerhard von Rad, in his contributions to the article "eikōn" (*Theological Dictionary of the New Testament*, ed. Gerhard Kittel, Vol. II, trans. G. W. Bromiley [Grand Rapids: Eerdmans 1964], p. 392, refers to the practice of earthly rulers to set up their images in their absence to assert their majesty. Friedrich Horst ("Face to Face," p. 265) draws on a different Ancient Near Eastern parallel, namely the creation of Enkidu in the image of Anu and of Gilgamesh. While there are no overtones of a superman-idea in the Bible, as there are in Gilgamesh, Horst points out that the Gilgamesh passage "defines that which makes man as 'that which corresponds to' God." (Cf. *The Epic of Gilgamesh*, Tablet I, Col. II, lines 31 and 33.)

[7] Hans Wildberger, "Das Abbild Gottes, Gen. 1, 26-30," *Theologische Zeitschrift* 21 (1965): pp. 245-59, 481-501; reviewed by Westermann, *Genesis*, pp. 210f.

[8] W. H. Schmidt, *Die Schöfpfungsgeschichte der Priesterschrift*, Kap. III B 9: "Das achte Schöpfungswerk: die Menschen. Gen. 1, 26-28, *Wissenschaftliche Monographien zum Alten und Neuen Testament* 17 (1964), pp. 127-48; reviewed by Westermann, *Genesis*, pp. 210f.

[9] Wildberger, "Das Abbild . . .," pp. 495f. My translation.

[10] Westermann, *Genesis*, pp. 211-13.

[11] Similarly, no distinctive significance should be attributed here to the difference of preposition: *in* our image" (*béṣalmēnû*), "*after* our likeness"; (kidmûtēnû); cf. Westermann, *Genesis*, p. 201.

[12] Barth, *op.cit.,* pp. 183, 196-99. His position is adopted by Paul K. Jewett, *Man as male and female* (Grand Rapids: Eerdmans, 1975), pp. 35ff. See also my paper "Sexuality in the Old Testament" in this volume, pp. 68-83.

[13] Hans Walter Wolff, *Anthropology of the Old Testament,* trans. Margaret Kohl (Philadelphia: Fortress, 1974), p. 163.

[14] See above, p. 53.

[15] Wolff, *Anthropology,* p. 162.

[16] *Ibid.,* p. 164.

[17] See quotation, above, 53. So does Barth, *op. cit.,* pp. 200f.

[18] Of course, this is in keeping with Paul's view of Christ as the second Adam (1 Cor. 15:42-50). For further discussion of the New Testament's treatment of the image of God, see Kittel's article "eikōn" TDNT II, pp. 395-97. Friedrich Horst, "Face to Face," pp. 268-70; Barth, Ch.D. III/1, pp. 201-06; Wolff, *Anthropology,* 164f. Wildberger ("Das Abbild Gottes," pp. 496-501) points out the complexity of the traditio-historical relationship between the New Testament passages mentioned and Genesis 1:26-30. Cautious as his conclusions are, he nevertheless questions the assumption of a Platonic background. If a direct connection with Genesis 1:26-30 cannot be established, a common background for Genesis 1:26-30, 2 Corinthians 4:4 and Colossians 1:15 might be found in the Ancient Near Eastern references to the king as the image of his god. I for my part am convinced that the linkage of the New Testament passages in question to Genesis 1:26-30 can be affirmed more boldly. A helpful summary and perspective on the biblical data concerning the image of God in humanity is provided by John Reumann in his "Introduction" to C. F. D. Moule, *Man and Nature in the New Testament,* Facet Books, Biblical Series 17 (Philadelphia: Fortress, 1967).

[19] The same holds true for rabbinic Judaism; cf. "eikōn." *Theological Dictionary of the New Testament* II, pp. 392-94.

[20] Wolff, *Anthropology,* pp. 164f.

[21] This warning is expanded in my paper "Human Wholeness in Biblical Perspective" in this volume, pp. 61-67. A broader approach to a biblical understanding of the nature of humanity is sketched there.

[22] The present paragraph earned me much enthusiastic affirmation as well as heated challenge from many workshop participants. Both were rather unexpected for me at that time, but they illustrated the relevance of my statement. Let me emphasize that I have the greatest appreciation for the help a minister can and should draw from the social sciences. My warning is directed against the unconscious and untested adoption by ministers of philosophical assumptions, incompatible with the Bible, that often accompany helpful disciplines.

Human Wholeness in Biblical Perspective

To heal means to restore to wholeness. But what is wholeness? My first task is to ask that question of the Bible. To put it in different words: what is the Christian's model of a human being? Toward what design is the Christian to move in seeking his or her own wholeness and that of a brother or sister?

Genesis 3:5 lets us hear, in the words of the serpent, the basic temptation for human beings: ". . . you will be like God. . . ." Adam and Eve wanted very much to be like God. They overstepped the limits God had set them, that is, not to eat of the tree in the midst of the garden.

The same tendency is expressed by the tower builders of Babel, "Come, let us build ourselves a city, and a tower with its top in the heavens, and let us make a name for ourselves . . ." (Gen. 11:4). Human beings always seek to define themselves in terms of greatness, placing themselves as highly as possible in the universe, wishing to be like God, or even to dethrone God and enthrone themselves.

Christians have a subtle way of doing this piously, with the help of Scripture, by thinking of themselves first and foremost under the title "image of God." That phrase, important though it is (and we shall return to it), occurs very rarely in the Bible. It is not a good starting point for understanding ourselves, not because it is not true and biblical, but because it is misleading when taken in isolation, and because it tempts us to think of ourselves in some way or other as being "like God," just as the tempting serpent wants us to do. It is safer to start elsewhere.[1]

The Hebrew word for "man, human being" (including both male

and female: Gen. 1:27),the German *Mensch,* is *'ādām.* It is closely related to *'ădāmāh,* "earth, soil, ground," and could consequently be translated as "earthling." Genesis 2:7 pictures God making this "earthling" of dust from the ground. Genesis 3:19 repeats this fact, now in a punitive context: "You are dust, and to dust you shall return." In keeping both with his God-intended earthiness and with his sin-caused transiency, Adam's assignment after the Fall is stated in earth-terms once again: "God sent him forth from the garden of Eden, to till the ground from which he was taken" (Gen. 3:23).

Someone will probably object by now: But are you not omitting the divine breath? Does Genesis 2:7 not continue: ". . . and breathed into his nostrils the breath of life; and man became a living being"? Yes, it does. Adam, "earthling" became a "living being." That introduces us to a second key word characterizing humanity in the Bible. Adam, "earthling," is also a living *nephesh.* This Hebrew word has many English translations: desire, soul, life, person, self.

Its basic meaning, however, is "throat, neck." Humankind became a living "throat, neck."[2] That sounds strange, but we, too, use parts of the body to characterize the whole person. Thus we say: "She is a brain," or: "He is all thumbs." In a similar fashion, the Old Testament characterizes humanity not only as being of the earth, but as being a "throat, neck," or "all throat." And it does so many hundred times!

When we say *brain,* we mean intelligence, for the brain is the seat of intelligence. Similarly, the throat or neck is the part of the body that represents the passage for breath and food. According to Hans Walter Wolff, *nephesh,* therefore, means "needy man," the human as characterized by his basic needs, such as breath and food.[3] For these we pant and gulp all the time. When we have them, we have a certain wholeness; without them we cease to be.

Another biblical word that defines humanity is *bāśār,* "flesh." It is used some 150 times, always signifying human weakness. Thus *basar* stands for infirm, vulnerable humanity.[4]

Who is the human creature, according to God's design? We have considered three key terms so far: (*'ādām*) "of the earth"; (*nephesh*) "needy person"; and (*bāśār*) "vulnerable person." That is a humble picture. The Bible teaches us to understand human beings by understanding their lowliness, their need, and their weakness. That is not the whole story, but it is a good starting base.

The relevance of this base for a healing ministry is easily recognized. We understand our brother or sister whom we want to heal when we see him or her as lowly, needy, and vulnerable. This is partly so by God's original design, and partly by the perversion of that design through sin. But it describes human nature better than all lofty references to human dignity, reason, freedom, creativity, potential, gifts, and even to the much-cited image of God.

In answer to the question "Who is my neighbor?" (Luke 10:29), Jesus told the story of the good Samaritan. That Samaritan knew the man by the roadside, not because he knew his background, or had discerned his gifts, or visualized his great potential, but because he saw him as needy and vulnerable. And therefore, he could be a healer toward that man.

On another occasion, when the disciples tried to understand human nature and human sickness, they asked Jesus: "Rabbi, who sinned, this man or his parents, that he was born blind?" (John 9:2). And again, Jesus' response showed that he understood the man not in terms of his background, not even in terms of sin and righteousness, but in terms of need. That made Jesus a healer, not only in this instance but throughout his ministry.

Even with respect to Jesus himself we get the impression that the woman who anointed him with precious ointment (Mark 14:3-9) understood him better than the disciples who awaited his great messianic deeds, for she saw his need, while they projected his glory.

If we then ask, toward what image of wholeness we shall work in our efforts to heal, the answer must be a very humble one: We heal our brother or sister when we help him or her to abandon the striving to be great, to be "like God," when we help him or her to accept the God-willed limitations of being human, and when we help him or her to meet the everyday requirements for staying alive.

II.

Only now, having considered humankind's limitation, loneliness, need and vulnerability, can we turn to humanity's calling. Being the image of God (Gen. 1:27) clearly means a status in the world that lifts humans above the rest of creation. In what way it does so has been interpreted variously.[5] I believe that it refers to a function assigned to humanity rather than a quality possessed, such as reason, conscience, or immortality. This function is that of representing God visibly, just as the images of the gods were meant to represent those gods in the Ancient Near East and to administer the earth as God's steward. Humankind is created by God as "earthling," a part of the earth. Adam is one of the works of God's six days of creation, a brother to the stones, plants, and animals. What lifts humans above these is not higher quality and lordship, but higher calling and responsibility. That a lowly creature, one of God's many works, can be called out from among the rest and given a special task with respect to the rest, that is God's grace in the context of the creation story.

And that grace is at work in God's government of history as well. Humanity in its lowliness, limitation, and need is the potential instrument to carry out God's purposes. Here we turn, in our search for the model human image, from what humanity needs to what humanity can do.

We might call this the theme of God's unlikely choice. It is unusual, unexpected, and marvelous that Abraham, who left the security of his homeland and his kindred, should start a great people and receive a great name in contrast to the tower-builders of Babel, whose joint efforts at achieving greatness came to nothing.

It is equally unusual, unexpected, and marvelous that the further "heroes" in God's story should be Jacob, who cheated his brother; Joseph, the spoiled and haughty dreamer; Moses, the Egyptian-educated escaped murderer; David, the lustful adulterer; Jeremiah, too young to be a prophet; Peter, the disciple who denied his master; Paul, the persecutor of Christians, afflicted with a "thorn in the flesh"; and above all, Jesus himself, the king born in a stable and executed on a cross.

These are merely some highlights in a story which make it clear that human greatness in the Bible is not a matter of fulfilled potential but of weakness called into service. There are no real "heroes" in the Bible, only anti heroes. While classical antiquity and Western literature and history are full of heroes that were undone through one tragic flaw, the Bible is full of inadequate people who rose to greatness through divine empowering. That is the story of divine grace in the image of humankind in the context of history.

It is mediated largely through the doctrine that humanity is not only *'ādām,* "earthling," *nephesh,* "throat, gullet, life," *basar,* "flesh, weakness," but also *rûah,* "spirit."[6] But humanity is not inherently "spirit." *Rûah,* "spirit," is first of all God's spirit, which can enter and empower persons to do what could not have been done out of their own capacity. In the New Testament *pneuma,* "spirit," functions in the same way. The gifts of the Spirit, referred to by Paul (Rom. 12:6; 1 Cor. 12:4), are therefore *charismata,* "gifts of grace" (*charis* means grace) worked by God's empowering Spirit rather than natural endowments or inherent human potential. They are the things a believer can do in spite of his or her limitations, neediness, and vulnerability.

And, very importantly the divinely empowered, *rûah*-filled person, acts not as an isolated achiever of personal heights, but as a collaborator in God's larger plans for the benefit of all humankind. Biblical greatness is always greatness in and for the human community, furthering the movement of that community toward God's future or kingdom.

What are the implications of this model of "greatness" or human fulfillment for our healing ministry? We remind ourselves that the first step in helping broken people is to restore them to the wholeness that comes when basic limitations are accepted and basic needs are met. In fact, wholeness is no more than that. The Bible's ideals for human existence under God seem sometimes amazingly low. Hear some classical formulations of them:

> He has showed you, O man, what is good;
> and what does the Lord require of you
> but to do justice, and to love kindness,
> and to walk humbly with your God?
> (Mic. 6:8)

Or, of the messianic end time:

> They shall sit every man under his
> vine and under his fig tree,
> and none shall make them afraid.
> (Mic. 4:4)

Jesus says:

> I came that they may have life, and have it abundantly.
> (John 10:10)

A simple everyday life, with its basic daily needs met, and with grateful subordination to God's will, is all that the Bible requires for human wholeness.

Our Western society tends to impose a different model on us. It has the form of a pyramid. The lowly, inconsequential existence of the masses forms the base. From that base each individual attempts, in a solitary struggle and by means of his or her own strength and endowment, to rise as far to the top as possible. Wholeness, the full life, the life that counts, is the life at the top. This life is, by definition, denied to the greater number and given only to the select few. To help a particular human being, therefore, to achieve fullness of life, is to spur him or her on to climb as high as possible.

By contrast we are healers of the broken, in biblical perspective, if we meet their basic needs and then help them to accept their limitations as a meaningful part of God's economy for their lives. At the same time this must not end in a fatalism that seeks no more.

Every person, no matter what his or her endowment, must and can be open to a call from God toward greater tasks.

Take a man who has been hurt seriously in a car accident. It becomes very evident that he is *nephesh,* life-breath that can be snuffed out; that he is *basar,* vulnerable flesh that can be cut up and torn. To be a healer toward him means to sew up his wounds and nurse him to a level of physical well-being where his basic needs are met.

But some physical handicaps remain, together with a bitterness of spirit that rebels against what has happened. The common Western view of life affirms his bitterness. He has indeed been impeded in climbing to the top of the pyramid. His life has been burdened by factors that will make it more difficult, or even impossible, for him to climb on to greatness, fame, riches, or whatever the top of the pyramid may symbolize for him. Thus his life will fall short of that fullness or wholeness which he might have achieved otherwise.

Christian healing aims at wholeness of a different sort. It, too, will sew up his wounds and nurse him to health. But it will, further, proceed to help him to see that his potential for greatness, understood now not as the top of the pyramid, but as usefulness as an instrument in the context of God's plans, has not diminished. Christian healing will make real to him God's word to Paul: "My grace is sufficient for you, for my power is made perfect in weakness" (2 Cor. 12:9). If he can appropriate this, against the background of Christ who served and suffered, not only to forgive sinners, but also to release sufferers from their apparent rejection, isolation, and hopelessness, he will indeed become whole again, even if he should never walk without a limp.

Notes

[1] For a fuller discussion of this topic see my paper "Created in God's Image," in this volume, pp. 51-60.

[2] Of course, I do not mean to suggest that the derived meanings ("desire, soul, life, person, self") should be disregarded in favor of the etymologically more original "throat, neck." Nevertheless, the continued use of that original concrete denotation in passages such as Isa. 5:14; Ps. 107:5, 9 and Prov. 25:25 shows that it cannot have been far from the Israelite's awareness even when *nephesh* was used in more derived senses. The same applies to the other Hebrew terms used here.

[3] Hans Walter Wolff, *Anthropology of the Old Testament,* trans. Margaret Kohl (Philadelphia: Fortress, 1974), pp. 10-25. I am also indebted, in what follows, to Wolff's broader treatment of "The Being of Man," pp. 7-79. It has not been my aim here, however, to present a comprehensive discussion of all dimensions of humanity's being. Instead, I have singled out those aspects that seem most relevant to the healer's concern.

[4] Wolff, *Anthropology,* pp. 26-31.

⁵ For a survey of interpretations see my paper "Created in God's Image" in this volume, pp. 51-60.

⁶ For further discussion see Wolff, *Anthropology,* pp. 32-39.

Sexuality in the Old Testament

The problem that faces the theologian studying this subject is that which besets biblical anthropology generally, namely, the difficulty of distinguishing confessional content from the Ancient Near Eastern context. In other words: Where does the Old Testament, when it speaks about the human situation merely report how things were in Israel in ancient times, and where does it proclaim, teach, and give perspective as to the nature of humanity in the light of biblical faith? Perhaps the two ways of speaking ought not to be distinguished at all points, and yet it might be helpful to divide the treatment of our subject into two parts, descriptive (psychological and sociological) and theological, in that order.

Sexuality in Israelite Society

The first part of our paper, then, will survey how sexuality manifested itself in the behavior of individuals and groups in Old Testament Israel. Our emphasis is to rest on that which was, rather than that which ought to have been. As the biblical records do not concern themselves in detail with the psychological history of individuals, the survey will be based primarily on the data concerning the social institutions that surrounded and gave expression to sexuality, although certain psychological insights will emerge from these data. Since a number of authoritative studies on the institutions of Israel are available, [1] our survey is summarizing in nature and claims little, if any, originality.

Life in ancient Israel was patriarchal. The basic living unit was the "father's house" (*bêt'âb*), which in turn was embedded in the large family or clan (*mišpaḥāh*) consisting of those "united by common blood and common dwelling place." 2 Such families combined to form larger tribal units. This social structure derived from Israel's seminomadic background. After the occupation of Palestine in the late second millennium B.C. and the adaption of life to village and town communities, it changed somewhat, making room for smaller units of living together, yet this never resulted in the near autonomy of the nuclear family consisting of father, mother, and children as we know it in our North American society today.

In earlier times, the patriarch, the head of a father's house, had almost unlimited powers, subject, however, to the jurisdiction of the clan elders "in the gate." Gradually these jurisdictions became less absolute. In David's time already, around 1000 B.C., appeals to the king in judicial matters were possible, so that the authority of the patriarch—and the collective authority of the village elders—could be bypassed (2 Sam. 14:1-8; 15:1-6). Jehoshaphat introduced further possibilities of appeal (2 Chron. 19:4-9). All of this pertained to grave cases of judgment, however; in the less weighty decisions of daily life we can safely assume a hierarchy of patriarchal rule dominated everything.

This male rule characterized not only the family, but all facets of society. During the time of the monarchy only one ruling queen, Athaliah, is documented, and she was a usurper who held power only until the traditional forces could expel her (2 Kings 11). Other governing functions were equally reserved for men, as was the extremely important institution of the priesthood. In Israel, in contrast to many other ancient peoples, there were no priestesses or other female cult functionaries. We know of some women who performed leadership functions, to wit, Miriam (Exod. 15:20; Num. 12) and Deborah (Judg. 4-5). In each case, however, we find that they were charismatic rather than institutional leaders. 3 As such they will be discussed in the second part of the paper.

Marriage in ancient Israel can be understood only in relation to the larger, patriarchally determined family unit. One could even go so far as to say that the atypical forms of sexual existence such as the unmarried life, as well as sexual deviations, such as adultery, find their measure in it. This is not to deny evidence of individuality and individual responsibility in Israel even in her earliest times. Such individual responsibility always defines itself against the group of which the individual is a part and toward which his individuality retains a certain tension, both then and today. For the Israelite of old, that group was first and foremost the father's house and the clan.

Marriage was considered a normal part of everyone's life and was entered into at a rather early age. Choice of mate was much more a matter of family agreement than of personal attitude and inclination, although the Old Testament does report instances where love played an important role, or where the will of the bride-to-be was consulted. Thus Rebekah was asked whether she wanted to marry Isaac (Gen. 24:57); Jacob preferred Rachel to Leah, even though Leah was the older and would have been first in line (Gen. 29). Michal loved David (1 Sam. 18:20) and was loved, in turn, by Palti-el, to whom she had been given and who walked after her weeping when Abner took her away to return her to David (2 Sam. 3:16). It is probably safe to say that the whole range of emotions characterizing the marriage relationship today was present in ancient Israel, but that it did not provide the basis upon which marriages were contracted nor the yardstick by which they were evaluated.

The psychological satisfactions sought in marriage were generally those of security within the family clan structure, provision of daily needs and services, and many children to bring esteem in community affairs and to perpetuate one's name. Psychological suffering was caused, conversely, by being barren, by remaining or becoming childless, and by the insecure position in society that resulted from being a widow or an orphan. Several provisions, such as sub-stitution of a concubine by a barren wife,[4] the levirate,[5] and the institution of gō'ēl[6] aimed at relieving, in part, the conditions just mentioned. This is also true of the extensive body of legislation and wisdom admonitions in the interest of the widow, the orphan, and the sojourner.

Polygamy was permitted, as long as it was properly concluded. While it flourished at certain royal courts, partly for political reasons, and was practiced here and there outside of court life, it never became widespread or characteristic of the Israelite marriage situation. A simple reason must have been the availability of women. Beyond this, however, the Israelite view of marriage was a predominantly monogamous one, as is shown clearly by the admonitions of the wisdom books (Prov. 5:15-20; 31:10-31) and Malachi 2:13-16, but even more forcefully by the fact that the relationship between Israel and God, with all its claims of exclusiveness, could be pictured as a marriage relationship (Hos. 1-3; Jer. 2, here engagement; Ezek. 16).

In all of these matters—the place of women, the nature of the marriage relationship, the practice of polygamy—it is well to remember that the sociolegal definitions of any area of life represent certain outer limits beyond which lies the forbidden; they are better indicators of the direction in which the concerns of a society extend than characterizations of everyday practice. Thus society was structured by clan-families having their center of authority in the patriarch. This social structure was a treasured institution. It does not mean, however, that women did not enjoy a good deal of respect and authority under the assumed, though not necessarily strongly felt or continuously emphasized, overriding authority of their husbands or other male guardians. The Ten Commandments, for example, list the wife with a man's possessions, emphasizing her inferior sociolegal status, but children—and this certainly means adult children, not infants—are commanded to honor father and mother equally (Exod. 20:17 and 20:12). The "ideal wife" of Proverbs 31:10ff certainly appears to be the household manager. Women spoke freely with men, even with the king, and if they had acquired the reputation of being wise, they were consulted far and wide (2 Sam. 14; 20:14-22). We must not, then, assume that the everyday life of an Israelite woman was one of degradation and humiliation, much less one approaching slavery, even though she bore much of the household drudgery—as do most women today!— and was inferior to men in certain sociolegal respects.

Unmarried life figured only as an exception. As psychological compatibility between marriage partners was not a necessity and as finding a partner was not left to the intangibles of psychological lovemaking, almost everyone could be provided with a partner, precluding our situation where many remain unmarried against their wishes. Jephthah's daughter bewailed "her virginity," the fact that she had to die before having entered into marriage (Judg. 11:37-40). Tamar remained single in her brother Absalom's house because she had been violated by Amnon (2 Sam. 13:20). Jeremiah's unmarried state was to be a sign of the calamities that were to come upon the people (Jer. 16:1-9). Such instances, then, confirm the fact that married life was considered the norm for everyone, a norm broken only under exceptional circumstances of an undesirable nature.

Nothing meritorious or saintly attached to remaining unmarried, nor does the Old Testament know of it as a charismatic gift (cf. Matt. 19:12; 1 Cor. 7). Eunuchs (*sārîsîm*) are mentioned in the Old Testament, but they are usually identified as foreigners or as nameless officials at the royal courts. According to Isaiah 56:3 they were excluded from full participation in the cultus (cf. Deut. 23:1).

In 2 Kings 20:18 (parallel Isa. 39:7) the possibility that the king of Babylon may take Israelite young men to be eunuchs in his palace is stated as a threat. Eunuchs were certainly not an institution germaine to Israelite views, even if some Israelites may have become eunuchs now and then during the monarchy.

Divorce was permitted on the initiative of the husband (Deut. 24:1-4; cf. Isa. 50:1; Jer. 3:1, 8; Hos. 2:2). Adultery is indicated as a possible cause in Jeremiah 3:8, but the law of Deuteronomy 24:1-4 seems to imply lesser causes, for it is assumed not only that the woman would go unpunished but will marry again, while adultery was to be punished by death (Deut. 22:22). It is important to note that divorce is not to become an easy means to get rid of a woman whom a man has abused or treated in some exploiting or maligning way that would leave her at a disadvantage in society (Deut. 22:13-21; 28, 29).[7] The Book of Proverbs encourages faithfulness to the "wife of your youth," however (Prov. 5:18; cf. Jer. 2:), and Malachi 2:13-16 makes this into an absolute demand, stating that the Lord hates divorce.

Deviations from the norms of sexual behavior were largely evaluated in terms of their effect on marriage and family. Adultery, that is illicit sexual intercourse with or by a married woman, was strictly forbidden (Exod. 20:14; Lev. 18:20; 20:10). An engaged girl was subject to the same rules in this respect (Deut. 22:23-27). A dual standard prevailed, as men were not always held to the same restrictions as far as relations to unmarried women were concerned. To visit a prostitute was forbidden largely because of its religious associations with Canaanite cult prostitution (Deut. 23:17), but it was not always condemned or punished severely. Judah visited a prostitute (Gen. 38). The Book of Proverbs warns against dealings with a "strange woman," but on the basis of her wiles, not of legal threat. Adultery, on the other hand, was punishable by death (Deut. 22:22-27).

Virginity was highly prized. According to Deuteronomy 22:14ff. a girl who had become a willing partner to fornication was to be put to death. Rape of a virgin imposed on the man the duty to pay a price to her father and to take her to wife without the right to divorce (Deut. 22:28, 29). Practice did not always follow these strict demands, however. Amnon was not executed by law for violating Tamar (2 Sam. 13), though he fell prey to vengeance, nor was Judah for visiting a prostitute (Gen. 38).

Homosexuality or sodomy (Gen. 19: cf. Judg. 19) was forbidden and punishable by death (Lev. 18:22; 20:13). The same was true of intercourse with a beast (Lev. 18:23; 20:15f; Deut. 27:21). There are laws against various other practices related to the area of sex, such as the prohibition to marry within certain degrees of relationship (Lev. 18:6-18; 20:10-21), or to approach a woman during her menstrual period (Lev. 18:19). It is impossible to list here every such detail. Perhaps we should mention the subject of masturbation because it figures so prominently in sex education today, often under the name of "Onanism," with reference to the behavior of Onan (Gen. 38:1-11). The point of that story is, however, that Onan failed to fulfill the obligation of levirate marriage, not that he practiced masturbation. On the latter subject the Old Testament is silent.

It is necessary to conclude this section of our paper with a caution: when we speak of a sociological study of Israel's institutions, we must not appear to be duplicating for ancient Israel what the modern sociologist does for contemporary structures. The main reason for the impossibility of doing that is the fact that we are gleaning our information from data ranging over a long period of time and collected on the basis of altogether different principles of selection than those that the subject under discussion would demand, while the student of contemporary society can gather the directly relevant data along carefully established principles of selection. We will have to be satisfied to discern certain basic outlines of the social concerns and institutions of ancient Israel.

Sexuality in the Old Testament's Theology

In remarkable contrast to the conformity of Israel to her Ancient Near Eastern environment, sociologically speaking, stands the distinctness of her theological valuation of sexuality. Basic here is the consistent and central affirmation that God is neither male nor female. This was not a self-evident aspect of the definition of deity, which could be taken for granted almost unconsciously, as it is for us. It was a radical rejection of sexuality as the central divine-human fact, as the basis of life and religion, a rejection, in other words, of the fertility cult of the nature religions surrounding Israel. [8]

In these religions the gods were the forces of nature perceived as personal: storm-god, sun-god, and others. As the impact of these forces upon human life was felt to be a multiple one, there were many gods. The multiplicity was weighted however; some powers were felt to be of greater prominence as were, consequently, their divine embodiments. The central place of importance was held by those deities who were the "patrons" of the life-giving and life-sustaining powers of fertility, such as Baal, the god of rainstorms in agricultural, but rain-deficient Canaan, and Anath, his female consort.[9] Similar divine pairs characterized other nature religions. The union of god and goddess would safeguard fertility of fields, flocks, and humans and could be celebrated and enhanced by its imitation on earth through "sacred" prostitution at the shrines. The context of understanding was that of sympathetic magic: a properly performed ritual act on earth would be multiplied in its effectiveness by the divine powers.

In contrast to this faith based on the fertility cycle of nature, Israel gave a very different answer to the question: Where does man meet God? The answer was not in the repetitive reproductive aspects of nature, but in unique experiences of groups and individuals, that is, at certain significant junctures in history. These highlights of "revelation" illuminated human life from the center of things— God—and authenticated all history as subject to the ongoing guidance of God, as salvation history (*Heilsgeschichte*).

While God is certainly affirmed in the Old Testament as creator and controller of nature, including the biological nature of humans, the central and significant confrontation of humanity with God does not come primarily through the medium of the cycle of nature but in and through history. The relationship is, therefore, formulated primarily in historical-political metaphors: it is a covenant, patterned on the international covenant between a great nation and a lesser vassal. Only fairly late in Israel's history does Hosea wrest the terminology of love and family from Canaanite monopoly to apply it to God's relationship to Israel. God, the faithful husband, continues his faithfulness to an unfaithful, adulterous wife, Israel (Hos. 1-3).[10] The use of such sexual language is evoked directly by the need to affirm that the God of Israel is also the sovereign of natural fertility, and that fertility-sexuality is not a realm to be left to the monopoly of Baalism. After Hosea, the relationship of God to Israel could be presented figuratively as that of love, sex, and engagement and marriage (Jer. 2:2; Ezek. 16:23; Isa. 54:4-8), though it never displaced the political metaphor of covenant in the Old Testament.[11]

While "man" is created in the image of God (Gen. 1:26, 27), this must, consequently, be taken to focus on humanity, not on masculinity or femininity.[12] God is neither male nor female. "Man" stands before God as human being/ *Mensch* (*'ādām*), not as man, male human being/ *Mann* (*'ish*) or as woman, female human being/ *Frau* (*'ishshāh*). Sexuality belongs to the created order and stands second to humanity. We are first and primarily *'adam-/Mensch* and only in second place *'ish/Mann* and *'ishshāh/Frau*. [13]

In this light the position of woman, which we have characterized, sociologically, as inferior in a patriarchally-ruled society, is acknowledged to be equal. She is human being, *'ādām/Mensch*, just as her male counterpart (Gen. 1:27), and she stands before God as such. Both man and woman are responsible moral agents. Eve is as responsible as Adam to obey God's command and as responsible as he for breaking it (Gen. 3). The law is as binding upon women as upon men, and the prophets accuse women for covenant-breaking just as they do men (cf. Amos 4:1-3; Isa. 3:16-26). God expects faith of women. Sarah should have lived by trust in God's promise just as Abraham, and she becomes guilty when she rejects faith (Gen. 18:9-15). God uses women to be the instruments of special guidance, as is evident in the accounts of Sarah, Rebekah, Rachel, Hannah, Ruth, Huldah, and others. Particularly interesting is the fact that women, though generally excluded from institutional leadership, appear as charismatic leaders, such as "prophetesses" or "judges" (Exod. 15:20; Judg. 4:4; 2 Kings 22:14-20). The understanding seems to be: While we can order our society according to our own (patriarchal) lines, we cannot prescribe whom God must choose and endow with spiritual gifts; and theologically a woman is as capable of that as a man.

It is true that the patriarchal system has circumscribed the participation of women in worship: they are not allowed to be priests. Only the men are to appear at the central sanctuary three times a year (Exod. 23:17). Certain parts of the temple are not accessible to women. These restrictions pertain more to the sociological channels of communication with God, however, than to the content of that communication. As to the latter, woman is equally capable of prayer, of divine guidance, divine election, of faith, of guilt and forgiveness.

Our emphasis so far has been on the theological priority of being human as over against being male and female. This may seem to play into the hands of those who are interested in assigning to sexuality a lowly, or even a somewhat sinful role. We need to proceed now to show that this is not true of the Old Testament. It may be well to point out immediately that an ascetic condemnation of sex is really the reverse side of the divinization of it. Both ascribe central importance to it, whether for good or for evil. The ascetic [14] who seeks elimination of sex from his life in order to gain merit shares with the Canaanite who elevates to divinity the belief that sexuality is the center from which life must be understood. This is idolatry in the Old Testament, for God alone is the center. It leads to a warped view both of life generally and of sexuality in particular.

Human sexuality shares with that of animals the blessing "Be fruitful and multiply" (Gen. 1:22, 28). Children are repeatedly called a blessing. Human sexuality has meaning beyond procreation, however. In Genesis 2:18-24 the motive for the creation of woman—and therewith of the duality of the sexes—is to provide man with "a helper fit for him,' for "It is not good that the man should be alone." The whole account is permeated by the emphasis on the kinship between man and woman, their belonging together, their "rib-closeness," as we might say. Procreation is not at the center of this passage, although it is referred to, no doubt, in the statement that they shall "become one flesh," and is the fullest expression of their belonging together. That the marriage relationship extends beyond procreation is also borne out by the value placed on lifelong faithfulness of the partners to each other, as we find it in the admonitions not to reject the "wife of your youth" (Prov. 5:15-20; Mal. 2:13-16), but even more in the comparison of faithfulness in marriage with covenant faithfulness to God (Hos. 1-3; Jer. 2:2; Ezek. 16).

This emphasis on the centrality of the recognition of the partner of the (other) sex as a companion fit to be a helper because he or she is a part of one's self is substantiated by the use of the verb "to know" (*yāda'*) for sexual union. *Yāda'* is "to know" in the common meaning of that term. It is also the verb used to describe the relationship to God: the faithful know God; the unfaithful do not know him. God knows his own, but the unfaithful, God does not know. [15] It means, then, that the ultimate goal of sexuality is a "coming to know" one's partner. We should not think of the use of this verb as a euphemism only; it actually characterizes and defines sexual union. [16]

The fact that the fullest relation to one's sexual partner can be designated with the same term, "to know," as the fullest relation to God indicates clearly that sexuality belongs to the central aspects of one's being, to the highest levels of one's personality, if we can speak of such levels at all. It is not to be relegated to some lower physical aspect of a person in contrast to some higher spiritual aspect which relates to God. Such a division of human personality, imported into Christian thinking from Platonism, is absent from the Old Testament in any case. Each person is one unified self or personality, and one's sexuality is a divinely ordained component of that self. [17,18]

One further aspect of our subject needs to be emphasized:

sexuality extends beyond marriage. Marriage is unquestionably its ultimate expression both in the Old Testament and elsewhere. Adam and Eve are the prototype of a married couple—one man and one woman given as helpers and companions to each other, recognizing each other in their belonging together and producing offspring. Adam and Eve are also man and woman in a corporate sense. In that sense also they recognize each other as helpers to each other who, in their togetherness, rule and subdue the earth and raise a new generation. One man and one woman, in marriage, are created to be helpers for each other, but men and women in society are that to each other also. [19] One can observe the deterioration of genuine humanity in situations where the sexes are artificially separated for prolonged periods of time: for instance, in prisons, army camps, and mental hospitals. Where sexuality, being male and female, is restricted to marriage only, marriage becomes seclusive and selfish, and life outside of marriage takes on the false face of an artificial neutrality that betrays genuine humanity. In the Old Testament the corporate responsibility of the male segment of the community to the female segment, and vice versa, is continually asserted or implied. The greater cohesion of social groupings and the sharper sociological distinction of the realms of the two sexes preserved it in a way that is not to be taken for granted in our more fragmented and individual-centered society.

Some Implications for Today

While it is the specialized task of the New Testament scholar, the systematic theologian, and the Christian ethicist to define in detail the relevance of the Old Testament to the subject at hand as well as generally for the Christian today, I would probably disappoint some expectations if I would not at least indicate in outline some of my thoughts with respect to the implications as I see them. I must insist strongly, however, that I am speaking here primarily as a Christian, and not as a student of the Old Testament. This part of the paper is, in other words, much more subjective and personal than the foregoing and claims much less to be a statement of the results of the research of Old Testament scholarship.

My division of the discussion of the Old Testament situation into a sociological and a theological part shows my conviction that the Christian shares with the Old Testament its theology, but not the ritual or ethical applications of that theology to ancient times. [20] The New Testament, and the Christian church, work out a new set of specifications on the basis of a shared theology, an ethic that will largely overlap with that of the Old Testament, but will not necessarily be identical. Thus both the Old Testament believer and the Christian may hold that one should not marry one's sister (Lev. 20:17), but not because the Christian considers the Old Testament law in this respect as binding. That this is so becomes clear when we remind ourselves that we do not consider the law to regard the leper as unclean (Lev. 13) to be binding on us, even though it stands in the same corpus of laws as the law against marrying one's sister. I consider it helpful, therefore, to separate the sociological situation in ancient Israel, created and/or upheld by law held to be divine in origin,[21] from the theology that defined and defines the faith.[22]

I do not think, consequently, that we should scan the Old Testament for laws on marriage, divorce, adultery, or the position of women in order to apply them as the Word of God to our time. Jesus does not do this either. He recognizes that Mosaic Law allows divorce, for example, but on the basis of the story of the creation of man and woman (Gen. 2)—that is, on the basis of the theology of sexuality—he sets up a new perspective for his followers (Matt. 19:3-9). Of course, it is good and instructive to know the Old Testament laws and to test carefully what New Testament ethics might say on the same subject. Our concern should be to find adequate expression of the biblical view of human sexuality in our time. My study of the Old Testament's perspective on the subject directs my attention—perhaps in a subjective selectivity—to the following:

1. Sexuality must not hold the dominant place in a Christian's understanding of humanity. The human race finds its proper focus in God; everything else, including human sexuality, is "in orbit." On the negative side this calls for a rejection of certain Freudian emphases as well as certain forms of asceticism that want to give to sexuality an equally central, though negative, place. On the positive side it offers a theological basis for a positive, nonprudish togetherness of men and women in their status of equality before God and their far-reaching equality of capacities and of needs. The biblical doctrine of humanity actually means the emancipation of woman. Up to a point Christianization has always meant that, be it in the Roman Empire or on the mission fields of our time. At some points the church has stopped short of drawing the full consequences of the biblical perspective, however, or has followed grudgingly in the steps of secular reformers.

2. The distinction between the sexes ought to be acknowledged and expressed. Pieter de Jong is right when he emphasizes the constancy of sexual difference over against the changing cultural

expressions of that difference.[23] To give a crude illustration: there is no *theological* reason why men should wear trousers and women skirts and not vice versa. The opposite situation would express distinction just as well. But there is no theological reason why that distinction should manifest itself in clothing at all, rather than in other ways. However, every society should acknowledge the distinction of the sexes in sufficiently many areas of life and sufficiently tangibly to safeguard a sense of awareness of this basic nature of humanity which is full of realism and meaning for human togetherness. The signs of the distinction must characterize each society in the long run; they are in most cases not to be imposed legalistically upon every individual at every moment. In the example given above the differentiation of clothing, if that is one of the signs of sexual distinction, need not mean that one must be particularly concerned that each woman wear female garments at each moment; or, more simply, it is quite in order for a gallant gentleman to offer his coat and hat to his lightly-clad and shivering lady!

This somewhat trivial and perhaps even ludicrous example illustrates a principle of widest implications. As mental exercise the reader might want to think it through with respect to "male" and "female" psychological traits. The value to be safeguarded is the quality of complementarity of life together, of being companions and helpers to each other, both individually, in marriage, and corporately, in society.[24] Where this is abandoned in favor of a regimented uniformity, a basic theological order of creation has been violated. Actually the loss of this distinction seems less real a threat than its misinterpretation, and that in two directions.[25] On the one hand the intended life together in the tension of sexual duality (male and female) is threatened by a legalistic externalization of it into matters of dress and decorum. On the other hand there lurks the danger of over-accentuation of it by a playing up of the rivalry of the sexes in their urge toward domineering or alluring the other, a rivalry which points to the effect of the Fall on sexuality, rather than to its God-intended nature.[26]

3. The goal of human sexuality is not exhausted in procreation. Human sexuality, unlike that of animals, has as its aim a relationship in which man and woman are companion and helper to each other. Their belonging together will result in procreation, but it also possesses a value, dignity and purpose in its own right. The Roman Catholic emphasis on procreation as the only ligitimation of sexual intercourse represents a limitation of the biblical purpose of sexuality. However, we must hasten to add that such a criticism does

not involve wholesale approval of all contraceptive means and practices. The divine blessing of procreation and the sacred gift of the child must be upheld. [27]

4. The sexual duality of human life is not limited to or exhausted by the marriage relationship. Human beings live as male and female in all situations; their relationships to others are never sexually neutral. The unmarried person also shares in the duality and is fully human, and the married person does not find sexual duality limited to marriage, although certain aspects of it are. This needs to be acknowledged, especially in Protestantism. It then poses the question how both a false veneer of sexual neutrality and an improper accentuation of sexual differences can be avoided. The relationship of siblings to each other may offer a practical model here, admittedly one upheld only by the strongest taboos.

5. Perhaps the most dangerous and most potent threat to a biblical approach to sexuality comes from the modern counterparts of the ancient nature religions. As the fertility cults of old beckoned their worshipers to find wholeness and salvation in fitting themselves harmoniously into the cycle of nature, various modern views of life also invite us to find our values in "that which is natural," to live "according to the laws of nature," especially in matters of sex. This elevation of the cycle of nature to divine authority is subtle and alluring just as was the Baalism of Canaan, and it calls for a decision between Yahweh and Baal.

Notes

[1] First and foremost, Roland de Vaux, *Ancient Israel* (New York: McGraw-Hill, 1965), 2 vols. An extensive bibliography on marriage, family, and related subjects can be found there, Vol. I, pp. xxvii-xxix. Ludwig Koehler's *Hebrew Man,* translated by P. R. Ackroyd (Nashville: Abingdon, 1957), though brief, offers a coherent picture of the web of Hebrew life. For an authoritative and stimulating treatment which accentuates the otherness and distinctiveness of ancient Hebrew understanding of life, as compared to modern attitudes, see Johs. Pedersen, *Israel, Its Life and Culture* (London: Oxford University Press, Vols. I-II, 1926; first published 1920). Two most significant works on our subject appeared after the completion of this paper and could, unfortunately, not be considered: Hans Walter Wolff, *Anthropology of the Old Testament,* trans. Margaret Kohl (Fortress, 1974); and Norman K. Gottwald, *The Tribes of Yahweh: A Sociology of the Religion of Liberated Israel, 1250-1050 B.C.E.* (Maryknoll, New York: Orbis Books, 1979).

[2] Roland de Vaux, *Ancient Israel,* vol. I, p. 20. The "father's house" (*bêt'âb*) was the living community which embraced the three or four generations (cf. Exod. 20:5!) descended from the same patriarch. It was the basic economic unit. The family-clan *(mishpāḥāh)* was the association of several father's houses for the purposes of protection. In nomadic times it was made up of adjacent groupings of tents and in settled life it basically constituted the town or village community.

[3] The term *charismatic leader* comes from the Greek word *charisma,* "spiritual gift," as used for example, by Paul in 1 Corinthians 12. It is used widely in biblical

scholarship to designate persons who were endowed by God with special capacities to carry out his will in particular crises. Thus Saul becomes the charismatic leader who rises to the occasion when the people of Jabesh-gilead plead for help (1 Sam. 11). The "judges" and the prophets of the Old Testament are generally considered to be such "charismatics." In contrast to the "charismatic leaders' stand the institutional leaders, men who are duly appointed to fill an established and continuous office, such as that of king, priest, governor, etc. "Charismatic" should not be associated in any specific way with the modern charismatic movement.

⁴ Thus Sarah gives her Egyptian maid Hagar to Abraham (Gen 16:1ff.). See Roland de Vaux, *Ancient Israel*, Vol. I, p. 24 for further discussion.

⁵ The *levirate* is the institution that the brother of a man who has died childless ought to take his widow "to build up his brother's house" by having a son with her. That son was considered to be the offspring of the deceased (Deut. 25:5-10; cf. Gen. 38 and Matt. 22:24-27). See Roland de Vaux, *Ancient Israel*, Vol. I pp. 37f. for further discussion.

⁶ The word *gō'ēl* is the present participle of the Hebrew verb *gā'al*, "to redeem, to act as kinsman": "one who redeems, acts as kinsman." In the closely-knit Hebrew clan-family each member could count on his relatives, in a defined order of priority, to take up his cause and fend for him. To act as kinsman might mean to enter into levirate marriage, to buy back a relative sold into slavery, to buy some land to keep it in the family, or even to perform blood vengeance. The role of Boaz with respect to Ruth, in the Book of Ruth, is a good illustration of the *gō'ēl*-function.

⁷ A similar concern for the woman is evident in the law that a captive woman, having been taken to wife, could not be sold when no longer wanted but had to be set free (Deut. 21:10-14).

⁸ Nontechnical, but authoritative accounts of these religions may be found in the following: John L. McKenzie, *The Two-Edged Sword* (London: Geoffrey Chapman, 1965; first published 1956), Ch. III: "The Gods of the Semites." G. Ernest Wright, *The Old Testament Against Its Environment* (Chicago: Alec R. Allenson, 1950), especially pp. 16-19. H. and H. A. Frankfort, John A. Wilson, Thorkild Jacobsen, *Before Philosophy* (Baltimore: Penguin Books, 1949 and later). Originally published as *The Intellectual Adventure of Ancient Man* (Chicago: University of Chicago Press, 1946).

⁹ Anath is Baal's consort in Canaanite literature. In the Old Testament she appears infrequently, her place as Baal's female partner having been taken by Asherah, a different female deity in Canaanite writings. The nature gods, like the forces they embody, are somewhat fluid as to their personal identity.

¹⁰ Even at that, Hosea's use of sexual language to draw an analogy between his own marriage and the "marriage" of God and Israel serves the purpose of illustration only; it lacks the "sacramental" realism with which an event on the human scene was seen as a reflection of divine reality in the ancient nature religions.

¹¹ It is misleading, therefore, if William Graham Cole begins his book—perhaps the most voluminous treatment of sex in the Bible—by presenting Hosea's characterization of the relationship of God to Israel, namely that of a husband to his unfaithful wife, as the proper starting point and climax of love in the Old Testament and goes so far as to say that "...all the developments in early Hebrew thought are in some sense preparatory to and gathered up in the career and the message of this wronged husband." *Sex and Love in the Bible*, (New York: Association Press, 1959), pp. 15f. The false perspective thus introduced is mitigated only somewhat when he contrasts Israel's sex attitudes and practices with those of her neighbors (*Ibid.*, pp. 193-229), and it is made three times worse when he sets Hosea's demand for "knowledge" of God into a simple equation to a Freudian demand for a "normal *vita sexualis*" as prevention of neurosis (*ibid.*, p. 277).

¹² When Pieter de Jong says, "The plurality in the life of man is a reflection of

plurality in the life of God," this must be rejected emphatically, at least for the Old Testament, even if it is supported by reference to Karl Barth. Pieter de Jong, "Christian Anthropology: Biblical View of Man," *Sex, Family and Society in Theological Focus,* edited by John Charles Wynn (New York: Association Press, 1966), p. 63. (The reference to Barth is to *Kirchliche Dogmatik,* III, 2 [Zollikon-Zurich: Evangelischer Verlag, 1948], SS. 242ff.). The Old Testament is not concerned with explicating Yahweh as Trinity, but with differentiating him from Baal. Even the cautious and finely nuanced exposition by Phyllis Trible "The Text in Context" *God and the Rhetoric of Sexuality,* (Philadelphia: Fortress, 1978), pp. 15-21, esp. the last paragraph, seems to me to burden the phrase "male and female he created them" (Gen. 1:27) with the wrong function. Rather than reflecting the nature of God in however indirect a sense, this phrase should be seen, I believe, as a safeguard against reading '*ādām* in the preceding verses as a male term. After all, the priestly writer of Genesis 1-2:4a must have known the use of "Adam" with male personal name overtones in Genesis 2:4bff.

[13] Helmut Thielicke rightly warns against a tendency in some quarters "to ignore the sex difference, which then produces an abstract concept of 'man' which has been stripped of all reality," but agrees that "the theological ontology of human existence must not go so far as to imagine that it can express the idea of *imago Dei only* by means of this sex differentiation." *The Ethics of Sex,* translated by J. W. Doberstein, (New York: Harper & Row, 1964), p. 6. We trust that the further pages of this paper will preserve proper balance with respect to the reality and theological significance of sexuality on the one hand, and its noncentral position in the Old Testament when compared to its place in the surrounding fertility cults, on the other.

[14] We refer here only to that brand of asceticism which sees the reduction or elimination of sex as absolutely desirable; we do not mean the charismatic call to the single life which some feel (cf. Jeremiah, Paul, and Jesus himself), nor the discipline of abstention for a time (1 Cor. 7:6).

[15] This is pointed out correctly by Otto J. Baab in his informative article "Sex, Sexual Behavior," *The Interpreter's Dictionary of the Bible* (New York: Abingdon Press, 1962), Vol. 4, p. 300. The whole article offers an easily accessible summary of biblical information, though its treatment of the *theology* of sex is extremely scanty.

[16] See Otto A. Piper, *The Christian Interpretation of Sex* (New York: Charles Scribner's Sons, 1953), pp. 52ff., for a profound discussion of sexual union as "knowing."

[17] The contrast between the biblical view of humanity and the Platonic view is a generally understood and accepted gain of more recent biblical scholarship. It is well presented in the article by Pieter de Jong (*op. cit.*). For a fuller presentation of the Old Testament view of human personality see the excellent discussion by Walther Eichrodt, *Theology of the Old Testament,* translated by John Baker (Philadelphia: Westminster Press, Vol. II, 1967), pp. 131-50: "The Components of Human Nature."

[18] In discussions pointing out the dignity given to sex in the Old Testament it has become customary to point to the open and unrestrained treatment of sexual love in the Song of Solomon. It is common knowledge, however, that this book has been admitted to the biblical canon only on the basis of an allegorical interpretation. While it elucidates some aspects of ancient lovemaking, its theological significance for our present study is peripheral.

[19] If one neglects this corporate meaning, one is led to views such as the following: "What is, in fact, conveyed in sexual intercourse is a knowledge both of one's self and of another. No man really knows what it means to be a man until he has experienced sex with a woman; and every woman is similarly innocent until she has

had relations with a man" (Cole, *op.cit.,* p. 276). Did Jeremiah or Paul not know what it means to be a man? We hold that they did, and that they were companions and helpers to woman in a corporate sense, even though not in the individual sense of marriage.

[20] Sometimes it is said that the ethical laws of the Old Testament are authoritative for the Christian, while the ritual laws are not. Such a distinction is not biblical. The Old Testament does not distinguish between "ritual" and "ethical" commands but intermingles them thoroughly in the same codes. We should, instead, distinguish between the basic theological perspectives, on the one hand, and their detailed application or acknowledgment in specific times and situations, on the other.

[21] If we say that law which was considered by Israel to be divine in origin is not always binding on us, this is not a denial of such divine origin. It merely means that we must not assume that whatever God commanded to some people under some circumstances was meant to be universal law. On the other hand, detailed applications arising from the same theology will not be in basic contradiction to those of other times and places, if one acknowledges a consistent, "faithful" God.

[22] Cf. Thielicke, *op. cit.*, p. 108, where he contrasts the legal regulations with the "kerygmatic core," the latter being the basis for later interpretations.

[23] Pieter de Jong, *op. cit.*, pp. 80ff.

[24] Cf. Thielicke, *op. cit.*, pp. 3ff. for a discussion of the theologically basic nature of this "Mitmenschlichkeit," this I-Thou-duality of the sexes.

[25] There seems to be an innate tendency in humanity to counteract a regimented uniformity of the sexes. Even certain communistic attempts at reduction to "equality" have been short-lived.

[26] Cf. Thielicke, *op. cit.*, p. 8

[27] See my essays "Quality of Life: A Biblical Study" and "Biblical Perspectives on Youth" in this volume, pp. 118-33 and 109-17, respectively.

Male and Female Roles in the Old Testament

Genesis 1 to 3 are the best known chapters of the Old Testament equalled in popularity only by the Ten Commandments and Psalm 23. They deserve their fame and are, therefore, properly highlighted by special treatment. On the other hand, they have often unduly overshadowed, or even usurped, the significance of the Old Testament as a whole. [1] For that reason it is appropriate to focus on the rest of the Old Testament and hear what this bulk of literature has to say on the subject of male and female roles. Now, I do not see a substantive difference between Genesis 1 to 3 and the rest of the Old Testament; it is their popularity and overinterpretation which frequently gives these chapters an apparently different and higher significance.

Let us turn, then, to a consideration of what it meant to be male or female in Old Testament Israel. I am deliberately stating the subject historically, rather than theologically. I shall ask what the roles of the sexes actually were in ancient Israel. [2] However, I shall then also ask briefly where Old Testament teaching affirmed or transcended ancient Israelite reality. Finally, I will conclude with a few evaluative thoughts concerning the Old Testament situation, comparing it with certain modern perspectives.

Human Before God

What did it mean to be male in ancient Israel? To start with that question immediately raises a basic objection: Can we start here? Must we not ask the prior question: What did it mean to be human, no matter whether male or female? Indeed, that is the proper starting point, and the answer—in its most general form—is simple.

To be human, or to be man in the sense of the German *Mensch,* means to be responsible to God. Whether this responsibility was heeded or disregarded, whether the response to it took one form or another was secondary. Before God, male and female stood together: God had created both, was expecting loyalty from both, punished both for transgressions, made forgiveness, blessing and promises available to both.

Before God, humanity is first of all "human being," and only secondarily male and female, just as God himself—in contrast to all the deities of the surrounding nations—is neither male nor female. God can be referred to in both male and female images, even though male images and masculine grammatical forms predominate, for social and linguistic, rather than theological reasons.[3] To see the plurality of male and female as having an analogy in the threefoldness of the Trinity—even if proposed by as venerable a theologian as Karl Barth[4]—seems unacceptable when one considers the century-long struggle of Israel with Baalism, that Canaanite fertility cult which made precisely this sexuality with its implications for fertility, its ontological center.[5] No, in the Old Testament, God is neither male nor female, and God confronts humanity, first of all, in his common humanness. The distinctiveness and complementarity of the sexes, though basic to all interaction on the human plane and created and blessed by God, rests on a solid basis of common humanity. In other words, man and woman have more in common than separates them. However, their differences are for that reason no less real, and they must draw our attention now.

Boys and Girls in Ancient Israel

A distinction between boy and girl set in almost immediately after birth: the boy was circumcised, receiving in his body the sign of the Abrahamic covenant (Gen. 17). No such initiation rite into the religious community existed for the little girl. In keeping with this, throughout most of Israel's history, there was greater openness towards intermarriage if the woman rather than the man was a foreigner.[6]

The childhood of boys and girls was not marked by any significant differentiation except the naturally greater association of son and father, daughter and mother. That led to a tendency for the boy to tend the flock and work in the field, while the girl would help her mother around the house. These lines were not sharply drawn, however; girls did work in the fields, and boys would help their mothers. As to parental authority, the father had a certain formal precedence, but father and mother are frequently named side by side, as in the commandment to honor father and mother (Exod. 20:12). Neither boy or girl received formal schooling; both acquired the necessary skills by observation and practice. Both had to share in the workload of the family from early childhood on.

Childhood ended early and abruptly with puberty for both boy and girl. A specific ceremony comparable to the later Jewish Bar Mitzvah is not known from the Old Testament, and the assessment of maturity may have taken different forms in different places.

The Role of the Man

Ludwig Koehler[7] has outlined simply and forthrightly what it meant to become a man, namely, participation in four great orders of life: those of cultus, justice, marriage, and war. (1) The cultus was not relegated to priests and Levites; its performance was incumbent on every adult male. Three times a year, ideal legislation demanded, he was to appear before the Lord at the central sanctuary (Exod. 23:17). In the bringing of tithes and sacrifices he had his specific role. Ritual cleanness was incumbent on him at certain times. As to ethics, he was the upholder of the law in his own household. The education of the young in matters of faith was also his responsibility (Deut. 6:20ff).

(2) The second great order of life for the Hebrew man was marriage. That he would marry was assumed as a matter of course, just as it was for each woman. Marriage was intitiated by the man, or between families. Since it was not left to individual courtship or to the development of subtle psychological affinities, much of the premarital and marital anxieties of today were unknown. That does not mean that love was not present between partners; we can assume that all the shades of interpersonal tenderness known to us were known to the Israelites as well.[8] It does mean that the forces which initiated a marriage and sustained it were primarily social, and only secondarily psychological. Polygamy was permitted in Israel, but apart from the royal court and certain ruling circles it must always have been practiced sparingly. Toward later Old Testament times it is definitely discouraged.[9] Children were the expected result and blessing of marriage—the more the better, especially if they were sons. That preference is undoubtedly related to the fact that sons stayed within the household, while daughters married outside.

(3) The upholding of justice was the third great order of life in which each Hebrew man participated. While the king's court served as court of appeal, most cases were settled "in the gate," that is, in the

assembly of male adults which could easily be called together in the open area just inside the town gate. The elders presided, but each member of the town or village assembled could raise his voice in accusation, defense, witness, and decision making. [10]

(4) Finally, each Hebrew man shared in the right and duty of defense. We must not hear this statement as carrying that ethos of "blood, honor, and heroism" which has surrounded military service from the ancient Romans to modern nationalistic and imperialistic states. [11] For the most part, Hebrew life was farming life in village and small town. Defense often meant little more than to perform a watchman's night duty or to protect the herds and flocks from wild animals, thieves, and robbers. Added to this were conflicts with neighboring towns, regions, or tribes. Only occasionally did a wider emergency call the Israelite farmer to arms for a time. Professional royal armies did exist from David's time, but they must have remained relatively small, and service in them was a matter for only a few.

Participation in the cultus, in marriage, in the dispensing of justice, and in defense of the community—that was what distinguished a Hebrew man as a man. It would be wrong to say that this was his role, if by role we mean his characteristic daily activity and behavior. The chief mark of his daily life was work, mostly unspecialized work as a peasant, or lightly specialized work as an artisan. But this did not make him a man, for work began for him as a child, and it was shared by the woman.

In each of his four distinctive roles he could "advance," so to speak. In the religious realm, the ideal was the "righteous" or "blameless" man. In marriage, it was his goal and reward to see his children and children's children grow up and perpetuate his name. In the affairs of the community, he might rise in wisdom and influence and sit among the elders in the gate. As a warrior, his skill and strength might be admired, though heroism in war attracted but limited glory and was not an end in itself.

The Role of the Woman

The role of the woman differed in many, though not in all respects. Like her husband's life, hers was one of daily work. With him she shared the duties of raising and educating the children. She was neither veiled nor restricted to house and yard, as women have been in many societies. A certain anxious and prudish concern for guarding her in the name of chastity, which came to characterize later rabbinic Judaism, is absent from the Old Testament. [12] She met the other women at the village well, talked freely with men, had some scope to develop her own entrepreneurial skills (Prov. 31:10-31), and had access to some of the professions of the time, such as those of midwife, mourner, and a few others.

The special task and dignity of the woman in Israel was childbearing. She had no need to worry about getting married: society looked after that, just as it did for the man. Her anxiety concerned her ability to bear children. Barrenness was the threat that hung over the young woman's life until she had given birth to her first child (Gen. 16:2, 30:2; 1 Sam. 1:5). Beyond that, her dignity and self-assurance grew as she became the mother of many. This was, in brief, the distinctive feature of her female role, although it did not in any way exhaust the variety of occupations that filled her life.

The realms of the cultus, of the maintenance of justice, and of defense and warfare were not directly accessible to her; generally speaking she participated in them as a member of the family, rather than as agent for the family. There are instances, to be sure, where women led in battle, were renowned for wisdom, or proclaimed God's word as prophetesses.

Evaluative Comments

My approach to our subject has been descriptive, outlining how it was in Israel. Let us ask briefly whether the Old Testament also teaches that it should be so, that is, whether it claims that the roles as described are normative. In this connection we must, first, remind ourselves of the concrete nature of the Old Testament: it does not generally theorize, philosophize, or dogmatize. God is not proclaimed in doctrines, but in stories; Israel tells of her experiences as a people and shows how God's power, leading, promise, testing, punishment, or redeeming permeated this story. Similarly, the Old Testament does not theorize about the nature of humanity. Genesis 1 to 3, the chapters excluded from this anaylsis, come closest to doing so. Israel lived her human role, with its male and female dimensions, and confessed that in that life it was possible to experience God and that through that life it was possible to respond to God and to praise God. In other words, the roles just described are seen in a positive light, though they are not idealized. Man's efforts are resisted by the thorns and thistles in his field. Woman's life is beset by the pain associated with her most dignified function. This was the consequence of sin. Nevertheless, life was under God, and it was good. There was no despair about the human condition as such, though there were agonizing laments about particular calamities. To this extent we can say that the Old Testament affirms life as lived in Israel, if it was lived well, i.e., the life of those who found approval in Israel.

Nevertheless, the prophets proclaimed hope for a new life to come when the "day of the Lord" would appear. These prophecies foresee a change from present injustice to future justice, and from present strife to future peace. A change in the roles of sexes, however, either toward different roles or toward a sexless existence, is nowhere predicted. We must assume, then, that this area of life is not judged by the Old Testament as having suffered particular perversion. On the other hand, we should not read an idealization of every feature of male or female existence into this observation. Before God, the sexes have a togetherness and equality that far outshadows the social situation. Herein lies an implicit challenge to the socially conditioned aspects of Israelite life which tend toward inequality of the sexes. [13] This situation is no different from the New Testament, where the ideal of equality (Gal. 3:28) and the social demands of the times in the Pauline churches (1 Cor. 11:2-16), stand in a certain tension.

Concluding Cautions

Our final section shall be devoted to a few cautions which ought to be raised, lest we evaluate the Old Testament situation on the basis of modern viewpoints, and thereby unavoidably misread it. Two areas may serve to illustrate the problem: (1) From a present-day North American middle-class standpoint, one may wonder whether Israelite women had "fewer chances in life" than the men. Their lives centered in the home. They did not have access to the public and leadership functions associated with cultus, justice, and war. Underlying such a perspective, however, is the high valuation which a capitalistic, entrepreneurial, individualistic, pioneering society places on movement and power. Did an Israelite woman really wish to go to the central sanctuary in Jerusalem, with its arduous and dangerous journey? Did she envy her husband when he rushed off to the gate to debate a case, or grabbed for his weapons to go to war? The Old Testament gives no evidence of such feelings. But further, did the Israelite man perceive these "chances" of his as enviable? Or did they place heavy burdens on him? To be sure, they were endowed with dignity, but was that not precisely because they were taxing, arduous, and fraught with danger?

(2) Many women today may point indignantly to the supposed

stereotyping and restricting of women to the role of mother and childbearer. But again, we have to bring to consciousness certain modern assumptions: many modern Western women do not value childbearing highly. Professional careers offer an alternative to the mother-and-housewife role. World overpopulation places in question the blessedness of many children. In the modern economy, children are a liability, instead of an asset. Social security is provided in ways other than the security of the family. And the safer and easier ways of childbirth and infant care diminish the sense of bravery and accomplishment of having given birth to and raised many children. The reverse was true for the Hebrew woman. We can be sure that her craving for children (Gen. 30:1) was not a sublimation of other desires, and that her rejoicing in children was not a surrogate for other satisfactions denied her. While other areas of easy misapprehension could be added, these may suffice to indicate the problem.

What, then, does an assessment of male and female roles in the Old Testament hold for us? The gains can be multiple. (1) As a historical study it is intended to throw some light on the life of Old Testament Israel. (2) From a theological vantage point, it attempts to outline how God chose to reveal himself in and through one particular ancient form of social existence, with its time-bound particulars but also its persistent self-definition with reference to God. (3) For our own time, with its renewed attempts to understand the roles of the sexes right, a study such as this might offer long-range perspective. It might invite us to see the meanings and values attributed to the sexes among other people, a people singled out by God for a very special role in his plans. If we are sensitive, we will respect these meanings and values, and they in turn will help us to balance our own views and preferences, to protect us from thoughtless or one-sided innovations, and to challenge us to persist in our search for the God-intended definition of human nature and society.

Notes

[1] A striking recent illustration of this is Paul K. Jewett, *Man as Male and Female* (Grand Rapids: Eerdmans, 1975). In this theological study, which subscribes to a high view of the Scriptures, a voluminous discussion of the *imago dei* (Genesis 1:27) stands over against an almost complete disregard of the remainder of the Old Testament.

[2] Particularly valuable and authoritative reference works on this subject are: Ludwig Koehler, *Hebrew Man*, translated by Peter R. Ackroyd (Nashville: Abingdon, 1975); Roland de Vaux, *Ancient Israel* (McGraw-Hill Paperback; New York: McGraw-Hill, 1965), Vol. 2, pp. 19-61: and Hans Walter Wolff,

Anthropology of the Old Testament, translated by Margaret Kohl (Philadelphia: Fortress, 1974), especially pp. 166-76.

³ This point is made well by Phyllis Trible in her provocative, if at times a bit forced, article "Depatriarchalizing in Biblical Interpretation," *Journal of the American Academy of Religion* XLI/1 (March 1973): pp. 30-48. Some of the female images for God, cited by Trible, are: Isaiah 42:14b; 49:15; 66:9, 13; Psalm 22:9-10a (midwife); Numbers 11:12. Cf. her more recent book, *God and the Rhetoric of Sexuality* (Philadelphia: Fortress Press, 1978). See also my article "Sexuality in the Old Testament" in this volume pp. 68-83 on this point and as background to this essay generally.

⁴ *Church Dogmatics,* III, 2, pp. 323f. This view is echoed, for example, by Pieter de Jong "Christian Anthropology: Biblical View of Man," *Sex, Family and Society in Theological Focus,* edited by John Charles Wynn (New York: Association Press, 1966),p. 63; and by Paul K. Jewett, *op.cit.,* who says: "As God is a fellowship in himself (Trinity) so Man is a fellowship in himself, and the fundamental form of this fellowship, so far as man is concerned is that of male and female" (pp. 13f). See my discussion above, p. 81, note 12.

⁵ Nontechnical, but authoritative accounts of Baalism and other Ancient Near Eastern nature religions may be found in John L. McKenzie, *The Two-Edged Sword,* (London: Geoffrey Chapman, 1965); G. Ernest Wright, *The Old Testament Against Its Environment* (Chicago: Alec R. Allenson, 1950) especially pp. 16-19; H. and H. A. Frankfort, John A. Wilson, Thorkild Jacobsen, *Before Philosophy,* (Baltimore: Penguin Books, 1949 and later); and John Gray, *The Canaanites,* (London: Thames and Hudson, 1964).

⁶ Cf. the story of Ruth. An exception was the time of Ezra and Nehemiah.

⁷ Koehler, *Hebrew Man,* pp. 74ff.

⁸ Cf. the Song of Songs; Genesis 24:67; 29:16-20; Deuteronomy 21:15-17; 1 Samuel 1:8; 2 Samuel 3:16; etc. The relationship of love to marriage in Israel is discussed helpfully by H. W. Wolff, *Anthropology of the Old Testament,* pp. 169-73.

⁹ The approximately equal number of men and women in any society is sufficient to limit polygamy. That monogamy was considered normal is borne out by passages such as Proverbs 5:18; Isaiah 54:6; Malachi 2:14f; Joel 1:8, and especially by the fact that the exclusive relationship between God and Israel is repeatedly pictured in analogy to marriage (Hos. 1-3; Jer. 2:2; Ezek. 16).

¹⁰ Cf. Koehler, *Hebrew Man,* Appendix: "Justice in the Gate."

¹¹ Cf. my article "War in the Old Testament," *Mennonite Quarterly Review* 46 (1972); pp. 155-56, reprinted in this volume, pp. 173-86.

¹² Cf. de Vaux, *Ancient Israel,* Vol. 1, p. 30. For the situation in rabbinic Judaism, see Louis M. Epstein, *Sex Laws and Customs in Judaism,* (New York: KTAV Publishing House, 1967), first published 1948.

¹³ Phyllis Trible puts it well: "I know that Hebrew literature comes from a male dominated society. . . . Nevertheless, I affirm that the intentionality of biblical faith, as distinguished from a general description of biblical religion, is neither to create nor to perpetuate patriarchy but rather to function as salvation for both women and men," (*op.cit.,* p. 31).

Education in the Old Testament and in Early Judaism

I.

Education as we think of it was unknown in Old Testament Israel. No school system existed, although some scholars claim that literacy was widespread.[1] Learning did take place, however, and at times, perhaps, in ways less lost in massive educational bureaucracies and more appropriate to the needs of the people than it does today.

What else is education than "a conversation between generations"? I heard this definition years ago, and I do believe that it describes well the heart and soul of that vast realm of endeavors. The Old Testament offers us some very basic models of such conversation, models that are effective today also, but can be seen more clearly in their forthright simplicity in Old Testament times. They are the models of parent and child, wise man and "fool," master and disciple, and priest and member of the congregation of Israel.

1. *Parent and child.* This is the primary learning relationship among all peoples, and even among many animals. Such learning begins at birth, and for the Israelite son or daughter, who continued to live in the context of the "father's house" (*bêt'âb*) or extended family,[2] it had no formal conclusion. The "curriculum" of this schooling consisted of the things needful to know for the survival and flourishing of the individual and the social group. A distinction between learning and work, such as we know, did not exist. Learning was largely imitation by doing. As children outgrew the first infant years, boys imitated the ways of their fathers and the other men, while girls watched their mothers and the other women.

Life in Old Testament Israel was not prudishly segregated, however.

Adulthood was marked for the man by the right to participate in four great orders of life: marriage, justice, warfare, and cultus.[3] A girl achieved womanhood through marriage and childbearing. Exact ages and specific ceremonies of passage are not reported to us.[4] And we should remember that the achievement of such marks of adulthood did not mean economic, vocational or social "independence," as we think of it, for the young man remained a part of his father's house, while the young woman joined the father's house of her husband.

"Religious education" was not set apart as a separate compartment of learning.

> When your son asks you in time to come, "What is the meaning of the testimonies and the statutes and the ordinances which the Lord our God has commanded you?" then you shall say to your son, "We were Pharaoh's slaves in Egypt; and the Lord brought us out of Egypt . . ."

In this way the classical statement in Deuteronomy 6:20-21 incorporates religious education into the everyday conversation between parent and child (Exod. 10:2; 12:26, 27; 13:8; Deut. 4:9; 6:7; 32:7, 46). We can be sure that such learning was considered just as important for individual and group survival as the arts of ploughing the field, grinding flour, or making a garment. And in this area, perhaps even more than in other realms of life, learning remained open-ended, for father and mother also continued to learn from the priests and the sages, as we shall see shortly.[5]

2. *Wise man and "fool."* The individual household was embedded in the clan (*mishpāḥāh*) or village. This expanded social context offered further scope for learning. L. Koehler has given us a masterful description of the ancient Israelite "village circle" (*sôd*).[6] It was the gathering of the men of the village after the day's work was done, while the women and girls were still occupied with the household chores. They would meet under a big tree, or at the well, or at the open place by the gate. No one was forced to come, but everyone wanted to be there, to enjoy the fellowship, to exchange the news of the day, to hear the stories of someone just back from a journey, to sing the familiar songs and, last but not least, to engage in that mental activity[7] which we may call "popular wisdom" or "folk wisdom" in contrast to its more sophisticated relative called "court wisdom."

The village circle is the life setting of many of the proverbs and riddles we find in the Book of Proverbs, beginning with chapter 10.

After the bustle of news exchange had settled down, one of the elders might raise his voice:

A glad heart makes a cheerful countenance.

This was a challenge which another was quick to take up:

But by sorrow of heart the spirit is broken (Prov. 15:13).

Then another voice:

A wise son makes a glad father.

And the reply out of the darkness of the evening:

But a foolish son is a sorrow to his mother (Prov. 10:1).

And another challenge:

Three things are too wonderful for me; four I do not understand.

After some silence, a voice might venture forth with a first answer:

The way of an eagle in the sky.

A second voice:

The way of a serpent on a rock.

A third voice:

The way of a ship on the high seas.

Then, finally, the clincher:

And the way of a man with a maiden (Prov. 30:18-19).

This could go on and on. The old men took the lead, but from time to time a younger voice from the outer edges of the circle would dare to make itself heard.

Of course, such proverbs were not always made up on the spot. They were transmitted from generation to generation, and each encapsuled in its terse form the results of long and perceptive observation of the patterns and interrelationships placed into life by God. In a sense, this wisdom, based on empirical observation, constituted the Israelites' natural and social sciences. There is one difference, however. While our sciences formulate into laws what must *always* happen in the controlled environment of an experiment, the proverbs of the wise put in focus what will *often* happen in the less controlled setting of daily life. That is the differences between wisdom and science.

Much of this wisdom was "secular," by our definition, dealing with wealth and poverty, work and leisure, neighborly relations, marriage, agriculture, and other topics. But again, the religious sphere is not separated from daily life. The wise knew well that human observation was limited in its capacity to understand the world. They acknowledged the mystery of God's ways:

Many are the plans in the mind of a man,

but it is the purpose of the Lord that will be established.

(Prov. 19:21)

Further, they taught righteous living:
  Better is a little with righteousness
  than great revenues with injustice.
            (Prov. 16:8)
But the real religious significance of this education lay not in
explicitly religious statements like these, but in the assumption
underlying all wisdom, namely that it is based on observation of the
order of *God's* world. And by including such proverbs, the Old
Testament acknowledges that revelation of God can indeed come
through empirical observation.

3. *Priest and member of the congregation of Israel.* The
educational setting of the ancient Israelite extended beyond the
family and the village circle, however, to include the sanctuaries
staffed by the professional teachers, the priests.[8] While we often
associate priests primarily with sacrifices and liturgical acts, we
must not overlook the fact that their other chief function in Israel
was to be guardians and dispensers of *tôrāh,* that is, instruction.
Deuteronomy 33:10 summarizes their dual commission:
  They [the Levites, that is, the priestly
  tribe] shall teach Jacob thy ordinances,
  and Israel thy law;
  they shall put incense before thee,
  and whole burnt offering upon thy altar.
Their special guardianship of *tôrāh* is also stated clearly in Micah
3:11; Jeremiah 18:18; and Ezekiel 7:26.

Tôrāh may be derived from the verb *yārāh,* "to throw," and even
"to cast lots" (Josh. 18:6). It may thus be related to the giving of
oracles. However, its Old Testament usage suggests that it derives
rather from the root *yārāh,* "to show, teach," so that its original
meaning is "instruction."[9] Its usual translation as "law," though
fixed by long tradition, is hardly appropriate for the Old Testament
period itself and obscures the basic teaching function of the priests.

For the longest stretch of Israel's existence in her land, such
teaching was concentrated at the temple of Jerusalem. Three times a
year every Israelite male was required to "appear before the Lord"
(Exod. 23:14-17; 34:18-23; Deut. 16; Lev. 23; Num. 28-29), that is,
make a pilgrimage to the place where the Ark of the Covenant was
kept. We can be sure that this requirement was fulfilled only
symbolically, as some persons and families from across the land
made the pilgrimage. For some, it may have been the desire of a
lifetime to set foot inside the temple at least once. Nevertheless, the
temple was the goal of pilgrimages on the part of many people on the

occasion of the three great pilgrim feasts: Passover/Unleavened Bread; Harvest/Weeks; and Ingathering/Booths, held in early spring, at midsummer, and in late fall, respectively (Isa. 30:29; Ps. 122; cf, Luke 2:11-51).

These feasts lasted for eight days each. They were marked by great liturgical events in which the whole congregation participated. At these high points the great acts of God in Israel's history such as the exodus from Egypt, the crossing of the Sea, the preservation in the wilderness, the occupation of the land under Joshua, and the election of David must have been recited and celebrated. Such celebration, with its recitals and symbols, was in itself highly educational.

During the festal week, however, there must have been many occasions for instruction in smaller groups. H. Kraus postulates that such instruction must have pertained to two areas: Yaweh's Torah and Yahweh's acts in creation and history. [10] He considers Psalm 119 to be the most impressive document of Torah instruction. Study of this sort may have been carried on in small groups. Kraus proposes the further interesting theory that the seven-day account of Creation (Gen. 1) might have corresponded to seven days of the festivals in such a way that the works of one day of creation may have been studied on each day of a festival week, accompanied by psalms such as Psalm 8. [11] The acts of God in Israel's history were surely told and retold, again accompanied by psalms, such as Psalms 105; 135; and 136, for poetry and song were important teaching devices (Deut. 31:19), as were the symbols of the temple structure and its liturgies.

Whatever were the details, we must assume that the pilgrim feasts were significant "short courses" in religion, not to mention the general educational value of a trip to Jerusalem and an encounter with many people from all parts of the land. Private trips to the temple on other occasions will also have taken place. At the center of such education stood the priests. That their teaching function was seen as a "conversation between the generations," in analogy to the parents' role, is shown by the occasional use of the term "father" for them (Judg. 17:10; 18:19). [12]

4. *Master and Disciple.* Until now we have considered forms of education to which all or most Israelites were exposed. Now we must turn to what we might call exclusive and specialized education. Most people in Israel were peasants and/or shepherds or herdsmen, even if they lived in towns. They learned their skills by observing their parents and neighbors, as we have seen above. There were some vocations requiring special skills, however, and such skills

were acquired in a sort of apprenticeship to a master who was accomplished in them.

Earlier we considered "folk wisdom," dealing with various life issues on the basis of accumulated experience. Learning by observation could also take place with respect to a particular and limited area of life, such as pottery making, carpentry, midwifery, and others. [13] A person accomplished in such specialities was called "wise" (ḥākām). Our Bible translations render the word, if used in this context, as "able" or "skilled," but it is important to note that there is continuity of designation between those "skilled" in various crafts and those "wise" men and women who coined our proverbs. Craftmen's skills were learned, as we said already, from experienced masters. There is some evidence that there were guilds in Israel. [14] Often a skill was handed down in a family, so that the master-disciple relationship coincided with that of parent and child. But this was surely not always the case. The head of a guild was called "father" (1 Chron. 4:14), showing once again how the parent-child pattern was the basic model of learning. [15]

The priesthood was hereditary. It required extensive training. Little is reported of this, but we must assume that certain older priests will have instructed the younger ones in the sacred lore of Israel and in such matters as are recorded in the Book of Leviticus. From an earlier time we have the story of Samuel's apprenticeship to the priest Eli (1 Sam. 1-3). In 2 Kings 12:2 we have the interesting note that the priest Jehoiada "instructed" the young king Jehoash who began to reign when he was seven years old. Thus it appears that priests may have given instruction even to some outside of the priestly lineage on a one-to-one basis.

A variety of special skills, from writing to statecraft and diplomacy, were required by the royal court and the government service. Thus the royal court became a center of the particular kind of learning which we may call "court wisdom," in contrast to "folk wisdom" and to the wisdom or skill of craftsmen. It has been suggested that there were formal schools for scribes at the royal courts of Samaria and Jerusalem, on the analogy to such schools in Egypt, Mesopotamia, and elsewhere. However, there is no explicit evidence for this.

Nevertheless, kings had their "wise men" as advisers (1 Sam. 16:15-17:23), and these undoubtedly had their disciples whom they trained in the arts of writing, statecraft, and diplomacy, but also in proper etiquette and in wise behavior at court (cf. Prov. 16:10-15). The young kings themselves were in need of such training and will have had their special mentors, as mentioned above in connection with Jehoash and Jehoiada. Joseph fulfilled such a role toward Pharaoh and is consequently called a "father to Pharaoh" (Gen. 45:8). That the king himself could become a wise man is best illustrated by Solomon, the "patron saint" of wisdom in the Old Testament (1 Kings 3; 4:29-34). Through such activity the royal court became a center of learning, a higher academy, so to speak, where wise men (and women?) taught, but also preserved the wisdom handed down (Prov. 25:1).

Finally, we know that the master-disciple relationship existed in the realm of the prophets. Elijah had his disciple Elisha (2 Kings 2), who in turn had Gehasi (e.g., 2 Kings 4:11ff), and was generally seen as a father figure by the "sons of the prophets" (e.g., 2 Kings 6:1-7). Perhaps the clearest example of a master-disciple relationship is that between Jeremiah and Baruch (cf. Jer. 36; cf. also Isa. 8:16). Characteristically, the master is called "father" in various such contexts (2 Kings 2:12; 13:14), for learning in Israel, as now, is a conversation between the generations.

II.

If education in the Old Testament is a conversation between generations proceeding in four exemplary models, the question concerning the dynamics and the mood of such interchange must arise. Was there a smooth and peaceful flow of learning from the older generation to the younger, or was intergenerational communication marked by frustration, rebelliousness, and erratic results? [16]

In order to respond to this question, we must first define more closely who the teaching and the learning generations were. Of the four educational models discussed, only the parent-child model involved young children in a significant way. The other three models approximated more closely what we would call "adult education," granted that adulthood began relatively early in ancient Israel. J. Conrad, in the only extensive study of youth in the Old Testament known to me, [17] draws the significant intergenerational boundary between "the young generation," which has not yet assumed its full significance in upholding society, and the "older generation," consisting of those who carry the full responsibility for the life of the community. In other words, the "young generation" is marked by its "unfinished, becoming" quality and must be seen in terms of the *telos* or goal toward which it is developing. [18] Conrad delineates three perspectives on the goals of the young generation. [19]

1. From the traditional perspective of the patriarchally structured clans, the young generation was valued as the carrier of the clan's biological and social future. This value was achieved simply by being, without any educational aims and achievements. Of course, it was taken for granted that children and young people would acquire the skills necessary for living and practice these diligently.

On the whole, we can assume that young people submitted rather matter-of-factly to the authority of parents and elders and accepted readily their traditional skills, values, and way of life, including their religious faith. After all, an individual did not have any real alternative as to lifestyle in a homogenous clan-centered society. While the prophets warned continually against a deviation from God's ways on the part of the people, there was little danger that individuals would break away from the norms of society. Disobedience on the part of children did not have that ominous and foreboding quality which it acquires in our pluralistic society, and father's firm hand was enough to deal with it effectively (Prov. 23:13f.; 29:15). There was legal provision for a communally imposed death sentence against a "rebellious son" (Deut. 21:18-21). Such a situation must have been very exceptional, however, and no instance of an actual verdict to this effect is reported to us.

There must have been serious tensions between the generations, however, as is evidenced by the repeated commandments and exhortations to treat parents properly (Exod. 20:12; 21:15; Prov. 28:24; 30:17). Kings were in a better position to express their individuality, and consequently we witness many sharp contrasts in the policies, lifestyles and religious attitudes of fathers and sons of the royal house of David (cf. the drastic contrasts as we move from father to son among these kings: Ahaz, Hezekiah, Mannasseh and Amon, Josiah, Jehoiakim). The disturbed social conditions after the fall of Jerusalem and in the Babylonian Exile may have widened the scope of individual self-expression for many Jews (Ezek. 18).

On the whole, however, the assertion of the young against their elders was seen not only as wrong and counterproductive (Exod. 20:12; Prov. 15:5, 32; 17:25; 28:24; 30:17), but as a sign of divine judgment (Isa. 3:4, 5; Mic. 7:6). The destructive course of listening to the advice of the young and disregarding that of the old is graphically described in 1 Kings 12, leading to the division of the kingdom of Solomon. [20] It belongs to the possibilities of the sinful present order. On the other hand the restoration of harmony

between the generations will be a mark of the coming Day of the
Lord, when the new Elijah will "turn the hearts of fathers to their
children and the hearts of children to their father: (Mal. 4:5, 6; cf. 1
Kings 18:37).

2. From an educational perspective, presupposed already in the
commandment to honor father and mother (Exod. 20:12), but
particularly evident in the wisdom tradition, the aim and goal of the
younger generation was to lead the good, wise, and pious life (Prov.
1:7). The easy achievement of this ideal could not be taken for
granted. The very fervor with which the wisdom teachers
propagated the life of wisdom and warned of the life of folly (Prov.
1-9) shows that the younger generation (addressed in fatherly terms
as "My son!"; cf. Prov. 1:8; 2:1; 3:1; etc.) needed to be won for an
ideal that was not immediately self-evident or appealing to the
prospective learner.

The wisdom teachers struggled with evangelistic zeal to pull the
"fool" away from the brink of death to which the road of folly would
lead him, and to direct him toward life along the path of wisdom.
The latter was increasingly identified with *tôrāh*, until the two
became completely identified by the time of Ben Sirah (1:26, 6:37,
etc.). In this process they developed an "anatomy of foolishness,"
distinguishing between progressive degrees.[21] The "simple" (*pétî;*
e.g. Prov. 1:4, 22; 7:7), or "greenhorn" and the one "without sense"
(*hāsēr lēb;* literally: "empty of heart"; e. g. Prov. 7:7f.) were still
teachable. The "fool" ('ĕvil; e. g. Prov. 11:29) and the "fool" (*kesîl;*
e.g. Prov. 10:18) represent the hardened fool who resists teaching
and creates trouble. Finally, the "scoffer" or "scorner" (*leṣ;* e.g.
Prov. 29:8; 22:10; 3:34) and the "fool" (*nābāl;* Prov. and 1 Sam.
25:25; Ps. 14:1) are the arrogant fools, who say in their heart, "There
is no God" (Ps. 14:1). We see here the dedicated effort to achieve an
educational ideal that is religiously motivated and very sincere. It
stuggled against the odds of human sluggishness and sinfulness, but
it undoubtedly achieved some of the finest fruits of education in
ancient Israel (Ps. 1).

3. Finally, Israel did realize the limitations of a patriarchally
oriented educational system in which learning was expected to flow
from the old to the young. In part, this realization was based on
observation and common sense:

> Better is a poor and wise youth
> than an old and foolish king,
> who will no longer take advice.
>   (Eccles. 4:13)

The stance of Elihu in the Book of Job (32:6-10) must have been experienced from time to time. Here a young man politely awaited his turn to speak, but then he courageously contradicted the faltering attempts of Job's three friends to interpret Job's suffering. (Whether Elihu had something better to say is an open question.)

That the old is not always the better was also impressed on Israel by her history. Had it not been the Exodus-generation that had to die in the wilderness, while its children were allowed to enter the land? (Num. 14:29). It appears that the time of Jeremiah and Ezekiel, embracing the crisis of Jerusalem's destruction (578 B.C.), was especially cynical toward history:

The fathers have eaten sour grapes,
and the children's teeth are set on edge.
(Jer. 31:29; Ezek. 18:2f.; Lam. 5:7)

The prophets counteracted this mood by affirming that each generation had its own chance:

The son shall not suffer for the iniquity
of the father,
nor the father suffer for the iniquity
of the son.
(Ezek. 18:20)

There was another limitation placed on the absolute primacy of the older generation, namely the autonomy and the grace of God. Time and again, by way of an unlikely choice, God chose the apparently too young and inexperienced for his special tasks. We think of the election of Joseph (in contrast to his older brothers), Moses, Samuel (over against Eli), David (as compared to his older brothers, and over against Saul), and Jeremiah. In a sense, each new generation is God's new opportunity. Without abandoning her high view of the educational duties and capacities of the older generation, ancient Israel acknowledged that God, in his sovereignty and grace, could override normal patterns and choose the young and inexperienced for some of his greatest tasks. As long as those who teach preserve this insight, they retain a sense of wonder and mystery toward their students who, in a sense, are their inferiors, but who may far outdistance their teachers, not only in human learning, but also in God's plans for them.

III.

We must give brief consideration to the question whether the educational patterns, as described, are merely the time-bound customs of a small group of people of long ago, or whether they are inherently bound up with and proper to that theology which they perpetuated then and which we Christians hold to be God's word even for us today. It must be clear from the beginning, that many of ancient Israel's ways of teaching and learning belonged to a relatively unsophisticated, clan-centered, patriarchal agricultural society and have lost much of their usefulness for our cultural context. However, there are elements in what we have considered, I believe, that transcend their own time and culture and are worth our pondering if not our imitation.

1. I believe that the primacy of the parent-child model in education transcends specific cultural limitations. As mentioned earlier, we find it even among animals. Every society that considers the family structure foundational will remind itself that educational efforts and institutions outside of the family are merely extensions of parental right and duty. It has been a mark of absolutist and dictatorial ideologies and systems that they attempt to wrest this responsibility from the parents and transfer it to the state.

2. All real knowledge and wisdom is handed from the past to the future. Educational experimentation in our time with student-centered learning models, as well as the high value placed by our society on recent discoveries, may obscure this fact for us and suggest to us that significant knowledge lies with the young and "up-to-date," who have just left college or graduate school. This is deceptive, however. Even the latest discovery rests on the foundations of the past, and even the young teacher "speaks down" to the young generation of learners from the platform of the older generation, even if he or she is a young person, for he or she dispenses the knowledge of those who went before. That is why students will consider even very young teachers to belong to the older generation. "This is the first time I am discussing this problem with an older person," a student told me once when I was a very young college teacher. Upon checking the records I found that he was only two years younger than I was.

Erik Erikson has gone so far as to make this urge to care for the young by passing on one's values the mark of proper identity development of the middle-aged adult; he calls it *generativity*. [22] For the adult generations to talk with young people who move toward adulthood and to transmit knowledge and values in the hope that these will be received, cherished, and developed—that is not authoritarian in an antiquated and negative sense; it is healthy and responsibly human. Where it does not happen, society is perverted or sick. That such a flow of learning from the older to the younger should not be oppressive and authoritarian, but engage the mind, interest, and collaboration of the young, was already known in ancient Israel. The father's religious instruction was to be elicited by the questions of the son whose mind had been stimulated toward inner participation (Deut. 6:20-25; Exod. 12:24-27; Josh. 4:20-24).

3. As to method, much about education in the Old Testament is accidental and time-bound. One aspect that is inherent to biblical faith and should not be lost in Christian education is the centrality of storytelling in transmitting the faith. Deuteronomy 6:20 to 25 is once again a classical passage. Religious questions are to be answered by telling the story of God's great acts. The medium of the story is a part of the message; it cannot be replaced adequately by any other medium. God's revelation was experienced by Israel as a series of incidents or stories that flow together into a comprehensive story of God with humanity. No audiovisuals, no charts, no deduction of abstract doctrinal statements can or should replace that method in the Christian church. [23]

4. The wisdom emphasis of the Old Testament is a further value to be retained. By this I mean the empirical search for God's order in nature and in human life, without the assumption that the insights gained are valuable only if they can be demonstrated to be consistently valid under controlled conditions. In other words, and without any anti-scientific tendency whatsoever, the church needs to affirm that God gives us significant access to an understanding of the world in ways more humble, but much more comprehensive on the average, than our scientific efforts are likely to offer. We must not devaluate wisdom as a mode of understanding by limiting significant insight to what is "scientific." The attempt of the social sciences to restrict themselves to the model of the natural sciences should not be furthered by Christians.

5. The preservation of learning and practice, evident throughout the apprenticeship-centered education of ancient Israel, remains a desirable goal for us. Certainly we must resist an impatient pragmatism that presses for "practical applications" at every step of the way. However, a search for knowledge that is disinterested in its application to life and refuses to take responsibility for the practical consequences and applications of such knowledge is also out of step with a biblical understanding of humanity as the steward of God's world.

6. Finally, the Old Testament should remain our model in its refusal to separate "religious education" from "general education." The same parents who teach the child to walk, to talk, to tend the

sheep and to grind the flour are the teachers and models in matters of faith. While we cannot expect in a pluralistic society that communal institutions will perform the functions of the Israelite village circle, we must not allow our minds to separate any realm of knowledge from any other. We must counteract, by a comprehensive understanding of all knowledge as rooted in the one God (Prov. 1:7), the tendency of the various disciplines to seek their own autonomy in our time.

IV.

Briefly, and by way of an epilogue, I wish to point out certain developments in early Judaism thay may help us to connect the educational patterns of ancient Israel with those of New Testament times.

The great educational institution of Judaism is the synagogue. K. Hruby characterizes it as a place of prayer and teaching.[24] Its precise time and mode of origin are unknown, but it is widely accepted today that it emerged either during or shortly after the Babylonian Exile (598/587-539 B.C.), to meet the religious needs of the Jewish community that had lost its temple.[25] The first trustworthy reference to a synagogue comes from a relatively late Egyptian source, however, namely an inscription from the time of Ptolemy III Euergetes (246-221 B.C.).[26] By New Testament times, synagogues were found in Palestine and in many parts of the Roman Empire.

In spite of the meager reports of its origins, we can safely assume that the teaching functions of the synagogue consisted, from the beginning, of the reading of the Scriptures, their translation into the vernacular (Aramaic for Palestine; Greek for the diaspora), and their exposition in a homily. Jesus' participation in the synagogue proceedings of Nazareth must have been quite typical (Luke 4:16-30). It is likely that men and women were segregated, both in the second temple and in the synagogues. Women were not obligated to attend synagogue services, but they could do so and often did. They could also be called upon to read the Torah. Some of them became learned in the oral rabbinic tradition.[27] On the whole, the teaching function of the synagogue must have been akin to that of a Protestant preaching service, with a somewhat greater emphasis on the reading, as compared to the preaching.

The emergence of the synagogue was paralleled, and intertwined with, the development of the scribes, a group of specialists in the study of Scripture.[28] Their roots go back to two of the Old Testament's educational models discussed earlier. First, we observed that one branch of wisdom instruction at the royal court was the training of young men as scribes, in the secular sense, who would become the educated civil servants. Secondly, we recall that the priests were originally the custodians of *tôrāh,* that is, religious instruction. As the Babylonian Exile removed the need for a royal civil service, and as the new emphasis on the study of Scripture required increasing intellectual expertise, the learning of the wise and the educational duties of the priesthood must have merged to produce this new and important class of theologians and educators. Ezra was the scribe *par excellence.* Of priestly lineage, "he was a scribe skilled in the law of Moses" (Ezra 7:6). "For Ezra had set his heart to study the Law of the Lord, and to do it, and to teach his statutes and ordinances in Israel" (v. 10). From the emergence of the Pharisaic movement in the second century B.C., the scribes were associated closely with that movement, being its intellectual core. They became the lawyers and guardians of Scripture and produced the rabbinic tradition, the intellectual-theological backbone of Judaism through the centuries.

While the synagogue was the central institution dispensing religious instruction in early Judaism, it was not a school in the customary sense of the word. There were various more or less organized efforts at group instruction in preexilic as well as postexilic times. These were carried on at the royal court, among the prophetic groups, and among the people generally by priests and Levites (Neh. 8:7, 8).[29] Evidence for the existence of schools, however, comes only from rather late postexilic times. The first reference to a "school" (*bêt midrash* = "house of seeking/study") is found in Sirach 51:23. The Talmud credits Simon ben Shetach, a contemporary of Alexander Jannaeus (103-76 B.C.) with the demand that children should be sent to school (*bêt-hassēpher* = "house of the Book"),[30] and Joshua ben Gimla, high priest between A.D. 63 and 65, is said to have decreed that every town should have a school for children from six or seven years up.[31]

It seems that public education was well established among Palestinian Judaism at least by the first century A.D. Whether the later Jewish educational system of the Talmudic period and the Middle Ages, consisting of primary (*bêt sēpher*), secondary (*bêt midrash*), and higher schools (*jeshîvāh*), can be read back into this time, is very questionable.[32] It is interesting to observe, however, that these later Jewish schools, though offering instruction in reading and writing, had as their aim the instruction in Torah, rather than the pursuit of a general educational ideal.[33] Their curriculum consisted of reading from the Bible sentence by sentence, translating it into Aramaic, and memorizing what was read. Next came "Talmud," or oral interpretation, on the basis of the written Mishnah. The highest level of scriptural training, that of a rabbi, could be attained to in the "Jeshivah," the school operated by a rabbi. [34]

In spite of this well-structured three-tiered educational system, in the Talmudic period and even in the Middle Ages, Judaism considered the father to be the person primarily responsible for the education of his children, both in Torah and in a vocation. The schools were established as a help to fathers who were not in a position to carry out this educational mandate. [35]

With this observation we recall the primary educational model with which we began our survey of education in the Old Testament, the model of parent and child. And the father's model as a teacher was the great teacher of Israel, the Heavenly Father:

> Behold, God is exalted in his power;
> who is a teacher like him? (Job 36:22) [36]

Notes

[1] Roland deVaux states, "Writing was in common use at an early date." *Ancient Israel* (New York: McGraw-Hill, 1965), Vol. I, p. 49. Widespread literacy is also posited by J. Kaster, "Education, OT," *The Interpreter's Dictionary of the Bible,* Vol. E.-J., p. 34. The evidence for such claims is rather limited, however, and we must assume that many in Israel were illiterate.

[2] On the tribal structure of Israel see deVaux, *Ancient Israel,* Vol. I, pp. 3-23; and Norman K. Gottwald, *The Tribes of Yahweh: A Sociology of the Religion of Liberated Israel, 1250-1050 B.C.E.* (Maryknoll, New York: Orbis Books, 1979), esp. pp. 237-341.

[3] Following Ludwig Koehler, *Hebrew Man,* trans. by P. R. Ackroyd (Nashville: Abingdon, 1957), pp. 74ff. See also my "Male and Female Roles in the Old Testament," in this volume, pp. 84-91.

[4] There are certain exceptions. Num. 1:3, 18; 26:2; 2 Chron. 25:5 set twenty as the age for military service. Exod. 20:14 gives the same age for taxation. On the basis of these, together with the judgment in Num. 14:29; 32:11 and the table of values in Lev. 27:1-8, Hans Walter Wolff concludes that "in general the twenty-year-old counted as being completely responsible," *Anthropology of the Old Testament,* trans. by M. Kohl, (Philadelphia: Fortress, 1973), p. 121. A Levite began his service at the mature age of thirty (Num. 4:23). See Wolff (*ibid.,* pp. 119-127) on the Israelite's stages of life, and Koehler, *Hebrew Man,* pp. 52-54 on the age of marriage.

[5] Although the statement that Ishmael was circumcised at the age of thirteen (Gen. 17:22) has sometimes been taken to point to a special importance of that age for religious maturity, the Jewish custom of Bar-Mitzvah, at age thirteen, is a later development and cannot be supported from the Old Testament.

[6] Koehler, *Hebrew Man,* pp. 86ff.

[7] The nature of this mental activity is classically presented in Gerhard von Rad, *Old Testament Theology,* Vol. I, trans. by D. M. G. Stalker (New York: Harper, 1962), pp. 418ff. For a full treatment of all aspects of wisdom in the Old Testament

see von Rad, *Wisdom of Israel,* trans. by J. D. Martin (London: SCM Press, 1972).

[8] deVaux, *Ancient Israel,* Vol. II, pp. 353-55: "The Priest as Teacher."

[9] See deVaux, *Ancient Israel,* Vol. II, p. 354, and the standard Hebrew dictionaries.

[10] Hans-Joachim Kraus, *Theologie der Psalmen* (Neukirchen-Vluyn: Neukirchener Verlag, 1979), pp. 113f.

[11] *Ibid.,* p. 113.

[12] See also deVaux, *Ancient Israel,* Vol. I, p. 49.

[13] Thus Exod. 28:3 speaks of all those "who have ability" (lit.: "who have a wise heart/mind"), whom God has "endowed with an able mind" (lit.: "a spirit of wisdom") to make Aaron's garments. Exod. 31:1ff. describes how God's Spirit had made Bezalel and other "able men" (lit.: "all who have a wise heart/mind") the ability to make the utensils for the tabernacle (cf. also 35:10; 36:1, 2, 4, 8). Similarly, there is reference to all women who "had ability" (lit.: "women who have a wise heart/mind") to spin; Exod. 35:25. Ezek. 27:8, 9 refers to "skilled men" ("wise") outside of Israel who were pilots and those who could caulk the seams.

[14] deVaux, *Ancient Israel,* Vol. I, pp. 76-78.

[15] *Ibid.,* p. 77.

[16] On the subject of intergenerational relationships see Hans Walter Wolff, "Problems between the Generations in the Old Testament," *Essays in Old Testament Ethics,* edited by James L. Crenshaw and John T. Willis (Hyatt-Festschrift; New York: KTAV, 1974), pp. 77-95.

[17] Joachim Conrad, *Die junge Generation im Alten Testament* (Stuttgart: Calver Verlag, 1970.

[18] *Ibid.,* pp. 9-12.

[19] I am following Conrad in this threefold division in a general way, but the following sections are not a resume of Conrad's work. Cf. also my "Biblical Perspectives on Youth," in this volume, pp. 109ff.

[20] Wolff ("Problems," p. 84) treats this especially helpfully.

[21] Following John Paterson, *The Wisdom of Israel* (New York: Abingdon, 1961), pp. 64-68. Paterson may have classified too neatly; in many cases the terms for *foolishness* will have been used as synonyms. Nevertheless, the classification points to a mental effort on the part of the wise that is worth noting.

[22] Erik H. Erikson, *Identity, Youth in Crisis* (New York: W. W. Norton, 1968), p. 138f.

[23] Thus also Wolff, "Problems," p. 92.

[24] Kurt Hruby, *Die Synagoge: Geschichtliche Entwicklung einer Institution* (Zurich: Theologischer Verlag, 1971), p. 9 and n. 3.

[25] *Ibid.,* pp. 14-30; and H. H. Rowley, *Worship in Ancient Israel: Its Forms and Meaning* (London: S.P.C.K., 1967), pp. 213-45: "The Synagogue." Hruby explains how local worship services may well have been conducted at various places in Israel during the time of the second temple, or even earlier, and how such meetings may have developed into the synagogue (pp. 15ff.).

[26] Hruby, *Die Synagoge,* p. 19. This is a sober historical assessment. Rabbinic tradition, unhampered by questions of authenticity, traces the origin of the synagogue to Moses, or even beyond, *ibid.,* pp. 27-30. We note parenthetically that *synagogue,* like *church,* refers both to the building and to the congregation gathering there.

[27] On the participation of women in the worship of the temple and the synagogues see Hruby, *Die Synagoge,* pp. 50-55.

[28] A helpful account of the emergence of the scribes is given by Matthew Black, "Scribe," *The Interpreter's Dictionary of the Bible,* Vol. R-Z, pp. 246-48. Cf. also Kaster, "Education," p. 32.

[29] A good survey is offered by Kaster, "Education," pp. 30-33.

[30] Jerus. Talm. *Kethuboth* VIII, according to Donald E. Gowan, *Bridge Between the Testaments: A Reappraisal of Judaism from the Exile to the Birth of Christianity,* second edition, revised (Pittsburgh: The Pickwick Press, 1980), p. 301. See also Kaster, "Education," p. 33.

[31] Bab. Talm. *Baba Bathra* 21a; *ibid.*

[32] Gowan, *Bridge,* p. 301.

[33] Johann Maier, *Geschichte der jüdischen Religion* (Berlin/New York: Walter de Gruyter, 1972), p. 111f.

[34] *Ibid.*

[35] *Ibid.*

[36] On this point see Kaster, "Education," p. 33.

Biblical Perspectives on Youth

This essay has been developed with a particular view to the needs of the high school and Sunday school teachers. I assume that "youth" suggests to us that age after puberty during which the young person is still dependent on his or her parents but engages in a rather lengthy process of establishing economic and emotional independence. In Erik Erikson's terms[1] it is the period of life marked by the developmental task of identity formation and generally spans the years from twelve to eighteen, although it may well extend beyond eighteen, especially for those continuing their education beyond high school. In that case it may cut into, and overlap with, the next developmental phase, the age of intimacy.

Identity formation, or gaining a sense of "who I am," is achieved largely by bringing the given facts of one's life into confrontation with possible alternatives. Thus one's family is compared to other styles of family life; one's childhood faith is tested in the light of other denominations or religions; one's previous friends and activities are reconsidered, and sometimes—perhaps temporarily—rejected for other possibilities. The young person may become idealistically attached to a philosophy, movement, or lifestyle in his or her search for a true and satisfying self. On the other hand, he or she may camouflage the search for this ideal by an overtly cynical behavior or by slavish conformity to peer group ways. Erikson stresses the importance of granting youth a "moratorium," a time of tolerant acceptance while the young person experiments with modes of being that seem extreme or out of character in order to find his own self-identity. Such identity is marked by a reasonable harmony between past and present and between given realities and ideal aspirations. Where such a sense of identity is not achieved, "identity confusion" follows, that is, a sense of uncertainty about self, resulting in inconsistent behavior, difficulties in forming deep and lasting relationships (intimacy), or even "negative identity," such as a self-image as a failure or a delinquent.

I have spelled out in some detail, and with the help of Erikson's insights, what our time and society considers to be "youth." What then does the Bible have to say about "youth" as defined? The answer is: nothing! A period of "youth" as described was not known in Old or New Testament times. The reason for this lies in the fact that the basis for our experience of youth, namely the possibility of alternative modes of life and the time and freedom to choose among these, was nonexistent, or at best very slim.

Let us consider some pertinent facts. Serious work, and therefore economic usefulness, began early for the Israelite boy and girl. A certain economic worth is ascribed to them beginning with age five (Lev. 27).[2] On the other hand, economic independence in our sense was never achieved, for the economic unit was not the individual, nor the primary family, but the "father's house," that is, the extended family spanning three or four generations.[3] Professional differentiation was very limited, with most people engaged in agriculture. Whatever specialization existed was largely hereditary, so that personal choice of vocation was next to nonexistent. Thus the vocational-economic area of life did not offer any scope for individual identity formation in our sense.

The same is true of courtship and marriage. Most Israelites married relatively young.[4] Marriages were generally arranged between families rather than by personal choice. While the girl would leave her family to join that of her husband, the young couple would continue to live in the context of the extended family and be subject to the elders. Once again, there was little scope in this area for young people to choose between alternatives and therefore to work out their own identity.

The same holds true of the third great identity-provider in our time, the area of faith or of philosophy of life (*Weltanschauung*). While individuals could stray from the faith of the people by practicing magic or being delinquent in their religious duties, "conversion" to another religion, on the part of an individual, was unthinkable in Old Testament times. Israel was warned of turning toward Baalism often enough, to be sure, but that was a matter of group deviation, not of individual choice among alternative possibilities. In New Testament times this was somewhat different, but for the Old Testament period the religious realm offered no more scope for the development of a personal identity than did the realms of economics and of sexuality.

It is necessary to say all this in order to avoid misunderstanding. The intent is not, however, to invalidate our topic. Of course there were young people in biblical times, and the Bible has something to say about them. Let us turn to the Old Testament first.

Youth in the Old Testament

Joachim Conrad, in the only extensive study on the subject known to me, employs the term "the young generation" (*die junge Generation*) for the object of his research. [5] This "young generation" is delimited by the existence of an older generation and defined by comparison with it. That older generation in Conrad's approach is made up of those adults who are at the peak of their social power and influence and who direct the destiny of the social group. Conversely, the young generation consists of those who have not yet achieved their fullest social significance.

How is this young generation viewed? Conrad distinguishes three separate though not contradictory perspectives:

1. In the patriarchal-familial thinking of ancient Israel—and the same is true of the whole Ancient Near East—the young generation is valued as the replenishment and continuation of family and clan. This is its importance for the future, an importance achieved merely by being. To have a son to carry on his name is each Israelite's wish. The son's individuality recedes in comparison to his mere existence. The daughter's individuality is even less important, as her role in the perpetuation of name and family is a mediate one, namely to become the mother of sons.

2. Certain passages and sections of the Old Testament add to the concern for continuity a concern for the quality of that continuity. The commandment to honor father and mother "that your days may be long in the land which the Lord your God gives you" (Exod. 20:12) already evidences a concern for the quality of life lived by the young generation. The wisdom literature in particular addresses itself to the young, unformed and still pliable generation with a strong appeal to lead the right kind of life. [6] The emphasis falls on the individual who has to make choices. The future significance of the young generation is the perpetuation not simply of life, but of the wise, good and pious life, and this goal is achieved by wise decision making. We must hasten to note, however, that this choice is not the same as modern Western youth's sorting out of several real

alternatives of being (identity). It is the choice between the (known) right and the (known) wrong way.

3. Finally, Conrad points to a third perspective on youth, namely youth as potentially open to God's special call to become an instrument in salvation history. A great number of stories of significant biblical personages are preceded by the account of the person's call before birth, in early childhood, or at an age apparently too young for the task at hand. We need only think of Isaac, Joseph, Moses, Gideon, Samson, Samuel, Saul, David, Solomon, and Jeremiah. Whether special personal qualities are recognized or not, such a call of the young is always an expression of God's sovereign ability to overrule human standards and expectations, and of God's grace that is ready to use the weak and unqualified. Often the apparently unsuited youth is juxtaposed to an apparently much better qualified exponent of the older generation, as in the case of Samuel and Eli, or David and Saul. This perspective on youth as God's potential instrument is limited to the select few. Not everyone will, in fact, be called to special service. Those who are, are singled out not for personal achievement and glory, but for service of God in behalf of their people. Again, the goal is not an individually chosen identity over against other possible alternatives, but obedient acceptance of the only right way of response.

Youth in the New Testament

In the New Testament considerably less attention is given to what we have called, with Conrad, *the young generation.* However, certain Old Testament perspectives are continued, sometimes in modified form. Conrad's first perspective—the importance of offspring for the continuance of humankind, is tacitly acknowledged, as it is universally. The specific Old Testament concern for the preservation of name and family, however, has given way to the concern for personal eternal life and for the preservation of the family of faith, the church.[7]

The significance of youth as the age where the important decisions concerning the wise, good, and pious life are reached, is again acknowledged, even if somewhat peripherally. Jesus approves of the rich young ruler's effort to keep the commandments from youth on, even though he transcends it with a further calling to total dedication (Mark 10:17-22). Timothy's Christian upbringing by his mother and grandmother receives approving mention (2 Tim. 1:5). The "household codes" (*Haustafeln*) contain statements pertinent to right decision making for all ages, including youth (Col. 3:20, 21;

Eph. 6:1-4; Tit. 2:4, 6; 1 Pet. 5:5). On the whole, however, the new thrust of the gospel, recorded in the New Testament, has not yet settled into distinct forms and patterns of guiding the young, so that the comments pertinent to that seem more incidental than programmatic.

Conrad's third perspective on youth, that is, youth as potentially more subject to God's call than the established generation, seems most evident in the New Testament. Thus the special calling of John the Baptist, of Jesus, and of Paul before birth is recorded in each instance (Luke 1:13; Matt. 1:20; Gal. 1:15). The disciples of Jesus appear to belong to the "young generation," both as to their chronological age and their relationship to Jesus. Chronologically they must have been relatively young if we give any credence to the traditional dates of the deaths of Peter, John, and Paul. Their disciple-relation to Jesus, their "master," who himself was only approximately thirty years old, again places them into the young generation (cf. "little children," John 13:33). And, of course, they are the young who are especially called, not on the basis of personal qualification, but of God's sovereign grace. While Paul's famous equality-passage, Galatians 3:28, does not say that in Christ there is neither young nor old, one does gain the impression that such an understanding was in fact present in the early church, and that on the basis of God's free grace.[8]

It may be interesting to note in this connection that the New Testament, while reticent in its expressions on youth, contains weighty passages mentioning children, especially also in the ministry of Jesus (Matt. 18:1-6; 19:13-15; 10:13-16). One explanation undoubtedly derives from the fact that these references to children spring not from a concern with childhood, but from the need to explicate the nature of the kingdom of God, and that childhood is used to exemplify the humble and trusting attitude necessary for entering into it. However, there also appears to be the thought on Jesus' part that all children, and not only those selected for special tasks in God's service, are "called" simply by virtue of their childhood and their openness to God's future, in analogy to the new understanding of the priesthood as having broken all social limits and belonging to all believers.

Significance for Today

It is not easy to assess the significance of our survey for contemporary Christian theology and practice. What we observed were largely socially conditioned views and practices, although that does not necessarily make them theologically irrelevant, for the Bible's theology is expressed through the realities of socio-historical life. Nevertheless, it seems clear that, with the exception of the wisdom perspective, there is no explicit "theology of youth" in the Bible. Where statements on youth take on a theological coloring, the theological component is often not specific for youth, but forms part of a wider concern. Thus God often calls persons apparently disqualified on account of their youth, but this is in keeping with God's sovereign grace generally, a grace that chooses not only the young over the older, but also the poor over the rich, or the foreigner over the Israelite. In view of all this, the following applications to the contemporary Christian situation should be seen as suggestive rather than authoritative, or as counsel rather than doctrine. I shall list them in point form.

1. The fact that the Bible does not contain a specific theology of youth may be suggestive. While our time and culture sets youth apart, most ages and cultures have not done so, but have seen young people within the continuum of human life, which takes on distinctive features at each age without becoming fragmented into forms of existence dissociated from each other. Such also is the situation reflected in the Bible. I am not advocating that we disregard the cultural features of our situation. Nevertheless, the church may do well to brace herself at least somewhat against the tendency of our culture to set youth apart ever more sharply. In our ministry to youth (and to children) we do well to remember that young people are first of all people and only secondly young. We minister to older people as individuals, for example, but we emphasize almost exclusively group activities when we plan church programs for youth. Should we rethink our tendency to isolate and highlight the distinctives of youth over against the common human needs and qualities?

2. Conrad's first Old Testament perspective on youth highlighted the value of biological continuity. In the New Testament, this concern, though undoubtedly taken for granted, was superseded in part by the concern for personal life after death and for the continued existence of the church. The church could afford to press these new emphases, since a deep appreciation for biological continuity was solidly embedded in all cultures of that time. For us this is different. Growing world population; increasing concern for a high standard of living not dependent on children, or even hampered by them; a widespread loss of hope for the future; and the medical possibilities of birth control and abortion have made

human biological existence and continuity of questionable worth. Thus childhood and youth, while glorified on the one hand, are also regarded with much suspicion and antagonism in our time.

We do not have the space here to pursue the causes of this shift of attitude, nor can we extricate ourselves from our culture. The Bible should remind us, however, that human life is still God's good creation, that the continuation of humankind is still God's will, and that children are still a blessing. We need to work toward the "humanization" of children and young people. They are neither playthings nor monsters, but human beings in the process of becoming, just as older people are. While we need to understand their distinctive features in our culture, we must neither envy nor fear them, but love them as young brothers and sisters whose existence is natural, God-willed and good, and who have more in common with us than that which sets them apart as youth. Understanding for them is needed, but no special key or secret code, supposedly lost to those over thirty, is needed to communicate with them. A natural and joyful acceptance of the young, widely lost in our society, should be the aim of the church. Jesus' attitude toward children underscores this for us.

3. Youth as the time for right decisions leading to the wise and God-fearing life was the special emphasis of the wise men in Israel. The New Testament reports largely on a church occupied with first-generation concerns. In our time, the concern for setting young people on the right path of life and faith has become the almost exclusive preoccupation of the church's ministry to youth. Will our children accept the faith and ethics of their spiritual heritage? That is the great question of the church in our pluralistic society.

Neither the New Testament nor the early phase of the Anabaptist movement of the sixteenth century give us very overt and specific guidance in dealing with the "second generation." The wisdom literature of the Old Testament can be very helpful, but it needs to be supplemented by other Old Testament perspectives. Its strong emphasis on right choice and personal effort leaves it open to the danger of works-righteousness, as compared to the grace of God so evident in Israel's history of salvation. The same is often true of our Christian education efforts in church and home. As we lead our youth toward decision, commitment and responsibility, let us make doubly sure to inject a full measure of God's grace. It is grace that can lead the prodigal son back home again, but also grace that enables the father to wait when he can do nothing else, committing his distant son to God's care and working with the older son who has stayed at home. Parents and church leaders among us sometimes appear to lose perspective in this regard and assume not only full responsibility, but also full "command" in the matter of guiding their children and youths into the way of wisdom and faith.

4. Finally, both Testaments affirm that God loves to call the young into service, in spite of their youth and apparent lack of qualification. What teacher among us has not been uplifted and inspired by observing the beauty of faith and commitment in children and young people? God said to Jeremiah, "Do not say, 'I am only a youth'!" (Jer. 1:7) and Paul admonished Timothy, "Let no one despise your youth!" (1 Tim. 4:12). We also need to be open to recognize God's special calling to young people in our midst, and perhaps, in the context of a Christian "democratizing" of the divine call, to all young people.

On the whole, I believe, the church recognizes the potential of youth to be called into God's service. There is a temptation, however, to confuse such a divine call with natural endowment or talent. We encourage our young people to recognize their organizational, teaching, musical, academic, or artistic talents and to place them in the service of God and the church. Samuel, David, or Jeremiah, on the other hand, were called to do in God's service things for which they seemed unsuited at the time. Jesus' parable of the talents (Matt. 25:14-30) does not highlight the person with five talents and encourage that person to use them while disparaging the one-talent person. On the contrary, it points out, in keeping with the Old Testament, that God would be equally ready to praise the one-talent person as a good and faithful servant if the person had only trusted God to want him or her to be that. It is right and good that we encourage the use of special gifts in God's service, but we appropriate the marvelous grace of God only if we are open to God's significant activity through the apparently unsuited, including those apparently too young.

Notes

[1] Erik H. Erikson, *Identity: Youth in Crisis* (New York: Norton, 1968), esp. pp. 128-35.

[2] The meaning of this chapter, and the phases of life experienced by an ancient Israelite, are helpfully discussed in Ludwig Koehler, *Hebrew Man,* trans. Peter R. Ackroyd (New York: Abingdon, 1956), pp. 35 to 40; and Hans Walter Wolff, *Anthropology of the Old Testament*, trans. Margaret Kohl (Philadelphia: Fortress, 1974), pp. 119-27.

[3] For a full discussion of Israelite family and clan structure, see Roland de Vaux, *Ancient Israel* (New York: McGraw-Hill, 1965), Vol. I, pp. 19-61; and Norman K. Gottwald, *The Tribes of Yahweh: A Sociology of the Religion of Liberated Israel,*

1250-1050 B.C.E. (Maryknoll, New York: Orbis Books, 1979), pp. 237-392, with summarizing chart on pp. 338-41.

[4] Koehler, *Hebrew Man, loc cit.* See also my papers "Male and Female Roles in the Old Testament" and "Sexuality in the Old Testament" in this volume, pp. 84-91 and 68-83, respectively.

[5] Joachim Conrad, *Die junge Generation im Alten Testament: Möglichkeiten und Grundzüge einer Beurteilung* (Stuttgart: Calwer Verlag, 1970).

[6] See my article "Education in the Old Testament" in this volume, pp. 92-108.

[7] That the concern for individual salvation did not altogether disrupt the natural family bonds is evidenced by the fact that whole families were baptized and added to the church (Acts 10:24, 47-48; 16:33).

[8] This statement is made cautiously and tentatively. It is certainly true that the early church soon adopted the Israelite and Synagogal pattern of governance by "elders" (*presbyteroi*), who were undoubtedly older men as to age.

12
Quality of Life: A Biblical Study

Human beings have at all times cherished certain aspirations for their lives, the fulfillment of which would appear to them to make life satisfying, while their frustration would render human existence miserable and futile. The level and content of these aspirations are determined to some extent by individual views and ambitions, but to a much greater extent by the resources and traditions of the society in which an individual finds himself.

Most societies are variable in their definition of legitimate human aspirations. First, there is a constant adjustment of what is hoped for to what is possible in any given time and situation. Secondly, there are differing levels of aspiration which are considered proper to various groups within a society, resulting in class or caste structures. Thirdly, and of great importance for our present study, there frequently exist tensions between an officially prevailing theology or ideology on the one hand, and a divergent popular desire on the other. Thus an official ideology may require a people to live frugally and work hard for the promotion of its ideals, while the people chafe under this expectation and perceive it as a more or less intolerable burden. The attempt to define absolute and generally valid minimal standards of human aspiration, such as the French Revolution's trilogy of liberty, equality, and pursuit of happiness, or the United Nations' Declaration of Human Rights (1948) are relatively new in human history.

If we turn to the Bible with the question concerning the quality of life, we must conduct our inquiry on two levels. First, we have to ask what its people at various times perceived to be legitimate and necessary expectations for a meaningful and satisfying existence.

Secondly, we must transcend the time-bound and descriptive answer to inquire further which of these expectations of Israel or of early Christianity can claim to reflect divine norms of enduring validity, and which must be revised in the light of revealed ideals that were not, or not fully, realized in biblical times.

Such a task might be undertaken in two separate steps, but for our present purpose I propose to allow the two steps of the inquiry to intertwine. It is important, however, that we be mindful throughout not to identify unquestioningly what prevailed in biblical times with what constitutes the abiding biblical teaching. Thus the fact that ancient Israel suffered illness somewhat fatalistically as a decree of God—though not without the pious rebelliousness of the lament Psalms and Job!—does not mean that we, who know of the healing ministry of Jesus, should set our aspirations to health in the same way.

As to organization, I have divided our theme into four topics: (1) Life and Descendants. (2) Land and Property. (3) Freedom, Justice and Equality. (4) Personal Fulfillment.

Life and Descendants

Throughout the Bible, life is valued positively. It is a gift of God (Gen. 1, 2), both to humanity and to animals. It is given to human beings so that they may be God's image or representative to administer the created world (Gen. 1:26-28), an assignment of trust and dignity.[1] Work is included in this original and dignified assignment (Gen. 2:15). While humanity is not divine, and therefore experiences the limits of finiteness with respect to life and knowledge (cf. the trees of life and of the knowledge of good and evil, Gen. 2:9, 17), there is nothing negative about this, and it is perceived as such only by humanity's rebellious assertion of autonomy over against God.

This human rebellion constitutes humanity's sinfulness and tarnishes humanity's God-willed existence severely. Life and work on the land become burdensome (Gen. 3:17-19); dominion over the animal world turns into mutual enmity (Gen. 3:15); the blessing to be fruitful and multiply receives the admixture of pain in childbirth (Gen. 3:16); and the end of life, rather than constituting fulfillment, becomes untimely termination (Gen. 3:19; cf. the decreasing age of people, 6:3).

This characterization of life has been drawn from Genesis 1 to 3, which is probably the Bible's most explicit statement of theological anthropology.[2] The rest of the Bible, while less theoretical and explicit, supports this picture. To document this, we observe the following:

1. The basic goodness and dignity of life is expressed supremely by God's own continued concern for humanity, a concern that initiates the whole story of salvation, preserves a remnant even in the depths of human depravity and divine punishment, and expresses itself supremely in the self-giving death of God's incarnate Son, Jesus Christ.

2. While the story of salvation highlights God's concern for humanity, the Bible affirms this concern on a lower and broader level as well. Salvation is God's continued effort to raise people from the level of fallen humanity to the level of God's original and full intention for them, that is, for partnership in God's rule. Only some of the earth's multitudes enter by this narrow gate, however, and even these experience the fullness of God's kingdom only by way of signs or foretastes of God's presence, waiting for a greater eschatological fullness. Thus it may seem that the greater part of human existence on this earth has been abandoned from God's concern and relegated to a negative, God-forsaken status. But this is not so.

The Bible maintains, side by side with God's special work of salvation, that God continues to bless the ordinary life of all human beings in many ways. Thus there is no place for a haughty disdain on the part of the redeemed for the supposedly lower existence of ordinary humankind, for their God "makes his sun rise on the evil and on the good, and sends rain on the just and on the unjust" (Matt. 5:45). All life stands under God's care and is potentially redeemable. This is the theological basis for our respect for all life and our concern for its quality. Claus Westermann has expressed the relationship between blessing and salvation somewhat like this: God blesses all people in many ways, but some recognize it and respond, and this response leads to a relationship or covenant.[3]

3. When we ask concerning the quality of life, we are inquiring, in the terms stated, on the level of blessing, rather than salvation, although we must always remember that salvation—the restitution of our God-intended nature—hovers over all human life as a potential. How, then, does God intend human life to be blessed? That is to ask in biblical language what standards God has set for the quality of human life.

a. God wants us to live, and not to die. The Bible does not glorify any form of death, be it death to achieve glory, to defend the nation, to avert indignity and shame, to avoid hardship and pain, or whatever. It is very reserved even in its advocation of martyrdom. The death of Christ is the supreme sacrifice, but it is unique. Christians are baptized into Christ's death (Rom. 6:3, 4) in a figurative sense, but that is different than to die for Christ, let us say, in a holy war for the spreading of the faith, as we find it in many religious contexts, including the medieval crusades. It may be unavoidable to face death for one's faith, as Daniel, Stephen, Paul and others knew, and as the persecuted Christians of the first centuries did so bravely. Nevertheless, it is not the believer's sacrifice that God wants, but the substitutionary sacrifice of Christ (cf. Gen. 22).

b. God wants us to be fruitful and multiply (Gen. 1:28). Even after the Fall, children remain a blessing. Childlessness is a form of suffering endured temporarily by some, like Abraham and Sarah, Hannah, Elizabeth and Zechariah, to be broken by the even more striking blessing of a child chosen for God's special service. Many of God's new beginnings in the salvation of his people start with the report of the birth of a child (e.g. Moses, Samuel, John the Baptist, Jesus), and the fullness of the messianic age will be ushered in by a special child (Isa. 9:6).

While the Bible does not deal explicitly with abortion, we may note that life in the womb is assumed in a matter-of-fact way to be continuous with life after birth (Jer. 1:5; Ps. 139:13-18; Isa. 49:5; Matt. 1:20; Gal. 1:15). This is not negated by the fact that Exodus 21:22-25 places a higher value on the life of the mother than on that of the fetus. It is acknowledged that there are special times of crisis where a prophet (Jer. 16:1-4) or an eschatologically oriented group of believers (cf. 23:29; 1 Cor. 7) may be commanded or counseled as a sign not to marry, or to be without offspring. But that merely underscores the negative quality of childlessness, and the blessing of children. While we may well ask, in view of world population figures, what "filling the earth" may mean today, it is quite certain that an attitude hostile to the child as such, whatever form that attitude may take, is antibiblical.

c. God wants us to be healthy and reach a mature age. In the early chapters of Genesis (Gen. 1-11), man's progressive fall into sin is paralleled with a progressively diminishing length of human life. Thus sin is correlated with brevity of life, while the God-intended life is a life that reaches ripe old age. Moses, God's special servant, reaches the full measure of years set in Genesis 6:3, namely 120 years (Deut. 34:7). There is a reference to becoming "old and full of days" (Gen. 35:29; cf. 24:1), a state where a person is ready to die. The words of David's old friend Barzillai about himself express this state beautifully (2 Sam. 19:33-37). To see one's children's children grow up constitutes fulfillment and satisfaction.

Sickness is generally treated as a prelude to death; a reaching of death into life. The suffering it causes is not only due to physical pain and discomfort, but also to the fact that illness is generally understood, in some sense or other, as coming from God (Ps. 88). Sometimes the sufferer takes it as punishment for sin, while sometimes—notably in the case of Job—he refuses to do so and cries out at his incomprehensible lot. Even so, he does not resort to magic, as the Ancient Near Eastern people did, but clings to the very God whom he regards as the source of his trouble. ("My God, my God, why hast thou forsaken me?" Ps. 22:1). Thus he refuses to accept sickness and suffering as God's full and final will. The Book of Job justifies this hesitation by telling us, the readers, (but not Job), that his suffering was not a form of punishment, but a form of testing for which Job, as a particularly pious man, was judged worthy by God (Job 1, 2). Job himself was led to acknowledge that suffering must at times be left a mystery, beyond the reach of human reason (Job 40:3-5; 42:1-6). In the Suffering Servant passage, Isaiah 53, the Old Testament expresses with greatest clarity that suffering, far from being negative only, may in certain—though surely not in all—instances be regarded as God's special calling to a high and exalted ministry. The experiences of such suffering mediators as Joseph, Moses, and Jeremiah had already prefigured this teaching.

The New Testament confirms in various ways that sickness and suffering are not God's full and final intention for humanity. The prominence of healings among the miracles of Jesus underscores the fact that the rule of God (kingdom of God) means, among other things, release from sickness. In the fullness of the kingdom, suffering will have ceased (Rev. 7:15-17). Jesus makes a number of very explicit statements against the identification of individual instances of suffering and special personal sinfulness (John 9:3); Luke 13:1-5). Further, the example of Jesus' healing ministry and his teachings in his parables (the good Samaritan, Luke 10:29-37; the rich man and Lazarus, Luke 16:19-31) have undoubtedly been most effective in Christianity's effort to heal sickness actively now, an effort that seems to have been much less evident in Old Testament times. Above all, of course, it is Jesus' own passion and death which takes up the positive theme in suffering formulated in Isaiah 53 and carries it to its fullest possibility. Paul, in a similar if lesser manner, is led to accept his "thorn in the flesh" as having a special and positive intent from God (2 Cor. 12:7-10).

To summarize, the Bible teaches that God does not abandon humankind to sickness and suffering. In the context of a sinful world, God may use these to punish or to test. Often suffering must remain mysterious to us, but sometimes—especially in the cross of Christ—we may be able to see a positive intent even now. In any case, however, we may believe that sickness is not God's ultimate will, and we ourselves must strive to engage in a healing ministry as a sign of the coming kingdom.

Land and Property

Quality of life depends largely on having the resources to sustain it. This is true even if one does not wish to go as far as Karl Marx in making the struggle over material wealth central to all human endeavor. In the last analysis, all forms of wealth or property are derived from the land, its products and its resources.

Land is a theological theme throughout the Bible.[4] In the creation accounts (Gen. 1-3), the earth is designated as the garden to support humans and animals. Humankind is to till it and keep it (Gen. 2:15), and generally to administer it as God's image or representative (Gen. 1:26-28). Rebellion against God leads to a vitiation of this relationship and task. Man is driven out of the good garden, to eke out a living in the sweat of his brow, from a land full of thorns and thistles (Gen. 3:17-19). Scarcity of land and resources, and hard toil, have marked human existence throughout history.

The question of land ownership has dominated history, leading to inventiveness, migrations, and wars. Whose is the land? That is a perennial question. The Bible answers unequivocally: It is the Lord's. God alone can confer rightful ownership, but such ownership is never absolute. Israel was told:

> The land shall not be sold in perpetuity, for the land is mine; for you are strangers and sojourners with me. (Lev. 25:23)

"Strangers and sojourners" means as much as "landed immigrants" in our language, or more simply, "long-term guests." It emphasizes humanity's duty to treat the land as God's property. This precludes autonomous disposal and irresponsible exploitation. It also puts in question any absolute right of any person or group to any lands and resources, to the exclusion of others.

Israel received her own land as God's gift, promised to Abraham and inherited after a long period of sojourning in a foreign land and traveling through the wilderness. Israel's laws impressed upon her the need to exercise good stewardship of this land. Further, the laws threatened her with eventual loss of the land in case of poor stewardship, a threat repeated by the prophets and eventually realized through the Assyrian and Babylonian captivities. God's ultimate ownership of the land was to be acknowledged by rituals such as the offering of the firstfruits (Deut. 26:1-11). One of the basic principles of good stewardship was the equal distribution of the land. The second half of the Book of Joshua details laboriously how the land was parceled out to each tribe, clan, and family. There is something sacramental about this; every member of the covenant community was to receive his share of God's gift, the land. Laws like those of the Sabbath Year (Lev. 25:1-7) and the Jubilee Year (Lev. 25:8-55) were to remind Israel of the need to counteract the inevitable shift in property ownership by conscious measures.

The story of Naboth's vineyard illustrates a flagrant violation of this principle of equal distribution (1 Kings 21). The king wants the little man's vineyard and uses power and deceit to get it. This evokes divine condemnation through the prophet Elijah. About a century later, around the middle of the eighth century B.C., such oppression of the smaller farmer by the wealthy landlord seems to have become the order of the day, but it does not go unchallenged. The great prophets of the eighth century, notably Amos, Isaiah, and Micah, speak out against it in the name of the Lord:

Woe to those who join house to house,
who add field to field,
until there is no more room,
and you are made to dwell alone
in the midst of the land.
The Lord of hosts has sworn in my hearing:
"Surely many houses shall be desolate,
large and beautiful houses, without inhabitant. (Isa. 5:8, 9)

The commandments not to steal, and especially not to covet the neighbor's house and other property, are also meant for the protection of the weak. The penalty for the abuse and the hoarding of land, said the prophets, would be the loss of the land. Just as God had taken the land from the Canaanites in the time of Joshua to give it to Israel as a gift and a tangible token of the covenant, God would take it away from a faithless Israel which had broken that covenant through selfish abuse of the land.

What has been said of land pertains to all property. The Old Testament considers property, used rightly, as a gift and blessing from God. It condemns materialism, however. "Man does not live by bread alone. . ." (Deut. 8:3). The manna is to be gathered only for a day at a time (Exod. 16:19, 20). And in all consumer practices there is to be an element of graciousness toward the neighbor (Deut. 24:19-22). the Bible condemns hardheaded pursuit of gain (Amos 4:1; 8:4-6) as well as reveling in luxury, which is unavoidably at the expense of others (Amos 6:1-7). and we note especially that the condemnation of amassing wealth and luxury is not based solely on unjust ways of acquiring them. It is the fact of unfair distribution of wealth, and not only the mode by which it came about, that runs counter to our status as God's guests on this earth.

The teachings of Jesus and the New Testament bear out the same perspective. We recall quickly Jesus' concern for the poor as expressed in his ministry to their needs. We remember some of Jesus' key words such as:

Blessed are you poor, for yours is the kingdom of God. . . .
But woe to you that are rich, for you have received your consolation (Luke 6:20, 24).
. . . it is easier for a camel to go through the eye of a needle than for a rich man to enter the kingdom of God (Matt. 19:24).

We remember also the parable of the man who built his barns bigger, only to find that his life was asked of him that night (Lk. 12:16-21), and we recall the story of the rich man and Lazarus (Lk. 16:19-31), which makes it particularly clear that it is not the rich man's unjust acquisition of wealth that constitutes his sin, but rather the mere fact of the unequal distribution.

All this led the early church to attempt a community of goods (Acts 4:32-37; 5:1-11). The experiment failed, or at least it was abandoned as a binding model. Nevertheless, the story of the early church is one of mutual aid and concern, as Paul's efforts in support of the poor mother-church of Jerusalem evidence especially plainly (1 Cor. 16:1-4). We should also note, however, that material goods remain a gift of God; that we are to pray for our daily bread (Matt. 6:11); and that honest work to support oneself and one's dependents, over against pious idleness, is commanded (2 Thess. 3:6-13).

Neither Old nor New Testament attempt to quantify what constitutes a fair share of land and wealth, nor do they expect a society without any economic differentiation. The yardstick of a person's own right to material goods is the simultaneous well-being of his neighbor. That seems so simple that one wonders why it is necessary to make long speeches about it; yet how difficult it is to live accordingly!

Freedom, Justice, and Equality

This array of weighty words reflects some of modern Western man's basic expectations of a good life. Each of them represents a legal minimum. A rich and fulfilled life goes far beyond them in positive content, but freedom, justice and equality seem necessary minimal conditions for happiness and fulfillment to us. What does the Bible say? Of course, our question is not so much as to what extent biblical people actually enjoyed these conditions, but in how far the Bible affirms them as God's will for all human beings.

1. The expectations of *freedom* and justice authenticate themselves immediately as God-willed, if we consider their opposites: captivity and injustice. God's central self-manifestation in the Old Testament is the redemption of the oppressed Israelites from their Egyptian bondage. Through it God comes to be known as Israel's redeemer. God's new name, revealed to Moses (Exod. 3 and 6), was filled with content by redeeming acts, so that it resulted in the frequently used formula: "I am Yahweh (Jehovah/LORD) your God, who brought you out of the land of Egypt, out of the house of bondage" (Exod. 20:2, and frequently). The references to the saving acts of God in connection with Israel's exodus from Egypt fill the rest of the Old Testament. God is, by definition, the redeemer from bondage, and bondage, captivity, oppression, are thus indelibly stamped as evil.

In the New Testament, this definition of God as the redeemer from bondage receives cosmic dimensions. God, in Jesus Christ, redeems humanity from the captivity of whatever principality and power may hold humanity captive in its clutches. The fact that this cosmic redemption extends to the suprahuman and invisible powers of darkness, however, should not make us forget or brush aside that this is only a widening of understanding regarding God's redeeming activity, an activity which was paradigmatically expressed in God's freeing of a group of slaves from their earthly taskmasters. That Jesus did not mean to exclude limited and earthly bondage from God's redemptive will is shown by his repeatedly expressed concern for the oppressed and the prisoner (Matt. 11:5; 25:36). Both Testaments include freedom from captivity and oppression in their descriptions of the coming fullness of God's rule (the Day of the Lord, and the kingdom of God, respectively). (Isa. 9:4-5; cf. 42:7; 49:9; Mic. 4:4; Luke 4:18).

God, the redeemer from bondage and oppression, was to be the model for the Israelite in the treatment of neighbors. Having experienced release from captivity and oppression, one was to refrain from oppressing and enslaving one's neighbor (Exod. 21:16; Deut. 5:12-15; 24:7). The reality in ancient Israel did not conform fully to the ideal. There was slavery, although it appears to have been limited in extent and comparatively humane (Exod. 21:1-11; Deut. 15:12-18; 21:10-14; Lev. 25:25-38, 39-42). Where rulers like Solomon wanted to exact forced labor from their people, they met violent opposition (1 Kings 12:1-20). The prophets spoke out forcefully against selling the poor into slavery for debt (Amos 2:6; 8:6). Israel did subjugate some foreign people, however, and the Old Testament distinguishes, in matters of freedom, between an Israelite and a foreigner.

Jesus' ministry, as was mentioned already, was a ministry of redeeming all humankind from the bondage of the cosmic powers of darkness, Satan and his cohorts. However, the result of this redemption reached into the earthly forms of bondage, such as sickness and imprisonment, as we have noted already. The early church continued this ministry in many ways, but there, too, the ideal was limited by sociological realities. It is well known that the apostolic church, while embracing slaves as welcomed and desired brothers, did not reject totally the institution of slavery as it existed in the Roman Empire.

In spite of the imperfect implementation of freedom in Israel and in the early church, the liberating thrust of the will of God was clear, and at least partially effective in concrete situations, in both Testaments.

2. *Justice*, just as freedom from oppression, has the full theological support of the Bible, being rooted in the character of God who is the supreme and righteous judge (Gen. 18:25; Judg. 11:27; Ps. 94:2) and the advocate of all who suffer injustice.

"Justice," often paralleled by "righteousness," transcends the meaning of our term *justice*. While we tend to apply it primarily to legal justice, the Bible goes beyond that, though it includes legal justice. To do justice, or to be a just person, means basically to respond to situations of need in a helpful manner. God's justice consists of crushing the oppressor and helping the oppressed. God's representative, the king, is to be the primary example of God's justice. Psalm 72 states it classically:

Give the king thy justice, O God,
and thy righteousness to the royal son!
May he judge thy people with righteousness,
and thy poor with justice!

May he defend the cause of the poor of the people,
give deliverance to the needy,
and crush the oppressor!

For he delivers the needy when he calls,
the poor and him who has no helper.
He has pity on the weak and the needy,
and saves the lives of the needy.
From oppression and violence he redeems their life;
and precious is their blood in his sight. (v. 1, 2, 4, 12-14)

Job defends his righteousness and justice in similar terms:
I put on righteousness, and it clothed me;
my justice was like a robe and a turban.
I was eyes to the blind,
and feet to the lame.
I was a father to the poor
and I searched out the cause of him
whom I did not know.
I broke the fangs of the unrighteous,
and made him drop his prey from his teeth. (Job 29:14-17)

In the New Testament, the good Samaritan would be an example of doing justice, for he responded helpfully to the cause of the poor and needy.

However, this wider understanding of justice as "setting right" the affairs of the oppressed and needy does include the specifically legal-judicial realm. It is significant that all law in Israel, including the gradually evolved casuistic law practiced by the elders in the village gate, was "law of Moses," that is, a part of God's proclaimed will. All legal provisions and institutions to insure justice ultimately derive from God.

In actual practice, justice was not always achieved in Israel. Ample evidence for this fact can be found in the Psalms and the Prophets. The lament psalms contain two main causes for complaint: sickness and injustice. However, it is telling that these psalms are outcries to God as the final court of appeal.

God's spokesmen, the prophets, are vigorous advocates of justice. God's will for justice is undoubted. This becomes especially clear when we note that the theme of justice dominates the Day of the Lord passages which describe the fullness of the divine rule to come, or the kingdom of God. That rule will be one of justice, and consequently of peace. Isaiah says of the branch that shall come forth from the stump of Jesse:

He shall not judge by what his eyes see,
    or decide by what his ears hear;
but with righteousness he shall judge the poor,
    and decide with equity for the meek of the earth;
and he shall smite the earth with the rod of his mouth,
    and with the breath of his lips he shall slay the wicked.
Righteousness shall be the girdle of his waist,
    and faithfulness the girdle of his loins. (Isa. 11:3-5)

For the New Testament, this new David has come in Jesus Christ, who has begun his reign of righteousness in sign form now, but will complete it in its fullness in the end.

3. *Equality* in the biblical sense is rooted in the equality of all human beings before God. This begins with male and female, who together are created to be God's image (Gen. 1:27). It is further underscored by the monotheism of biblical faith. There is no hierarchy of divine beings, and no hierarchy of peoples. Israel's election has often been interpreted as divine favoritism, and was so interpreted by Israelites themselves at various times. But the Old Testament makes it abundantly clear (Deut. 7:6-8; 9:6-8; Amos 9:7, and many others) that this is a total misunderstanding of election. Israel is called to be an instrument through which all nations will be blessed (Gen. 12:3).

Similarly, all persons who stand out as great personalities in the Bible—Abraham, Moses, David, the prophets—derive their greatness from their instrument function. They are important to the extent that they carry out their calling to be God's servants for the benefit of their people. There are no heroes in the Old Testament, if by heroism is meant higher glory and loftier position on the basis of greater personal worth and achievement. The reversal of worldly hero worship in the ministry of humiliation by Jesus Christ (Phil. 2:5-11) clinches this observation.

We have already discussed the understanding of land and property claims in Israel, and their thrust toward equal distribution in keeping with need. There was no caste or class structure in Israel, at least none that found any social, much less any theological, acceptance. Of course, there were some differences in wealth and office, in keeping with the natural developments and needs in any human community. The Old Testament does not promote a doctrinaire egalitarianism. There were also flagrant abuses as in the case of Solomon's aggrandizement, and there was a short-lived movement toward an upper class of wealthy landowners from the mid-eighth century (the time of Amos) on. Such developments were fiercely condemned by the prophets and were named as a major cause for the fall of Israel (722 B.C.) and Judah (587 B.C.) to foreign powers. The exilic and postexilic community appears to have regained some of the equality inherent in Israel's faith and life.

The New Testament continues these trends. The full ideal is stated classically in Galatians 3:28:

There is neither Jew nor Greek,
there is neither slave nor free,
there is neither male nor female;
for you are all one in Christ Jesus.

As we know, this ideal stood in tension at various times with the social realities of that age. Slavery was not totally rejected, as we already noted. The role of women, though greatly elevated, could not escape the yardsticks of social propriety. And finally, the Jewish-Gentile tension created controversy for some time. Nevertheless, the ferment of equality of all people before God was present and active in the dough of society.

Personal Fulfillment

This heading embraces the sum total of modern Western aspirations in life. Will my life be such that it will have been worth living? Modern Westerns ask this question very individualistically. One perceives oneself, if not as an island, at least as a rather self-contained unit and expects that the fulfillment of one's life should be evident to, and experienced by, oneself. Further, one expects such fulfillment largely in terms that make one stand out from others. [5] If one can accomplish some uniqueness that makes one unexchangeable, one's personal fulfillment is enhanced. Thus such features as artistic creativity (in producing the new and unique) and inventiveness are often associated with fulfillment. The same is true of positions of authority and power not achieved by many, and thus setting their incumbents apart. Unusual, exotic experiences—from lion safaris to drug-induced psychic trips—are sought out in the quest for a fulfilled life. In the religious sphere, special "spiritual experiences" are often the goal. [6]

Such a list does not exhaust modern people's search for fulfillment, but it is sufficient to indicate its direction. Biblical persons were quite different in this respect. To the extent that we know of their life aspirations, they all had the characteristics of becoming *like* others, rather than different from others. Not uniqueness, but incorporation was the aim.

Ludwig Koehler states that entering adulthood meant for the Israelite man to be admitted to four great orders of life, namely those of marriage, of war, of justice, and of cultic worship.[7] Going beyond Koehler, we can point out that within each of these realms a man could move to a certain fulfillment of its ideals. Within marriage, a man hoped for children and children's children. To see them grow up was the joy of his old age. The realm of warfare offered one the possibility of being praised as a man of valor, but as we noted already, heroism never became an end in itself; the aim was not individual glory, but usefulness in the protection of the community. The war dead were neither envied nor celebrated, but mourned. In the realm of justice the adult Israelite could gain respect as a man of wisdom, who had good counsel to give, and who would eventually sit among the elders in the gate. In the realm of the cult, a man was responsible for his household, and as he applied the law of God, he might come to be righteous, like Job. Thus far for the man.

The Israelite woman's aspiration was to be a mother of many.[8] She did not need to worry about getting married, as the family arranged for that, just as it did for the man. But childlessness was a grave cause for suffering, since the raising of a family was her desired goal. In our world where overpopulation is a threat; where the pain and the danger of childbirth have been reduced by medical science; and where child mortality is drastically controlled, it is hard for us to appreciate fully the sense of bravery, of accomplishment, and of vital contribution to society which a mother of a large family felt in Israel. Her sense of fulfillment was in no way a sublimation for other achievements which were not open to her as a woman.

Thus both the man and the woman experienced fulfillment by becoming part of those realms and activities that sustained and protected the ongoing life of the community. Becoming a better part, rather than standing out individually, was their goal and fulfillment.

The New Testament continues this principle of incorporation, over against the modern promotion of a solitary self. Paul's analogy of the Christian as a member of the body (Rom. 12:3-8; 1 Cor. 12) is most telling here. One's aspiration as a Christian is to strive for one's eternal calling, but as one does so, one's life can be evaluated by one's harmonious functioning as a member in the body of Christ, the Church. Or, to put it differently, one's goal should be the exercise of one's spiritual gifts, yet these gifts are never understood as individualistic enhancement, but as qualities that make one useful in the furthering of the life of the community.

There is one other great difference between the biblical and the modern Western sense of personal fulfillment. The modern Western person tends to think quantitatively. Even when he considers the realization of his values, his concern is with amount and extent. If friendship is good, we must have many friends. If traveling is a worthwhile experience, we must see the whole world. If health is desirable, we must do away with illness. If the hungry are to be fed, we must plan in terms of the world's millions. Sometimes one wonders whether marriage is not threatened due to the same quantitative approach: If sex is good, sex with more than one person is better! Such a concern for quantity or coverage encounters the despair of ineffectiveness. If our relief donations cannot do away with hunger in the world, what's the use? If there always have been wars, one might as well give up striving for peace.

In remarkable contrast to this, we see Jesus walking the land for a few brief years, healing a few sick among his world's thousands, feeding a few people, teaching his twelve disciples. (When I have a college class of twelve, I wonder whether such a low enrollment warrants my efforts and my salary!) Where is Jesus' sense of effectiveness and relevance?!

Jesus stands in direct line with the Old Testament. Consider Abraham, who was promised that he would become a great nation and inherit the land. By the time of his death, he had *one* son (of the line of Sarah, that counted) and *one* plot of land (the field of Machpelah). In other words, he had reached fulfillment, not by quantitative fullness, but by having received a foretaste, or a sign, that God was at work in his life. Similarly, many psalmists praise God for *one* experience of healing or vindication, promising to serve God as long as they live. The important aspect of a fulfilled life was to have tasted of God's goodness, not to have "eaten it all the time."

Jesus established signs or foretastes of the kingdom.[9] Hebrews 11 spells out how the faithful live only in part by experiencing the goal, but remain pilgrims and sojourners on this earth. Perhaps it would help us not to lose courage in our efforts to raise the quality of life, if we could see ourselves as establishing signs of the kingdom, rather than as quantitatively changing the earth into the kingdom in our own strength.

Notes

[1] For more detailed discussion see my paper "Created in God's Image" in this volume, pp. 51-60.

² For a fuller interpretation of these chapters see my paper "In the Beginning" in this volume, pp. 41-50.

³ Claus Westermann, verbal statement in the context of the Sprunt Lectures, Union Theological Seminary, Richmond, Virginia, Jan. 31-Feb. 3, 1977.

⁴ For a fuller discussion see my article "The Biblical Basis for Stewardship of Land" in this volume, pp. 158-69.

⁵ On this subject see also my article "Human Wholeness in Biblical Perspective" in this volume, pp. 61-67.

⁶ On this subject see also my article "Which Way to God?" in this volume, pp. 9-14.

⁷ Ludwig Koehler, *Hebrew Man* trans. Peter Ackroyd (Nashville: Abingdon, 1977), pp. 74-84.

⁸ The following is spelled out more fully in my articles "Sexuality in the Old Testament" and "Male and Female Roles in the Old Testament" in this volume, pp. 68-83 and 84-91, respectively.

⁹ For an interpretation of the biblical significance of signs see my article "Sign and Belief" in this volume, pp. 15-26.

Part III
In Quest of Place

13
Geography of Faith

The Lure of Mother Earth

Rabbi Richard L. Rubenstein in an article subtitled "The Meaning of Place in Contemporary America," takes his reader up Mount Washington and surveys with him the city of Pittsburgh below.[1] He is impressed by two scenes in particular, one of them natural, the other man-made. There is, first, the "great meeting place of waters at which the Allegheny and the Monongahela rivers join to become the Ohio," and there is, second, "a magnificent view of Pittsburgh's economic and financial heart, the Golden Triangle."[2] He knows of no other American city save San Francisco that has so impressive a natural view. But the two foci of this view are at odds with each other. The great anonymous business corporations, "devoted to the successful exploitation of the earth's resources," have built their skyscrapers without intuitive empathy for the drama of the landscape, so that they stand there now in their vertical abruptness as a violation of it. America has no holy places, laments Rubenstein, and most Americans, especially professional Americans, lead a nomadic existence, without permanent attachments to places or regions, and without love for them.

Things are different, claims the rabbi, in other parts of the world. Rotterdamers knew how to rebuild their city after World War II. Paris has as its sacred heart the Cathedral of Our Lady of Paris and the Ile de la Cité on which it stands. Rubenstein recounts his sense of the sacred as he visited the Cathedral of Ibiza and, especially, the Cathedral of Our Lady of Chartres, where the crypt impressed him most of all. These are second only to the holy places of Palestine: the Church of the Nativity, with its cavelike entrance and interior reminiscent of a womb; the Harem el Khalil in Hebron, built over the traditional site of the Cave of Machpelah (Gen. 23), the burial place of Abraham and the other patriarchs; and the temple area itself, situated on the rock that tradition has called the navel of the earth. It will not surprise the reader at this point that Rubenstein becomes overtly psychoanalytic and associates these holy places, with their imputed symbolism of cave, tomb, and navel, with the security of the womb, to which humans long to return. To meet the sacred is to enter the womb, as it were.

It is not simply their capacity for Freudian interpretation, however, that makes places sacred; after all, America has caves and rocks enough. Holy places are not designated by humans at all, says the rabbi; they themselves make their inherent holiness known. Many of the holy places named above were built on sites of older shrines, so that at points successive religions have worshiped on the same spot. We understand now that it is the great mother goddess herself, worshiped under different names by many peoples and at many times, the goddess of fertility of humanity and earth, who apparently shows herself to those who can perceive her in the land.

What started at one level as an aesthetic and ecological concern in the face of the skyscrapers of Pittsburgh, turned then into a romantic trip to Rotterdam, Paris, Chartres, and the Holy Land and found its psychological common denominator in the Freudian symbolism of the return to the womb, has shown itself to be now, on the religious level, a divinization of the earth, a neo-Baalism. According to Rubenstein, however, this most primordial and persistent of religions is not available to Americans. Being nomadic in orientation, estranged from the land, and always on the move even if it be to the moon, America has missed discovering her sacred places; Pittsburgh certainly has, and it seems that other spots have equally poor chances of finding the holy. That we must live on the Freudian level is the rabbi's message to us. The fixed points of reference which every person needs so badly will not be available to us in our nomadic existence, other than inside us as we "discover resources for survival *within ourselves.* If we find any Archimedean point, it will be within. The security of home is only a memory. All we have left is the uncertain capacity to assume responsibility and direction over our own destinies. We cannot go home again."[3]

This Freudian gospel as a second best to the ultimate truth of Baalism, served by a rabbi with the age-old spices of Judaism, and made palatable to Americans with a green ecological icing, should be enough to call any Christian to his theological arms, provided that he takes the rabbi seriously enough to engage in battle. And we have to take him seriously, not because he is a popular writer and lecturer in contemporary North America, but because the various aspects of his article illustrate with the clarity of a textbook example the ideological approaches taken widely in our time to the question of our geographical existence. The following options emerge: (1) We can continue on that path which Rubenstein imprecisely characterizes as nomadic exploitation of nature, the path which is symbolically represented for him by the Pittsburgh skyscrapers as the headquarters of the great earth-exploiting corporations. (2) We can revolt against this nonrelationship to place and land either aesthetically or ecologically, by drawing on other modes of architecture or land use for our nostalgic dreams or for our reformer's models. (3) We can internalize geography so as to provide us with a stock of images of home, security, and holiness; these would not necessarily have to be Freudian. Such images are portable and can have value, therefore, for the nomad also. They offer the best available mode of relating ourselves to the land, according to Rubenstein. (4) We can attempt to sacralize the earth, the ground; to declare it holy and to seek an empathetic sense of unity with it, that is, to become nature worshipers. When we have come to be sufficiently attuned to nature, she herself will draw us to her bosom at those eternally sacred spots which we do not determine, but which are primordial and have their sacredness within themselves.

Every sensitive observer can find an extensive literature that moves along one or the other of these lines of approach to nature, place, and land, frequently progressing from concern for the preservation of the ecology as its appetizing starter to an outright neo-Baalism as its pagan end. [4] Is there not, the Christian asks, a theology of place that (1) neither exploits nor divinizes nature, and (2) neither internalizes geography so as to strip the actual geographical landscape of all theological significance, nor endows the landscape with a fixed and immovable theological meaning which declares certain places as sacred always and in themselves, so that they become the centers not only of pilgrimages but of holy wars and crusades? Leaving aside the first aspect, the quest for a truly Christian theology of nature, I direct my attention in this article primarily to the second point: What is a Christian theology of place? I ask whether Pittsburgh or Vancouver, the Mississippi or the western prairies, the farm where we grew up or the town where we attended school, are no more than the more or less exchangeable background scenery for Christian existence, or whether Christian existence can be expressed through them for us, just as it can be expressed—as Luther has helped us to see—through our vocation.

Christian theologians, by and large, have not occupied themselves with questions of humanity's geographical existence.[5] The Old Testament, to be sure, is vitally concerned with place and land. Its story can be told in terms of the land, from the promise to Abraham "To your descendants I give this land" (Gen. 15:18) down to the restoration of Jerusalem after the Babylonian Captivity, and further. The patriarchs are sojourners in the land. Moses leads Israel out of Egyptian captivity through the wilderness toward the Promised Land. Joshua begins its conquest, and David completes it by capturing Jerusalem-Zion. The land is Israel's inheritance from the Lord, the concrete and tangible expression of her covenant relationship to God. The prophets warn that covenant breaking will result in the loss of the land. Eventually a covenant-breaking people loses the land and has to go into Babylonian captivity, but there prophecies of hope are again in terms of a coming return to the land and a rebuilding of Jerusalem. Even the eschatological promises of God's ultimate reign are couched in geographical images. The land is always that specific land, the Land of Canaan, the geographical area of Palestine, the good and fertile land between the Mediterranean and the arid wilderness of Transjordan. Admittedly this land, with its various places and features, acquired a symbolic significance even in Old Testament times and became a religious reality which was not to be thought of as completely coextensive with any one set of boundaries at any one time. Nevertheless the theological meanings expressed in geographical terms never lost their moorings in concrete landscape; they never became only images of the mind.

In the New Testament much of the geographical terminology of the Old Testament (together with much of the latter's nongeographical terminology) is detached from specific and concrete realities and extended to worldwide dimensions. Israel is now the people of God anywhere; Jerusalem-Zion stands for the presence of God wherever that may be; Gog and Magog are the enemies of God from the four corners of the earth; to be a stranger and exile on earth, who seeks the city that has foundation, whose builder and maker is God, describes the Christian's existence in the world as he lives in the hope of eternal life. If we add to these developments the statements of Jesus that his kingdom is not of this world (John 18:36), and that the time shall come when people shall worship God neither in Jerusalem nor on Mount Gerizim but in spirit and in truth (John 4:21-24), we are not surprised that it has become a widespread, if not universal, assumption that geography has ceased to be theologically meaningful in the New Testament and for the Christian faith. In its stereotyped form this view can be stated thus: while the faith of the Old Testament was land-tied (a mark of its limitations), the faith of the New Testament is spiritual, which means primarily "inward, personal" to some, and "supernatural, otherworldly" to others, but "nongeographical" to most.[6]

Insofar as this view has prevailed, there is justification for the accusation of those who say that Christianity has become guilty here (as well as at other points) of desacralizing the earth; of literally and figuratively "de-secrating" it. But the alternative for the Christian cannot be neo-Baalism. Even a nature-embracing Christianity in the manner of Saint Francis will hardly be sufficient. Only a biblically-rooted theology of place and land will fill the need. Before we go out in search of such a theology, however, we must consider a question which interposes itself, namely that of the significance of geography as such for the understanding of modern humanity in the global village. There are those who claim that one's place today is of near-irrelevance to one's identity, both in one's own eyes and in the eyes of others. If they are right, concern for a theology of place is both anachronistic and superfluous. But is this really the situation of geography in our time?

The Myth of the Global Village

There were times, and not long ago, when a person's birthplace was the third most important item in identification, the first being his or her name and the second being his or her father's or ancestor's name. "I am NN; child of NN; from place NN" was the formula for self-introduction. Vocation ran a close fourth, with some flexibility of order among the elements following the name. In Canada even today the information which a person must give to a police officer on demand is name, address, and vocation. (The name, of course, includes the family name, which does the duty of the parent's or ancestor's name in our society.) Not only is a fixed address assumed here, but it is ranked with only three other items as having a certain primacy in identifying who one is.

The similarity is deceptive however. In many ages and cultures identification by place was understood to convey a fullness of characterization of a person by comparison with which the above-mentioned law preserves merely an empty shell. To know that one came from this village or that country meant to place one culturally, that is, to describe by implication many of one's mental and social—perhaps even biological—characteristics. This information in our time provides merely a convenience for the purpose of contacting a person. General mobility and the mixing of cultures effects a progressive erasing of the individuality of place and the continuity of attachment. The phrase "It could have happened anywhere" describes with increasing correctness much of our personal and group history. In the persuasive journalism of Alvin Toffler we read: "Never have man's relationships with place been more numerous, fragile and temporary."[7] For Christians it is tempting in these circumstances to assert, with seeming justification from the New Testament, that this is no loss to faith, for the significant spiritual events are either inward or otherworldly anyway.

Such currents of sociological development and theological thinking need to take note of certain counterindications to their assumed demise of geography. It is only recently that biologists and anthropologists have given much attention to the spiritual habits of animals and of humans. Robert Ardrey, in *The Territorial Imperative* (1966),[8] presents amazing findings about the behavior of animals in relation to their living space and their attachment to place, findings which cannot be disregarded as irrelevant for the understanding of human geographical behavior. Not only do various animals have well-defined needs in terms of space available to them and of distances between them, but such "territorial species" will mark off particular areas as their domain, doing this individually or in groups and resorting to most varied patterns. How behavior is related to territoriality, and how it is modified when patterns of territoriality are infringed upon, is equally significant. Ardrey argues that humans also are "territorial animals," acting with respect to place in a genetically determined pattern. This does not mean that humans are completely subject to biological determinism. Ardrey pleads for a distinction between a "closed instinct" which determines precise patterns of behavior and is found most purely in some insects, and an "open instinct," which allows much modification due to environment, and which is common in the higher animals. And yet there are biologically based patterns, he reports and argues (especially against cultural anthropologists), within which such learning takes place and which must not be disregarded.[9]

Edward T. Hall,[10] writing also in 1966 and exploiting also the findings of biologists regarding territoriality, applies them to human needs of space and sensitivity to distances. He points out the significance of locations and positions and attempts a cultural differentiation to show that Germans, Japanese, and Arabs, for example, tend to attribute different meanings to distances, positions, and locations.

Psychologists have also been concerned with the importance of geographical-spatial data for the self-understanding of humans. It is not enough, they realize, to philosophize abstractly about space and its relation to time through movement, and to contemplate humans as spatial, as well as temporal beings, where space means abstract dimensionality. The specifics of one's spatial surroundings become closely intertwined with one's experience. One lives in his *Eigenwelt,* that is, that private sphere which one constructs from elements of one's environment and elements within oneself. Infringement upon this *Eigenwelt* can lead to pathological conditions. Especially in schizophrenia, disturbances in spatial relationships become very obvious.[11] Eugéne Minkowski[12] speaks of "lived space" which is qualitative and personal. He illustrates from one aspect of space— distance. Geometrical distance extends between two points, regardless of the presence of houses or fields or woods between them. The mid-point between these two points would be half the distance away from each. But if we attach a personal goal to traversing a distance, the situation becomes different. If I set out to visit an art gallery several miles away but have to abandon my goal after traveling half way, geometrically speaking, I cannot say that I have made half my trip. The universal geometrical meaning of space is to be distinguished from the personal meaning which the same geography may acquire for a certain person. In the latter context, life normally has a certain spatial "fullness" for us. We experience people walking about on the same street with us, each pursuing his or her purposes, as belonging to us in a sense, tied to us through spatial awareness, yet separated from us by spatial gaps. By the way of contrast, Minkowski gives the illustration of a schizophrenic who assumed matter-of-factly that his psychiatrist and a priest, not otherwise associated with each other, had had consultation. There was a collapse of spatial gaps in the patient's perception of reality. (While Minkowski rules out any persecution delusion in this case, he considers such collapse of lived space to be a possible substructure of such delusions.)

The meaning of one's place can be assessed, finally, in philosophical terms. Jonathan Z. Smith outlines two basic but different approaches that can be traced through history: one sees the universe as open, the other as closed.[13] In the latter, man's task is that of "finding his place" in the universe; in the former, man is always on the move. In the latter, man is always at work to carve out a secure enclave for himself; in the former, man always tries to break out of the fences that want to contain him. One seeks order and meaning, the other movement and freedom. "The question of the character of the place on which one stands is *the* fundamental symbolic and social question. Once an individual or culture has expressed its vision of its place, a whole language of symbols and social structures will follow."[14] The social significance of one's understanding of one's place is illustrated by Smith with reference to money. In the open view of the universe—prevalent in North America—money is a means to transcend one's place, of freedom to escape from being locally bound. In a locative or closed society, money serves "to establish or re-enforce a sense of place." We have tried to demonstrate that, even in our present world of mobility, place and geography provide extremely significant perspectives for our understanding of human life.[15] We have done so by drawing eclectically on representative insights from the disciplines of biology, anthropology, psychology, and philosophy. But has this not been an exercise in demonstrating the obvious, in adducing scholarly testimony for a truth which everyone experiences and observes, and for which we could all bring supportive illustrations from various walks of life? The following personal observations are given at random.

Many of my college students grew up on prairie farms. By the time that the younger children of a family have reached college age, the parents are often ready to retire, which means selling or renting the farm. Conversations with students have shown me time and again that this move by the parents can mean a minor identity crisis for the children, even though they have already been away from home for some time without thought of returning home for any extended time. It is not enough to have the internalized security of their childhood home on the farm, though that is certainly important; these students discover that their identity is tied, in part, to the actual farm, so that a wound has to heal when that attachment is cut.

Another observation comes from my refugee life during World War II. Many people had to leave their homes. They found scanty accommodation in rooms requisitioned from residents of the places where they eventually arrived. How should they think of themselves in a new place? If a person in such circumstances could establish some identity between his or her former home and the new place, perhaps through setting up a picture or item from the old home, the new situation was reinterpreted as a "being at home," even if only in part (unless that object served as a fetish only). It matters how we understand our place, even at times of greatest "uprootedness."

A related phenomenon is evident in group movements. My Mennonite forebears have a history of migration, usually in groups, such as village populations. Often these were movements from older and more prosperous settlements into frontier wilderness. But the poor and struggling pioneer villages, not comparable at all to those left behind, were generally called by the same names as those that had been home in former times. Some village names have traveled from West Prussia to Russia and on to Paraguay or Canada. In each case a new place was interpreted as home, and the move as a movement home.

Finally, an observation about letter writing. North Americans, especially North American professionals, are nomads, according to Rubenstein and Toffler. They travel easily and lack permanent attachment. In one sense this is true, and yet not altogether. Many things fall into place when one realizes one quality of this readiness to move. Here letter writing is illustrative. One writes personal letters in order to keep in contact with people who have gone away. With my European background, it took me some time to discover why my North American friends would not write letters to me, except at times when special concerns warranted writing. Some had been close friends, and when we met again the old relationship seemed to be there still. Only after years did I discover what I believe to be the answer: in their view they had not really been away from me. Americans regard America as *one* locality, for certain purposes; almost like an area marked off as theirs in terms of Ardrey's territoriality. As long as one is in that territory, one is not away. One may make phone calls or drop in on neighbors, even if they are several hundred miles away, but one does not indulge in such a symbolism of distance as writing personal letters, unless, of course, there is some concrete occasion that warrants it. And in this attachment to America, Americans are not nomads in Rubenstein's sense; they may not love Pittsburgh with lasting loyalty, but they do love America, "from California to New York Island." One even wonders at times whether America as such is perhaps perceived to be that holy place which Pittsburgh is not.

Toffler's analysis of statistics of movement in America do indeed support the common observation that mobility is on the increase. [16] The conclusions which he draws from them, however, show a patent inner contradiction. While affirming on the one hand the profound impact of the change of home upon the individual, he pictures on the other hand a new breed of people who apparently move easily and joyfully at a moment's notice. These are for him, the new people of "super-industrial society, the way of the future." They often show, he observes, a loss of commitment, for commitment to anything, including place, depends on length of association. On second thought, however, he concludes that their commitments simply shift from place-related social structures to other, place-less ones, such as the corporation, the profession, or the network of friendship. But, we ask, if exposure to many places during a single lifetime results in lack of commitment to places as such, should one not expect exposure to many people—certainly a fact in every mobile urban existence—to lead to a loss of genuine human attachments altogether? That this is not so is borne out again and again. Exposure to many people requires greater selectivity in forming deep attachments; that a person lives next door does not now automatically result in the same interdependence which neighborhood meant in a farm or village setting. On the other hand, life among multitudes of people may lead to even deeper, and certainly more conscious, ties to those to whom one's loyalties reach out.

This may well be, I suggest, true of loyalty to places also. If Toffler speaks of the demise of geography, he really hits only a certain form of loyalty unreflectingly granted to some few places due to lack of exposure to others. The mobile modern person of the future, on the other hand, can be expected to become more consciously selective in geographical attachments. He or she will in all likelihood not be committed automatically to every spot on the map where he or she happens to spend some time. Those places which form the geographical coordinates for whatever meaning he or she has found in life may well be treasured more highly and more consciously. Then he would indeed be a nomad in the truer sense of the word, that is, one whose life would show a pattern of movement, but a pattern not unrelated to certain fixed points with reference to which one would interpret one's movements. The nature of the significance of geographical realities in modern life is undergoing momentous changes, but the fact of their significance is no less to be reckoned with. From the Christian perspective it is precisely the understanding of life as a pilgrimage which shifts geography into the circle of central theological concerns.

The Places Which the Lord Will Choose

If geographical realities have not ceased to define human life but have emerged into a changed but no less central role in modern times, their theological interpretation, far from being an anachronistic effort, needs renewed attention. How is my Christian existence anchored to the map? Or how is my "anchoredness" to the map to be understood in Christian terms? The Christian (and the Jew) must immediately reject as antibiblical all forms of neo-Baalism, including that of Rabbi Rubenstein. The Christian will be diffident of finding the holy spots of the earth where the mother goddess beckons to be worshiped; one would be serving at such spots not the God of Abraham, Moses, and Jesus Christ, but merely God's creation, as nature worshipers of old have done, "on every high hill and under every green tree."

Can the "sacred places" of Christendom, instead, command the Christian's loyalties and reward him or her with geographical anchorage? Jerusalem, Bethlehem, Rome, Lourdes, Canterbury, Geneva? Again Rabbi Rubenstein provides us with an insight. Upon reading his article we are at first surprised that he, a Jew, can sense the holy in Our Lady of Paris, in the Church of the Nativity, and in the Dome of the Rock. Is he so ecumenical in outlook that he can submit to the meaning of Christian and Moslem holy places just as well as to that of Jewish ones? Far from it, we discover. Since it is the mother goddess of the womb and the earth whom he discovers in all these, he does not understand these sacred places as being sacred in the context of the theologies of these religions. To find inherent sanctity in places, it becomes necessary to step outside the realm of biblically-oriented theology. The very concept of a statically sacred place with its inherent holiness not only withstands all New Testament theology, but has no ground in the Old Testament either. Outside of biblical theology all holy places are akin to one another so that rituals from various religions can be easily appropriated to the worship of the mother goddess, as Rubenstein correctly observes and illustrates. So-called Christian holy places, if their holiness is statically and inalienably tied to their location, derive their real legitimation from outside the realm of biblical theology, just as do those which claim overtly to be nature shrines.

Here the Old Testament is often seriously misunderstood. While humans according to biological predisposition, just as certain animals, may be bound by laws of territoriality, organize their behavior around a firmly staked out piece of ground, and defend it as their dearest possession, biblical faith does not sanctify a firm attachment to the ground, much less declare such ground to have been sacred from primordial times. That would be Baalism again, the worship of the god of the land, or Hitler-ideology of blood and soil. Biblical faith redeems from bondage, including the bondage of territoriality. But at the same time it shatters false securities, including those offered by territoriality. The doctrine of election in both Testaments pertains to places as it does to people, and election is for a time, so that an end may be accomplished.

Holy places in the Old Testament, therefore, do not claim primeval sanctity; they receive their holiness in the broad light of history. Their holiness is their election toward importance for a time to bring to pass God's purposes, and such a holiness is then conditional upon their functioning toward the fulfillment of those purposes. Throughout the Old Testament there exists a rich and many-sided theology of the land, [17] aptly illustrated by the meaning of the land in Deuteronomy. Formulated as farewell sermons of Moses, the Book of Deuteronomy addresses the Israelites as a people on the verge of crossing the Jordan. It sees the land of promise and of rest lying almost within reach. Its riches and its blessings are extolled in glowing terms, and Israel is instructed in the ways of life and worship in this land, which is God's land, to be given as a gift in fulfillment of his love and his promises to the patriarchs. But this land will be a touchstone, at the same time, as to whether Israel will be true to her covenant-bond with God, through serving God and God only with all her heart in loyal allegiance. If not, if she will desecrate this land by breaking the covenant stipulations in her dealings with God and with neighbor, the blessings of the land will turn into curses, the last and worst of which will be that God, who has given the land to Israel as a gift and a trust, will take it away again.

We can see here in only one Old Testament sampling how the land is not considered to be holy in itself. True, it is God's land always, and God can dispose of it, just as God is the sovereign over all lands, but whether this particular land will give Israel a special bridge to God, as it were, so that her life of faith can settle down here permanently to a religious territoriality, is another question. No, the land is a sacred plot by virtue not of any inherent sacredness but of God's choice of it as an instrument toward his purposes. If these purposes are thwarted God will lay aside that instrument.

The prophets, consequently, warn Israel that her covenant breaking will lead to loss of land and to exile, and the Deuteronomic History—extending through Joshua, Judges, 1 and 2 Samuel, and 1 and 2 Kings—is a grand theological survey of Israel's approximately 650 years in her land, to show how God once gave the land as a tangible token of the covenant relationship, at the time of Joshua, and how a history of persistent covenant breaking made God take it away again through Nebuchadnezzar in the year 587 B.C. Any concept of an eternal sacredness of the land of Canaan or of the city of Jerusalem constitutes a perversion of Old Testament claims. [18] When Judaism today reveres the Holy Land, the temple area, and other such places as memorials to God's historical revelation in the past, Christians can join in and add their own memorials. But when Judaism goes further and attributes to these places an eternal and inherent sanctity, we must object not only on New Testament grounds, but also on the basis of the Old Testament. [19]

The teaching of the New Testament in this respect must be of even greater interest to the Christian. What does it say concerning the theological significance of geographical data? A question that may well be asked first is this: Does the New Testament treat the sacred places of the Old Testament as holy places? Without reflection one would tend to answer in the affirmative. Does not Jesus' ministry take place in the same land in which Abraham sojourned, which Joshua conquered, over which David reigned, and for which the prophets wept? Was he not born in the city of David's birth, Bethlehem, and crucified in the religious center of Israel, Jerusalem? Surely this is a holy land, these are sacred places, where the acts of God become visible to people again and again, and where our eyes of faith should be directed even today, for holy history seeks out holy ground!

And yet we must reject this response. The holy geography of the Old Testament is not upheld as continuing to be holy in the New. While Jesus' ministry extends to approximately the same area as that of the Old Testament kingdoms of Israel and Judah, the meaning of this territory becomes a radically different one from that in the Old Testament. And this is not because the New Testament proclaims a faith which is either inward or otherworldly, and therefore not interested in geography. Hans Conzelmann[20] devotes a whole third of his *Theology of St. Luke* to a discussion of the theological significance of the geographical information in that Gospel, that is, of the places, the regions, and the manner of movement associated with Jesus. For in these we have to see an aspect of the Incarnation also, the Incarnation which is not to be limited to the person of Jesus of Nazareth, but extends also to his movements and to the places where he moved.

The briefer treatment here may serve as a sample of the rich and complex geographical theology of Luke and Acts. F. C. Grant, following Ernst Lohmeyer and R. H. Lightfoot, gives the following picture of the theological significance of geography in Mark: Galilee is the "Holy Land" of this Gospel, the land which, according to Isaiah 9:1, 2, dwelt in deep darkness, but has seen a great light (though the Old Testament reference is provided by Matthew, who preserves Mark's Galilean emphasis and elucidates it overtly through the Old Testament interpretation).[21] Being a Galilean, according to Mark, is almost synonymous with being a follower of Jesus. The opposition of Jesus comes from the scribes who came down from Jerusalem. And Jesus himself goes to Jerusalem to suffer and to die. In Galilee the good news is proclaimed, and there the fulfillment of the end time expectations is anticipated, so that the disciples are directed to go there immediately after the resurrection and to expect the resurrected Lord.

Note, first, how geography incarnates the message of election of that which is lowly: Galilee, the region on the far fringe, away from the center of Jewish religious activity. (Luke expresses election geographically also. Jesus, rejected by his home town Nazareth, makes his elected home, Capernaum, the center of his ministry, foreshadowing the movement of the gospel from Jerusalem to Rome, from Jews to Gentiles, a story which he will tell in Acts.)[22] Note, second, that Jerusalem, though significant in Marcan theology, has not at all that meaning which it generally had in the Old Testament. It is now not the place of the presence of God but, by contrast, the place where God's presence is not tolerated—a far cry from the idea of inherent and perpetual holy spots on earth! And, third, note once again in what manner the Old Testament's sacred places are seen in the New Testament. They are not holy places in perpetual continuity; instead, their Old Testament meaning, now still present as a mental image, contributes to the interpretation of new divine acts.

This dynamic becomes particularly clear in Matthew, where Old Testament localities are constantly adduced, not for their inherent theological significance, but for the purpose of interpreting typologically the new realities brought by Jesus. Thus Jesus' birth in Bethlehem authenticates him as the son of David; his Sermon on the Mount makes us see him as the promulgator of God's will in the light of Moses and Mount Sinai, and so forth. In the Gospel of John this use of Old Testament geographical features for the interpretation of Jesus becomes so focused that the significance of the Old Testament feature in question is often transferred to the very person of Jesus. Thus the cleansing of the temple (John 2:13ff) concludes with Jesus' reference to his body as the temple which will be destroyed and raised again, and in which God resides. When the Samaritan woman at Jacob's Well recalls sacred history and asks: "Are you greater than our father Jacob, who gave us the well, and drank from it himself, and his sons, and his cattle?" (John 4:12), Jesus affirms once more that he, not Jacob's Well, is the source of water that sustains life. And again the Pool of Bethesda in Jerusalem, with its reputed powers to heal, is set aside in its significance as Jesus heals the sick man (John 5:1ff). Or we think of the manna in the wilderness (John 6:31ff) to which Jesus juxtaposes himself as the true bread of life.

This observation, that the sacred geography of the Old Testament lives on in images of the mind which help to interpret life typologically, might confirm in us the stereotyped conviction that the New Testament is uninterested in the actual and external geographical features of its own setting, and that Christians throughout the world, consequently, also live in theologically insignificant geographical contexts, even though they may sing in the geographical images of the past "We're marching to Zion" or speak of their "Damascus Road experience." In that case an application—Christianized, to be sure—of Rabbi Rubenstein's counsel to rely on one's internalized resources might be the final insight resulting from the search for the theological significance of places. [23]

The function of interpreting new divine acts typologically through reference to the Old Testament's geographical data and their meanings is but one of two ways in which geographical features become theologically important in the New Testament, however. The other has also been alluded to already: the New Testament proclaims overtly and repeatedly the significance of new places for faith, or reinterprets former holy places, like Jerusalem, so as to give them a new theological meaning. The Gospel of John, the Gospel where Old Testament geography is practically absorbed into Jesus, elevates new places, such as Cana, Bethany and Nazareth, to theological importance. [24] Nazareth may illustrate the process. D. Mollat has rightly said that Nazareth, and in a sense all Galilee, is the carrier of the *scandalon* of the Incarnation in the Fourth Gospel. [25] The motif question: "From where is Jesus?" receives the paradoxical answer: "He comes from Nazareth, he is a Galilean; and yet he comes from above, he is the Christ, the Son of God." Expressions like "Can anything good come out of Nazareth?" (John 1:45f) and "Search and you will see that no prophet is to rise from Galilee" (John 7:52; cf. v. 41) are countered with evidence for the divine sonship of Jesus of Nazareth. Only in John does the superscription on the cross include the name of Nazareth, embodying the fusion of contempt and exaltation which it incarnates in this Gospel.

The New Testament, then, abandons the concreteness of sacred Old Testament geography not toward inwardness or otherworldiness, but toward a new theological significance of new (or old) places, a new significance which emerges from new acts of God in history. In this light we must also read Jesus' statement that the time will come when people shall worship God neither in Jerusalem nor on Mount Gerizim, but in spirit and in truth. These words do not take faith off the map; they redeem it from static attachment to certain holy places alone, so that the whole map can now become potential territory for God's election toward his ends.[26] There is an analogy here to the priesthood of all believers. If we say that holiness does not inhere in certain persons, but that persons can be sanctified through God's choice of them for carrying out God's purposes, we must now equally say that holiness (or theological significance in the meditation of God's will and presence) does not attach inherently to certain places, but that every place can become the scene of God's self-manifestation in our time. Of course, the Christian understands this in the context of God's transcendence. Just as the assertion that God can be revealed today through people should not be inverted into the claim that people are divine in an immanental sense, the claim that God can choose any place as the place of self-manifestation should not be inverted into an assertion of divine immanence everywhere.

Tenting in the Land of Promise

Just as the Christian must not dissociate the Church from real people and make it into an altogether invisible entity—which is not to deny all need for a doctrine of the invisible Church—the Christian must not detach the Church from geography.[27] The Church is always somewhere; it has its geography not only of institutional extent but also of divine presence and activity. Each Christian in turn has ties to spots on the map where he or she has experienced these, and cannot, therefore, accept Rabbi Rubenstein's call for nothing more than portable, internalized meanings. While agreeing with him that we should not search for inherently sacred spots in America, whether Pittsburgh or others—they would be centers of Baalism anyway, just as those of Europe and Palestine become in Rubenstein's interpretation—the Christian should be open to the sacredness of places in the lives of groups and individuals because God has used places (in addition to people and events) to reveal himself to them. Christians have ties to many and various spots on the map. A Christian's history with God literally takes place on farms and in cities, in fields and forests, in countries and continents. The land of Canaan flowing with milk and honey, Zion, the beautiful city of God, but also the great and terrible wilderness, are still theological images of deepest meaning, but they take on embodiment for the Christian today not in geographical Palestine, but in that geographical setting where God's leading is experienced. [28]

A visit to Palestine may help the Christian to appropriate more fully and to clarify as to detail the geographical images of sacred history. While the possibility cannot be excluded that such a trip may in itself become for him or her an act or sign of God's leading, there is no more guarantee that this will happen than on many another trip. Biblical geography helps to interpret one's relationship to God as it provides images that can express the meaning of one's own life's path; as geographical reality the present geography of Palestine cannot claim any greater special significance than other places. [29]

The dynamic shown to be operative between the Testaments, and posited to be operative between the Bible and the present, is also at work between our own individual past and our own present. Just as biblical geography remains with the believer in the form of images that help to interpret the geography of our own pilgrimage of faith, so the places that had meaning for our Christian existence in our earlier years become increasingly transformed into mental images which we carry with us to help comprehend the meaning of our present place. To revisit our childhood home, for example, has a dual function for faith: (1) It performs a hermeneutical clarification. We clarify and reappropriate our images of security, parental love, early human relationships, first devotional experiences (assuming now that these had been present in childhood). (2) We allow these images to be expanded or reshaped. Thus, for example, the parental home, once symbol of security but now inhabited by strangers, comes to acquire the wider meaning that earthly securities are for a time only. This new relationship to place interprets again our present place both in its capacity to sustain and give security and in its character as a stopover on a journey, but never as the center of a circle to which all points on the circumference stand in a constant relation.

Notes

[1] Richard L. Rubenstein, "The Cave, the Rock and the Tent: The Meaning of Place in Contemporary America," *Morality and Eros* (New York: McGraw-Hill, 1970), pp. 164-82.

[2] *Ibid.*, p. 166.

[3] *Ibid.*, p. 182.

[4] Not many writers will go to such extremes as Everett E. Gendler, who attempts to discover a goddess Adamah (Earth) in that common Hebrew word in the Old Testament: "The Return of the Goddess," *Ecology: Crisis and New Vision,* ed. Richard E. Sherrell (Richmond, Va.: John Knox Press, 1971), 131-43. Yet even so circumspect a theologian as Conrad Bonifazi, in his attempt to bridge the estrangement between humanity and things, does not escape an immanental nature-mysticism. *A Theology of Things* (Philadelphia: Lippincott, 1967). Our own attempt, we hope, should help to "place humankind firmly on the earth," yet in the context of the biblical doctrine of a transcendent God who chooses to reveal himself in humanity and in nature without becoming coextensive with either.

[5] In contrast to the philosopher who concerns himself with "space" understood as abstract dimensionality, or the psychologist who tends to use "place" metaphorically to describe the reference system of a person, whether inward or outward, the geographer is interested in specific regions or localities that make up "the variable character of the earth surface," according to Richard Hartshorne, *Perspective on the Nature of Geography* (Chicago: Rand McNally, 1959), pp. 12-21. The once prominent distinction between physical and human geography has shown itself to be artificial. Even purely physical features are selected for study by the geographer according to the interest they hold for people, while human features, such as buildings or railroads, contribute significantly to the particular character of a place or region. The past must interest the geographer also, but "Such historical studies are essentially geography rather than history as long as the focus of attention is maintained on the character of areas . . ." (Hartshorne 107; cf. also 35, 36-47, 79f). In Hartshorne's definition, then, "geography is that discipline that seeks *to describe and interpret the variable character from place to place of the earth as the world of man"* (47, italics his). For our purpose we might extend the geographer's definition of place just slightly into the historical dimension, of which Paul Tournier reminds us when he says that "a real place is not only a geographical location. It must also be located in history" *A Place for You* (New York: Harper and Row, 1968), 60. In this connection we disavow, to avoid all misunderstanding, any interest in upholding any version of environmentalism, that is, the understanding that an area has determinative influence on its population. The interest of our study lies precisely in preserving the significance of geography for faith without making humanity a captive of the land. (On environmentalism, see Hartshorne, p. 55ff.)

[6] That the significance of geography for faith could not be suppressed in spite of its neglect in formal theology, is demonstrated by the flourishing of shrines and pilgrimages in Christian piety, as well as by such reassertions of the need for holy places as the Crusades represent. The lack of theological guidance in such questions must be blamed for the rank growth or uncontrolled emotionalism of these phenomena, as well as for their frequently perverse goals and practices. In a secularized form tourism preserves the witness to humanity's geographical existence.

[7] Alvin Toffler, *Future Shock* (New York: Bantam Books, 1971), p. 75.

[8] Robert Ardrey, *The Territorial Imperative* (Laurel Edition; New York: Dell, 1966).

[9] We are not concerned here with a critical assessment of Ardrey's theses; our interest lies solely in his testimony to the fact that territoriality has become the subject of significant research and discussion among biologists and social scientists.

The same applies to the selected topics drawn from other disciplines in the paragraphs immediately following.

[10] Edward T. Hall, *The Hidden Dimension* (Doubleday Anchor Book; Garden City, NY: Doubleday, 1969), first edition 1966.

[11] Tournier devotes *A Place for You* to a discussion of the significance of place, from the standpoint of a Christian psychiatrist. Cf. also Wayne E. Oates, "Spiritual Territory and Sick Religion," *When Religion Gets Sick* (Philadelphia: Westminster, 1970), pp. 101-21.

[12] Eugéne Minkowski, "Toward a Psychopathology of Lived Space," *Lived Time* trans. Nancy Metzel (Evanston: Northwestern University Press, 1970) original French edition 1933, pp. 399-433.

[13] Jonathan Z. Smith, "The Influence of Symbols upon Social Change: A Place on Which to Stand," *Worship* 44 (1970), pp. 457-74.

[14] *Ibid.*, p. 469.

[15] See above, no. 9.

[16] Toffler, *Future Shock,* pp. 74-94.

[17] Among writings specifically concerned with the theology of the land in the Old Testament the following may be mentioned: Gerhard von Rad, "There Remains Still a Rest for the People of God: An Investigation of a Biblical Conception," *The Problem of the Hexateuch and Other Essays,* trans. W. E. Trueman (New York: McGraw-Hill, 1966) original essay 1933, pp. 94-102; by the same author, "The Promised Land and Yahweh's Land in the Hexateuch," *ibid.* original essay 1943, pp. 79-93; by the same author, "The Deuteronomistic Theology of History in the Books of Kings," *Studies in Deuteronomy* trans. David Stalker (London: SCM 1953, 1956), pp. 74-91; by the same author, "Die Verleihung des Landes Kanaan," *Theologie des Alten Testaments I,* 4th edition (Munchen: Chr. Kaiser, 1966), pp. 309-17; Hans Wildberger, "Israel und sein Land," *Evangelische Theologie* 16 (1956), pp. 404-22; Patrick D. Miller, Jr., "The Gift of God (The Deuteronomic Theology of the Land)," *Interpretation* 23 (1969), pp. 451-65; Josef G. Plöger, "Die Aussagen über 'ereṣ and 'ādāmāh im Dt und ihre theologische Interpretation," Literarkritische, formgeschichtliche und stilkritische Untersuchungen zum Deuteronomium (Bonn: Hanstein, 1967), pp. 60-129. Cf. also the entries 'ereṣ (Land) and 'ādāmāh (Earth in the *Theologisches Wörterbuch zum Alten Testament* edited by Botterweck and Ringgren. For geographical terminology in the Old Testament, see Armin Schwarzenbach, *Die geographische Terminologie im Hebräischen des Alten Testaments* (Leiden: Brill, 1954). The Old Testament in the volume mentioned in number 19 below are also pertinent.

[18] When the so-called Jerusalem or Davidic Theology speaks of the "eternal" election of that city, it highlights God's unswerving faithfulness to his promises. It is a perversion, even in Old Testament terms (Jer. 7:26) to make of it an "eternal security" doctrine for Jerusalem.

[19] The understanding of the significance of the land, of Palestine, and of the city of Jerusalem forms a pivotal concern in Jewish-Christian dialogue. The major issues are reflected in *Jüdishes Volk-Gelobtes Land.* Die biblischen Landverheissungen als Problem des jüdischen Selbstverständnisses und der christlichen Theologie, herausgegeben von W. H. Eckert, N. P. Levinson, und M. Stöhr (München: Chr. Kaiser, 1970). We do not wish to deny all and every theological significance of Jerusalem and Palestine for the Jew and the Christian. That land has, of course, been central in the sacred history of both, and to "remember" (in a fullness of meaning that transcends our English word) is of theological significance in the Bible. We wish merely to recall the Christian (and perhaps this may be even more necessary with respect to the Jew, with his deep appreciation for the theological meaning of land) to a reconsideration of the theological significance of land in biblical perspective, so as to prevent a sliding into nature worship, or neo-Baalism,

as we saw it illustrated by Rabbi Rubenstein's article, though we might have adduced equally unbiblical attitudes towards the Holy Land and its various localities from Christian documents.

[20] Hans Conzelmann, *The Theology of St. Luke* trans. Geoffrey Buswell (New York: Harper & Row, 1961), original German edition, 1953.

[21] Frederick C. Grant, *The Earliest Gospel* (New York: Abingdon, 1943), pp. 125-47.

[22] Conzelmann, *Theology of St. Luke,* p. 34.

[23] Internalization of meanings, at one time attached to geographical realities, but now carried as mental images by a group or an individual, is a valid process in the transmission of meanings and values, of course, and is not questioned here. Cf. the works of Tournier and Oates, cited above, for the psychological significance of such internalization for the Christian.

[24] We cannot take up in this paper the complex relationship between "geographical fact" and the theological employment of geographical terminology, whether factually accurate or not. In connection with the Gospel of John the most recent trend seems to be a greater appreciation of the historical reliability of its geographical data. Cf. Raymond E. Brown, *The Gospel According to John* (Vol. 1, The Anchor Bible; Garden City: Doubleday, 1966), xlii-xliii; and R. D. Potter, "Topography and Archaeology in the Fourth Gospel," *Studia Evangelica,* Papers presented to the International Congress on "The Four Gospels in 1957" held at Christ Church, Oxford, 1957, ed. Kurt Aland et. al. (Berlin: Akademie-Verlag, 1959), pp. 329-37; as compared to the representatively distrustful position of C. C. McCown, "Gospel Geography: Fiction, Fact, and Truth," *Journal of Biblical Literature* 60 (1941), pp. 1-25, especially pp. 18f. Over against McCown, even a most cautious investigation into the "geography of the historical Jesus" would suggest that Jesus' actual movements were not unrelated to his message, that is, that Jesus proclaimed his message not only through word and sign, but also through his stays and movements, that is, through a theologically telling choice of place. Thus Albrecht Alt has made it appear very likely that Jesus not only limited his Galilean ministry to the geographical boundaries of that area but that Jesus avoided also the Hellenistic towns within it, so as to limit his ministry to "the lost sheep of the house of Israel," (*Where Jesus Worked,* trans. Kenneth Grayston, London: Epworth, 1961), a self-limitation that becomes meaningful and understandable theologically in the light of T. W. Manson's essay *Only to the House of Israel?* Facet Books, Biblical Series 9 (Philadelphia: Fortress Press, 1964).

[25] D. Mollat, "Remarques sur le vocabulaire spatial du quatriéme évangile," *Studia Evangelica,* pp. 322f.

[26] Thus also Tournier, p. 43; and J. J. von Allmen, "A Short Theology of the Place of Worship," *Studia Liturgica* 3 (1964), p. 156.

[27] *Ibid.,* p. 157.

[28] Tournier, adapting Buber's terminology, speaks of It-Places and Thou-Places in a person's life (13). And again he compares places of special personal meaning to the *kairoi,* the fullnesses of time: "There is a *kairos,* a moment in time when God reveals himself. Similarly he chooses places in which to reveal himself" (*ibid.,* p. 45).

[29] We would grant to it a status of *primus inter pares,* somewhat similar to that which later Christianity has accorded to the Early Church, or Gentile Christianity to the mother church in Jerusalem. (Cf. also above, number 19.) According to von Allmen (pp. 157f), the Church gathered for worship has reference, in terms of place, to four other places which are "echoed, approved, or anticipated" in it: the place of Christ's passion and death, the heavenly sanctuary, the Garden of Eden, and the heavenly Jerusalem. He does not, however, define with precision the way these "places" function theologically. Nevertheless we agree with him that the places of Christ's Incarnation have a primacy in the Christian's thinking, and yet not in such

a way as to be inherently sacred in the sense of nature worship, nor toward the end of despoiling the rest of the globe of theological significance.

The Biblical Basis of Stewardship of Land

Sojourners on Earth

A plot of earth, the Garden of Eden, was God's first gift to humanity. Man was made from that earth (*'ădāmāh*), as his very name (*'ādām*) signifies, and as Genesis 2:7 states: "God formed man of the dust of the ground (*'ădāmāh*)." That made him akin to the plants, for "Out of the ground (*'ădāmāh*) the Lord God made to grow every tree . . ." (Gen. 2:9), and "out of the ground (*'ădāmāh*) the Lord God formed every beast . . ." (Gen. 2:19). When Saint Francis of Assissi, in hymnic praise, proclaimed the sun, the moon, and the animals his brothers and sisters, he sounded a note struck in the story of creation.

In contrast to the widespread Ancient Near Eastern worship of divine mother earth, humanity was taken from under her sway and subjected to the higher authority of the creator of everything, including the earth. A demythologized earth was given back to humanity as garden, the Garden of Eden, to "till it and keep it" and "freely eat of it" within certain limits set by God (Gen. 2:15-17; cf. 1:30). Created "in the image of God,"[1] that is, as God's ruling representatives, human beings were blessed:

> "Be fruitful and multiply, and fill the earth and subdue it; and have dominion over the fish of the sea and over the birds of the air and over every living thing that moves upon the earth" (Gen. 1:28).

We note parenthetically that the blessing to fill the earth, and the permission to use its produce as food, was shared by the animals (Gen. 1:22, 30). And although the animals were subjected to man's authority (his naming them) and provided companionship (though not an ultimately satisfactory one) for him (Gen. 2:18-20), they were not given to him as food.

Humanity's rebellion against God, the so-called "Fall," is pictured in Genesis 3 and the subsequent chapters as a grasping for autonomy from God. To "be like God" and to disregard God's limitations by eating from the forbidden tree (Gen.3), to assume the right to kill one's brother (Gen. 4), and generally to seek human autonomy (Gen. 3-11) is the story of this rebellion. Sin, then and now, can be defined as humanity's attempt to act as master rather than steward.

The result is a reduction, though not a total loss, of God's intended commission and blessing. The land, the soil, is still man's place of life, scene of activity, and source of support, but his labors bear the stamp of servitude, the fertile garden is continually threatened by the inroads of the wilderness with the thorns and thistles, and his own earthiness becomes a sign of his mortality (Gen. 3:17-20). Humanity's relationship to the land becomes tenuous. Adam and Eve's expulsion from the garden (Gen. 3:22-24), Cain's lot as a "fugitive and a wanderer" ("And now you are cursed away from the ground . . ." Gen. 4:11) and the scattering of the builders of the Tower of Babel "abroad over the face of all the earth" (Gen. 11:9), link the theme of sin to that of homelessness and landlessness.

There is enmity now between human beings and their fellow creatures as represented by the serpent (Gen. 3:15), casting its disharmony even onto the companionship of man and woman (Gen. 3:16). The animals become—by way of concession to sin, though not without an element of grace in this—a source of clothing (Gen. 3:21) and food for humans (Gen. 9:3). However, humanity is to acknowledge God's ultimate sovereignty over life by abstaining from the eating of blood (Gen. 9:4), a practice incorporated into Israel's food laws (Lev. 17:10-16; Deut. 12:20-25) and affirmed even by the Apostolic Council in Jerusalem (Acts 15:20).

The story of Abraham initiates the theme of God's salvation of humanity. One ever-present strand in that theme is the restoration of humanity to a right relationship to the land. Uprootedness and homelessness remain a persistent mark of fallen humanity (Heb. 11:4-16). If accepted from God's hand, however, and lived under God's grace and leading, they can turn into a journey of faith and hope. That is the story of Abraham, who was called out of his homeland to become a wanderer with the promise of a new land which God would show him (Gen. 12:1-3). On this journey there are foretastes of fulfillment, stations on the way, tokens of belonging and rest. Abraham came to possess only one plot of ground in the land of his sojournings, and that was a burying ground (Gen. 23).

Abraham's descendants after him experienced other forms of homelessness: emigration, subjection and exploitation in a foreign land, escape, wanderings in the wilderness, and eventually conquest of the long-promised land of their forebears. Each of these stages was in its own way a contradiction of humanity's original destiny and commission to administer God's good land as stewards. Yet in each stage Israel experienced God's grace and leading, so that each could be seen as a way station toward the promised "inheritance" (as the land of Canaan is often called) and rest (Deut. 12:9).

But by what right, and in what sense, did Israel finally come to own the land of Canaan? Not by the right of the stronger or the more righteous is the Old Testament's persistent witness, but by God's grace (Deut. 7:6-8; 9:6-8).[2] The Book of Joshua, in its first half (Josh. 1-11), describes Israel's occupation of the land in a few stylized lines. While Christians are usually diverted from its message by the problems of cruel warfare, the book's own emphasis lies elsewhere. It characterizes Israel's weakness and God's initiative, so that all credit and glory fall to God, who alone is the victor, and who gives the land to a weak and undeserving people. How different a story from the self-glorifying national liberation stories that fill the history books of most nations! The second half of the Book of Joshua (Josh. 12-22) then describes in laborious detail how the land was distributed so that each tribe, clan, and family received its share in it. There is something sacramental about this distribution; as with the bread and wine in a Christian communion service, everyone was to have a part in God's gracious gift, the land, for it was the external token of God's covenant with Israel.

To possess the land, however, meant to hold it in trust after the manner of God's original desire. Israel was not to be its autonomous master, but God's representative and steward, ultimate ownership and authority remaining with God.

> The land shall not be sold in perpetuity, for the land is mine; for you are strangers and sojourners with me (Lev. 25:23; cf. Ps. 39:12; 119:19).

"Strangers and sojourners" means as much as "landed immigrants" in our terms, or simply as "long-term guests." It emphasizes Israel's duty to treat the land as God's property. What this meant in detail was spelled out in many of Israel's laws and institutions, together with the consequences of neglecting it. In other words, Israel as a people was again given a chance to live out, in a sinful world, the intended role for humanity as divine steward of God's land.

If this seems like a lengthy and general survey, we must remind ourselves that without this perspective we should totally miss the biblical meaning of such concepts as land ownership, possession, home country, land rights, and the like.

Israel's Stewardship of Her Land

What forms was Israel's stewardship of her God-given land to take? In a sense the whole Law of Moses, as expressed in the various law codes of the Pentateuch, constitutes the answer. It sketches the new life which Israel was to lead in the new land. It could be summarized thus:

> You shall love the Lord your God with all your heart, and with all your soul, and with all your might (Deut. 6:5).

When Jesus added, "You shall love your neighbor as yourself (Mark 12:31, citing Lev. 19:18), he merely made more explicit what was already included in loving God. For practical purposes this needed to be spelled out. The various laws did this, providing samples of love for God, either directly or by way of the neighbor, though these laws never attempted a coverage of life such as later rabbinic legal interpretation tried to derive from them.

For the Christian any consideration of Old Testament laws raises the vexing question of their relevance today. Without going into complexities, I believe a Christian can make these minimal assumptions: (1) While the specifics the laws require may be time-bound, the basic concerns along which they direct Israel's response to God—such as homage to his sovereignty, obedience, praise, concern for neighbor—are still shared by us. (2) Where we cannot accept the details required of Israel, we still do well to ponder their basic intentions and to ask by what specifics we might fulfill those intentions.[3]

Before we consider some aspects of Israel's land legislation, we need to remind ourselves again of the distinctive status of humanity as God's "strangers and sojourners" or "long-range guests" on the earth, as well as in the specific land that God has given them for a time. This theological definition of one's place on the map and relation to the land is distinctly biblical and must be distinguished from, and defended against, significant religious and philosophical alternatives.

Two of these may be highlighted for us, one ancient, the other modern. The first is Baalism, the religion of the Canaanites, one of the nature religions that characterized the Ancient Near East.

Nature, in her many forms and powers perceived as gods, was seen as divine. People feeling dependent on the gifts of mother earth, her rhythms and her fertility, worshiped her and sought her gifts. Israel felt this lure of the land through much of her history. Her laws warned against it (Exod. 10:2-6) and her prophets waged an incessant battle against it. Elijah exclaimed:

> "How long will you go limping with two different opinions? If the Lord is God, follow him; but if Baal, then follow him" (1 Kings 8:21).

And Hosea, about a century later:

> And she [Israel] did not know that it was I who gave her the grain, the wine, and the oil, and who lavished upon her silver and gold which they used for Baal (Hosea 2:8).

The danger of Neo-Baalism in our time is also very real. It comes in attractive forms, as Baalism did for Israel. How close we feel to God in our camp retreats by the lake, and how majestic is the sunrise at our Easter morning service! Ecological concern for the purity of our rivers and lakes, the preservation of species and the integrity of landscapes may be one of the sanest concerns of humankind in recent centuries. But how quickly do we worship nature instead of its Creator? The rising sun instead of the risen Son, whom it is to represent? Or turn to the purity of mother nature rather than to Jesus Christ for renewal? What seems so clean and invigorating shows its somber side when we see it developed to its full in a Hitler-ideology of blood, race, and soil, substituting the survival of the strong and pure for the biblical testimony that God graciously chooses the weak, liberates the oppressed, and forgives the sinful.

If divinization of nature, or Neo-Baalism, is one of our dangers, the opposite is humanity's assumption of ultimate authority over nature. We characterized it as the sin of Adam and Eve and their descendants. Deuteronomy warns Israel:

> Beware lest you say in your heart, "My power and the might of my hand have gotten me this wealth." You shall remember the Lord your God, for it is he who gives you power to get wealth; that he may confirm his covenant . . . (Deut. 8:17, 18).

This is the warning against human arrogance which sees the rest of the universe as things in the hands of humankind. The steward of God's gifts becomes the exploiter. Thus the pendulum of humanity's attitude to the earth swings from divinization to exploitation and back to divinization. But biblical stewardship is an alternative to both.

Humanity's status as steward or long-term guest of God on the land is maintained if God's ultimate sovereignty is confessed and upheld. To this end, Israel had many laws: (1) The return of the first fruits to God (Exod. 23:19; 34:26; Deut. 26:1-11; Lev. 19:23; Exod. 13:11-16) points to God as the real owner; (2) The prohibition against eating blood acknowledges that life, represented by the blood, belongs to God (Lev. 17:10-16; Deut. 12:20-25; cf. Acts 15:20). (3) The various food laws and other laws of clean and unclean, though complex in their background and difficult to interpret in detail, seem to call Israel to a recognition of certain God-given orders in nature, orders that allow man and woman certain freedom to use it, but also impose certain limits on them (Lev. 11; Deut. 14:3-21). (4) Food laws, laws of clean and unclean, and others pertaining to ritual purity and worship, belong to the wider complex of laws preserving a sense for the presence of the holy God in this world. The world is not divine, but the presence of God is real. God is gracious to allow himself to be experienced at certain places and in certain ways (Gen. 28:17; Exod. 20:24; Deut. 12:11; 1 Kings 8). Israel and her land were themselves to be a holy presence representing God in the wider world (Exod. 19:5, 6; Deut. 14:1, 2).

Humankind's status as steward or long-term guest of God was also to express itself in the use of one's land in relation to others, both human and animal. Again, many laws could be cited, among them the following: (1) The land was distributed fairly to each tribe, clan, and larger family (Josh. 1-11); furthermore this distribution was to be safeguarded, not only against common theft, (Exod. 20:15, 17) or moving the landmark (Deut. 19:14), but also against the wielding of economic or other power (Exod. 22:21-27; Lev. 25:35-38; Deut. 17:14-20); (2) While it was expected that imbalances of wealth and social status would develop in time, the laws of the Sabbath year (Exod. 23:10, 11; Lev. 25:1-7; Deut. 15:1-6) and the Jubilee year (Lev. 25:8-17) aimed at a periodic return to a fair-share situation. While they were ideal legislation, and probably never fully put into practice, they were not utopian, but exerted a very real impetus toward social justice, (3) The memory of Israel's enslavement in Egypt, and the awareness of one's own guest status in the land were to lead the Israelite to gracious magnanimity in the use of the land and its resources, giving special consideration to the sharing of wealth with the widow, the orphan, and the sojourner (Exod. 22:21-27; Deut. 15:7-11; 24:19-22). Even the animals were not merely to be exploited but should share in the goodness of God's land (Exod. 20:10; Deut. 25:4).

Whenever one deals with the do's and don'ts of the law for a while, one does well to recall that all the specific regulations are predicated on the understanding that God's creation is good; that Israel's specific land was God's gift to her; and that a certain level of enjoyment of health, material goods, and security from enemies is God's will for all people. These constitute divine blessing, a blessing that leads to *shalôm,* life in all its fullness. The Old Testament affirms fully God's present help in trouble, suffering captivity, wilderness; but these are never end stations in God's plan. There is no glorification of the spiritual over the material, no praise of asceticism, no glorification of poverty, and no theology of suffering for its own sake. God wants for everyone the good life, the life that can be enjoyed and that leads to rejoicing and praise (Lev. 23:39-43; Deut. 10:7; 16:9-12; 26:11). Sometimes it seems that our concerns for social justice, for stewardship of the land and its goods, turn into a glorification of austerity and of the very situations of poverty from which we rightly wish to relieve those caught in them.

The sabbath observance, though not linked exclusively to land, is in some ways the most powerful and telling ordering of the steward's life:

> Remember the sabbath day, to keep it holy. Six days you shall labor and do all your work; but the seventh day is a sabbath to the Lord your God; in it you shall not do any work, you, or your son, or your daughter, your manservant or your maidservant, or your cattle, or the sojourner who is within your gates (Exod. 20:8-10; cf. Deut. 5:12-15).

From here on Exodus and Deuteronomy differ in the motivation they provide. Referring to God's rest on the seventh day (Gen. 2:2, 3), the Exodus version (Exod. 20:11) links humanity's rest to God the creator. All of God's creative activity moves toward the accomplishment of God's purpose, when everything will be "very good" (Gen. 1:31). Human beings, as God's image and representatives, sharing with the Creator in the labors on earth, are to experience a foretaste of fulfillment, of purpose accomplished. Movement is not for movement's sake, or change for change's sake. The rest of the sojourner on the road foreshadows the final (eschatalogical) rest of God (Heb. 11:13-16).

Deuteronomy, on the other hand, identifies sabbath-keeping people with God the Redeemer (Deut. 5:15). Having experienced oppressive slave labor, and then God's redemption from it, the Israelite is to resist his exploitative tendency and grant rest to himself, to the people under his jurisdiction, and to the animals. The hard-pressing business mentality that can hardly outwait the sabbath is described and condemned in Amos 8:4-6.

The good gift of the land was given to Israel for stewardship. This gift was conditional upon the quality of stewardship exercised:

> See, I have set before you this day life and good, death and evil. If you obey the commandments of the Lord your God which I command you this day, by loving the Lord your God, by walking in his ways, and by keeping his commandments and his statutes and his ordinances, then you shall live and multiply, and the Lord your God will bless you in the land which you are entering to take possession of it. But if your heart turns away, and you will not hear, but are drawn away to worship other gods and serve them, I declare to you this day, that you shall perish; you shall not live long in the land which you are going over the Jordan to enter and possess (Deut. 30:15-18).

The Deuteronomic history (Joshua-2 Kings) and the books of the prophets tell the story of Israel's defection. Worship of false gods and oppression of the neighbor are the central foci in the accusations of the prophets against Israel. Eventually they announced that Israel's claim to the land had been forfeited and that God, who had given it to her as a token of the covenant in the time of Joshua, would have to take it away again. History justified this prophetic message; the Northern Kingdom (Israel) fell to the Assyrians in 721 B.C. and the Southern Kingdom (Judah) to the Babylonians in 587 B.C.

While this did not end the Old Testament story, it ended a chapter which demonstrated paradigmatically the challenge and the difficulties of being a people to whom the stewardship of a particular land was entrusted. The subsequent story continued to include themes of relationship to the land, even though other emphases (the law, sin and forgiveness, and eschatological expectation) sometimes gained preeminence over them.

New Testament Accents

It is clear that the New Testament devotes proportionately much less attention to land, its significance and its management, than does the Old Testament. This has led many Christians to believe that the land themes of the Old Testament belonged to the more material and time-bound encumbrances of the Old Covenant which were shed by Jesus and the apostles in favor of more spiritual concerns. "Spiritual" is then understood in a Greek philosophical sense as "inward" and/or "otherworldly."

John 4:19-24 is a favorite passage apparently justifying such a view. Only apparently, however, for when Jesus refers to the coming worship "in spirit and truth," rather than in Jerusalem or on Mount Gerizim, he is using *spirit* in the Old Testament sense: where the Spirit of God will move, that is, wherever God will show himself at work in the world. In other words, Jesus says that the temporary limitation of God's special presence to the land of Canaan and the temple in Jerusalem will give way to the potential "holiness" of all places on the globe.

Such a widening from Old Testament particularity to the New Testament's universality is fully in keeping with other instances of a New Testament development of Old Testament themes: the priesthood, an inherited prerogative of certain families in Israel, becomes the priesthood of all believers. Israel, the people of God by ethnic and historical association, becomes the sum total of believers. Far from depreciating the significance of geography for faith, Jesus throws the world open to such significance. All places and lands are now potential promised land, holy land, where God can manifest himself. That not only negates the false spirituality of the viewpoint referred to; it suggests also that the guidelines of land stewardship given in the context of Israel's occupation of the land of Canaan may well be broadened, not in their legal detail, but in their general significance, to stewardship of land on the part of believers anywhere.[4] For is it not more likely that Jesus' relative silence on questions of land expresses basic agreement with the Old Testament, rather than the opposite? We recall his affirmation of the basic meaning of the law as love of God and love of neighbor (Mark 12:29-31). The angelic hymn on the occasion of his birth proclaimed:

> Glory to God in the highest, and on earth peace [*shālôm*] among men with whom he is pleased! (Luke 2:14).

Let us spot-test the main points of land/earth-theology derived from the Old Testament for their New Testament relevance:

1. Is God still the ultimate ruler over the earth? Or has God abandoned interest in it in favor of a more "spiritual" domain? The main theme of Jesus' preaching and miracles is the kingdom of God. Jesus came to bring it with a heretofore unknown reality (Mark 1:15). He did signs of the kingdom. He taught his church to do such signs, and he taught us to expect God himself to bring in his kingdom, that is, his rule, with greater fullness (Matt. 24). However, we recall that the methods of Jesus in establishing God's rule on earth were methods of peace. In keeping with this, the possession of the earth/land is promised to the meek:

> Blessed are the meek,

for they shall inherit the earth (Matt. 5:5).

That is the New Testament counterpart to Joshua's conquest.

2. Was this kingdom a "spiritual" reality, in the philosophical sense, or did it involve tangible realities such as the land and its fruits? We recall that Jesus' works were largely works of caring for the physical needs of people: healing, feeding, lifting from oppression. His disciples followed in this. For a while they even considered community of goods to be a part of Christian living (Acts 4:32-37). While this was abandoned as a paradigm of Christian economics, the responsiblity for the physical well-being of the neighbor remained. It was exemplified clearly in Paul's promotion of the collection for the suffering Jerusalem church. We must take note here of the fact that the early church was no longer an almost exclusively agricultural community, and that principles applied explicitly to land and its produce in the Old Testament must now be applied more generally to property. Yet, is there property that does not ultimately derive from the land?

3. Was Jesus less concerned with acknowledging God's gifts of physical sustenance than other gifts such as forgiveness for sins? In answer we remind ourselves of his habitual prayer of thanks before meals, so that the disciples on the road to Emmaus actually recognized him by this characteristic practice (Luke 24:30, 31). We recall the inclusion of a petition for our daily bread in the Lord's Prayer (Matt. 6:11).

4. Was Jesus less concerned with equitable distribution of land and its goods than the Old Testament? In answer we recall the great number of words of judgment against the rich: "Blessed are you poor, for yours is the kingdom of God . . . But woe to you that are rich, for you have received your consolation" (Luke 6:20, 24). "It is easier for a camel to go through the eye of a needle than for a rich man to enter the kingdom of God (Matt. 19:24). And there is the story of the rich man and Lazarus (Luke 16:19-31), which makes it particularly clear that it is not the rich man's unjust acquisition of wealth that makes him guilty, but rather the simple fact of unequal distribution.

This may suffice to show that Jesus can in no way be understood to reject the basic principles of the Old Testament with respect to the nature of man's stewardship of land and its wealth.

In conclusion, we need to point out one further dimension of land theology in both Testaments. The Old Testament not only speaks of a Garden of Eden lost, of human existence as a pilgrimage, and of stations of rest on the way, but also of a garden restored. Nature herself, sharing in a state of sin, is to participate in a process of redemption also. The Old Testament, in its this-worldly perspective, freely paints earthly scenes of harmony in nature:

> The wolf shall dwell with the lamb, and the leopard shall lie down with the kid, and the calf and the lion and the fatling together, and a little child shall lead them. The cow and the bear shall feed; their young shall lie down together; and the lion shall eat straw like the ox. The sucking child shall play over the hole of the asp, and the weaned child shall put his hand on the adder's den. They shall not hurt or destroy in all my holy mountain; for the earth shall be full of the knowledge of the Lord as the waters cover the sea (Isa. 11:6-9).

This is paradise restored, full of harmony between humanity and beast as well as beast and beast (cf. Hos. 2:16-20). We can add to it passages of human peace under the dominion of God (Isa. 3:2-4; 9:2-7; 55:12, 13); of the blossoming of the wilderness, of flowing streams in the desert (Isa. 35; 43:18-21); and of the river of life proceeding from the temple of God (Ezek. 47). That these prophecies mix historical events and end-time expectations freely presents no unique problem, for the same is true of the theme of human redemption.

While Jesus is silent on this topic, Paul clearly affirms a redemption or restoration of nature:

> For the creation waits with eager longing for the revealing of the sons of God; for the creation was subjected to futility, not of its own will but by the will of him who subjected it in hope; because the creation itself will be set free from its bondage to decay and obtain the glorious liberty of the children of God. We know that the whole creation has been groaning in travail together until now (Rom. 8:19-22).

Christians face the question whether to understand the Old Testament passages as images of eternal life, or whether to expect a restored Garden of Eden on this our earth. I incline to the former. Revelation 7:15-17 appears to do so, and Revelation 22:1-5 takes such a view of Ezekiel's river of life, placing it into "a new heaven and a new earth" (Rev. 21:1). The eschatological Eden, just as the primeval Eden, transcends ordinary historical reality.

This, however, does not mean that the biblical doctrine of the restoration of nature has no significance for our daily life. The situation here is quite parallel to that of human restoration to God's will or kingdom. While the Old Testament pictures the fulfillment of human redemption in an earthly rule of God (or his law, or the

Messiah), extending from Jerusalem over all nations, the New Testament translates these events into God's eternity. But that eternal kingdom or rule of God begins in this world, as the sick are healed, the hungry fed, the prisoners visited (Matt. 11:1-6; 25:34-40). In a similar way, it seems to me, the beginnings of a restoration of the earth through good stewardship of it takes place in our historical situation and prepares the way for a greater, God-worked, universal redemption of nature.

Notes

[1] On human nature see my article "Human Wholeness in Biblical Perspective" in this volume, pp. 61-67. The significance of humanity's creation in the image of God is discussed in my essay "Created in God's Image" in this volume, pp. 51-60.

[2] For a discussion of war in the Old Testament see my articles "War in the Old Testament" and "Christian Perspectives on War and Peace in the Old Testament" in this volume, pp. 173-86 and 193-211, respectively.

[3] See the preface.

[4] For a fuller exposition of these thoughts see my paper "Geography of Faith" in this volume, pp. 137-157.

Part IV
The Burden of War

15
War in the Old Testament

If a Presbyterian can say that the Old Testament's image of God as warrior may be for the Christian "the real *skandalon* of the Old Testament,"[1] it is even more true that its war-filled pages have presented a persistent problem to those in the Anabaptist-Mennonite tradition. It has been the theme of war, more than anything else, that has led to a repeated devaluation of the Old Testament throughout our history as a peace church.[2] While all Christians must grant a degree of finality to the revelation of the New Testament, it is most important to define precisely in what sense the New Testament supersedes the Old, not only in its total claim, but also in specific issues.[3] In this article an attempt will be made to characterize in outline the Old Testament's theology pertaining to war, and to suggest a mode of relating this to the New Testament church.

War as a Topic in Old Testament Theology

Does the Old Testament concern itself with war *theologically* at all; that is, does it ask for an integration of the fact of war into its understanding of existence under God? Much attention has been given to the institution and the doctrine of "Holy War" in Israel since the appearance of Gerhard von Rad's basic study in 1951.[4] Theological treatments of the Old Testament's preoccupation with war in a more general sense are surprisingly rare, however. The Old Testament theologies accord this subject no more than fringe treatment in connection with some other theme, such as the problem of evil.[5]

One could ask whether the specifically confessional or kerygmatic interest of the Old Testament in this respect may not be limited to the doctrine of Holy War, so that a discussion of war beyond that doctrine might be relegated to the research into Israel's political and institutional history, or her ethnic and psychological characteristics, realms in which war has indeed received some careful attention. [6] We face here the problem that confronts the Old Testament theologian in many areas, namely, the difficulty of distinguishing confessional content from Ancient Near Eastern context introduced for purely descriptive, rather than normative purposes.

While it might seem plausible, then, to assume that war, apart from the Holy War doctrine, might be left to the non-theological disciplines, this would disregard the fact that war and war terminology enter into so many of the central theological themes of the Old Testament that a neglect of its theological dimension would be irresponsible. It can neither be expected, nor is it true, that a people which ascribed such central revelatory importance to its history could have considered an aspect of that history as prominent as war to be no more than accidental to the central core of its faith. The very formulation of the Holy War doctrine becomes explicable only as one sees it in its tension with the more general understanding of war which prevailed in the Ancient Near Eastern world and became effective in Israel as well. [7] On the other hand, it is true that the topic of war reached its most conscious formulation in the Holy War doctrine, while the broader meaning of war was never explicated with the same theological consciousness. We are therefore not in a position to trace an explicit and ready doctrine of war through the writings of the Old Testament, but must piece it together ourselves from the scattered evidence. For this reason we have chosen a synoptic approach, rather than the methodology introduced into Old Testament theology so effectively by von Rad. [8]

Once we grant theological status to the topic of war, we must still consider the question whether it warrants distinct and separate treatment. Should war not be seen as merely one of the many manifestations of evil, to be lumped together for the purpose of theological discussion with sickness, earthquake, fire, locust, plague, and flood? This, indeed, has been the practice of Old Testament theologians. [9] While the magnitude of the phenomenon would alone appear to warrant separate consideration, it is even more the historical nature of biblical revelation which we must invoke again. While God's sovereignty extends to all aspects of the universe, God reveals himself to Israel primarily as guiding the affairs of humanity. Therefore the disruption of the harmony of human life together takes on a significance distinct from, though not necessarily greater than, the evil perceived in nature. [10] And again it is the Holy War doctrine with which the Old Testament itself draws war into the realm of theological formulation by designating some wars as God's wars, begging thereby the question concerning the theological status of others.

War as a Theological Problem

War has been a phenomenon ever present in human society, and as such it fills the pages of the Old Testament also. While militaristic rulers and states have at various times glorified war and attempted to interpret it as noble and as pleasing to the higher powers, most people at most times have considered it a scourge and an evil, though they have generally failed to find ways of eliminating it for any length of time. The Old Testament shares this attitude with the rest of humanity. As Millar Burrows has said, "Much of the Old Testament represents the view of the peasant, who loses most and gains least by war." [11]

It is the peculiarly biblical image of God which turns war from a lamentable reality into a theological problem. This problem would not arise if the world were seen as determined by the interaction of more or less autonomous forces. As soon as one believes in a sovereign God, however, a God who rules with complete power and authority, one is faced with the problem of relating the fact of war to such a God. Does God want it and cause it? Does God have purposes with it? Are wars for the benefit of humanity? Are they consistent or capricious? Are there powers that oppose God and to whom God gives some leeway?

God's sovereignty is affirmed throughout the Old Testament. [12] God is in complete control, without rival or equal. In contrast to the ancient polytheistic religions which understood the world as being determined by many powers, powers engaged in conflict with each other and fluctuating between victory and defeat, the Old Testament sees its world as unified under the rule of one supreme God. Therefore even that which is perceived as evil must somehow be associated with that God; it must be ascribed to his will directly, or at least to his toleration. God gives life and takes life. Every death is actually a facet of God's rule which ordains for every human being to die. Some lives are taken through sickness, pestilence, or famine, and some through wars. [13] The sovereignty of God allows for no other conclusion.

The theological problem implicit in this sovereignty reaches full proportions when juxtaposed to God's consistent goodness and mercy which is, paradoxically, maintained at the same time and with equal conviction. "How can God allow . . . ?" becomes the question which reverberates through Israelite and Christian experience and history. Yet both Israel and the Church have preferred to live in the theological tension between God's sovereignty and God's goodness, rather than to seek its resolution by subordinating the one to the other. Waiting for the fuller answer has been the faithful person's response to suffering, whether it be that of Job, of the lamenting psalmists, or of Paul. This hesitation to ascribe to God everything that is, finds its expression, partly, in the doctrine of the Fall. [14] Humanity shares in the guilt for the evil experienced, though this does not explain the origin of evil, nor bring to an end the waiting for a fuller answer to that which one sees "in a glass darkly." Within this affirmation of disharmony between God's will and humanity's experience, war finds its place. Like murder, yes, even the killing of animals, war belongs to the Fall; it does not characterize the God-intended state of humanity. Even those wars designated Holy Wars in modern scholarship are not excluded here, as we shall see. But the roots of hope are here as well. The full assertion of the sovereignty and goodness of God must become manifest, and when that will be, when God's kingdom will come, war will be no more; it will be abolished together with fear, injustice, sickness, and the rest of evil.

These, then, are the theological coordinates within which war becomes a problem for biblical faith, and within which its solution is anticipated, even in the Old Testament. Instead of attempting to find a balanced doctrine or a uniformly advancing development in the Old Testament's treatment of war, we shall start with the continuing experience of war as a human reality accompanying Israel's history and shall try to point out the impacts, challenges and judgments to which it was subjected under the exposure to the central aspects of Old Testament faith.

War as a Human Reality

The Old Testament expects wars to take place. Israel's participation in war is taken for granted, on the whole. The commandment "You shall not kill" (Exod. 20:13) was never applied by Israel to the killing in war, but was reserved for what our society generally defines as murder. [15] Even sly murder can be praised when committed against an enemy (Judg. 3:15ff; 4:18ff). Cunning deceit and violence can bring honor when committed against national enemies (1 Sam. 27:8-12). Merciless warfare is generally accepted (2

Sam. 8:2; 11:1; 1 Kings 11:15f; 2 Kings 3:25), even though it is true that certain excesses of cruelty, such as mutilation of enemies, are the rare exception in Israel.

Yet while war is accepted as a fact of human life, and while some wars are presented as God's wars, the Old Testament extols the desirability of peace even for its own day. Abraham's willingness to resolve the tension between his clan and Lot's clan by his readiness to accept the poorer land receives commendation (Gen. 13:1-12). David may not build the temple because his reign has been filled with war and bloodshed; Solomon, a king with a peaceful reign, is to build it (1 Chron. 28:3). An excerpt from an Elisha story advocates what we might call "heaping fiery coals on the enemy's head" by kindness shown to prisoners of war (2 Kings 6:20-23). There is a long list of prophetic words condemning reliance on power and diplomacy, such as Isaiah 30:15, 16. [16]

For thus said the Lord God, the Holy One of Israel,
"In returning and rest you shall be saved;
in quietness and in trust shall be your strength."
And you would not, but you said,
"No! We will speed upon horses."
therefore you shall speed away;
and, "We will ride upon swift steeds."
therefore your pursuers shall be swift.

Ezra refuses a Persian military escort for the long and dangerous journey to Jerusalem, for he wants to trust in the Lord rather than in military power (Ezra 8:22).

No doubt, there is ethical refinement in a general sense, as the Old Testament story advances, a refinement which we must ascribe to the increasing permeation of Israelite life by the faith in a just and righteous God who acts reliably in the best interest of humanity. [17] Such refinement affected Israel's attitude to war also. It is probably unwarranted, however, to seek a steadily unfolding peace ideal in the Old Testament, at least as far as its own time is concerned. Nevertheless, there was a check upon unbridled human warfare and its idealization.

God as a Warrior

In view of what we have just said, it may surprise us to find that the Old Testament presents God himself as a warrior. [18] In the Song of Miriam or Moses (Exod. 15:1-18), one of the oldest and most focal chapters of the Old Testament, we have a celebration of the central act of salvation, the deliverance of Israel from the Egyptians:

> I will sing to the Lord, for he has triumphed gloriously;
> the horse and his rider he has thrown into the sea.
> The Lord is my strength and my song,
> and he has become my salvation;
> this is my God, and I will praise him,
> my father's God, and I will exalt him.
> The Lord is a man of war;
> the Lord is his name.   (vv. 1-3)

Passages in which God's activity is described in terms of victorious warfare could be adduced in great number. One of the most frequent designations of God, *Yahweh Sabaoth* or *Lord of Hosts,* almost certainly refers to God as the one at the head of the heavenly and earthly armies. [19] 1 Samuel 17:47 says "the battle is the Lord's," and Psalm 24:8: "Who is the King of glory? The Lord, strong and mighty, the Lord, mighty in battle!" The ideology of Holy War, to which we must give fuller attention below, centers in the conception of God as the great Divine Warrior. [20]

And yet we would misunderstand the Old Testament if we would read such characterizations of God as a glorification, or even an apology of warfare. Our problem pertains to the use of religious language. All our language about God is borrowed from some realm of human life. It is metaphorical. If we wish to express something about God's care and concern for man and his guidance of man, we look for a human relationship characterized by such qualities, and, having found one, say that God is our father and we are his children. Drawing our language from a different human realm, we can also say that God is our shepherd, and we his sheep. Since sovereign authority is central to the image of God in the Old Testament, and since the clearest demonstration of such authority in Old Testament times was the king, particularly as he defeated his enemies and returned victorious, it is terminology drawn from this realm which is frequently employed. God becomes the divine warrior who defeats his enemies in battle and returns victorious to ascend the throne of his dominion.

Such warrior language is intended to convey, metaphorically, God's sovereign control, not to glorify warfare. The goal of God's activity is never war itself, or victory itself, but justice and peace. God defeats Pharaoh to deliver a weak people from harsh oppression (Exod. 3:7-10). God drives out the Canaanites because of their sins (Gen. 15:16; Deut. 9:4, 5). Israel's goal is not conquest as such, but the inheritance, that is, the land of promise and rest from the enemies round about (Deut. 12:9). The pattern of the Book of

Judges illustrates the same (e.g. 3:7-11). The prophets announce God's wrath and punishment upon nations exploiting other nations (e.g. Nahum 3:1). God uses the Babylonians to punish Judah for her idolatry and injustice (e.g. Ezek. 9:1-10), and the Persian King Cyrus to free the Jews from the Babylonian captivity (Isa. 45:1-4). God is a God whose moral purpose is consistently bent on delivering the oppressed and punishing the oppressor. Justice and mercy are to be demonstrated in the military metaphors for God, not heroism or glory. Even the great final battle of the day of the Lord, when God will destroy his enemies, has as its goal the kingdom of justice and peace (Ezek. 39:25-29).[21]

That this is so arises clearly from two further considerations, namely Israel's view of the king and of the warrior, for it is from these, of course, that the Old Testament's language of God as "mighty in battle" has been derived primarily. Israel saw war as a reality and as a necessary means of defense and security. A king who waged wars that defeated the enemies and gave peace and protection to the land was esteemed highly and praised correspondingly. In contrast to the wars of aggrandizement, so characteristic of ancient and modern times, however, Israel's ideal of a king was that of the purveyor of justice who crushed the oppressor and helped the oppressed to his right (Isa. 11:1-5; Ps. 72). He was to be an instrument in God's hand. His power and success in war gains importance toward justice, not toward glory. Israel's ideal king, David, was forbidden to build the temple because of the many wars he had to wage; it was to be built by Solomon whose reign was more peaceful (1 Chron. 28:3).[22]

The war heroes are regarded in the same light. Israel praised its heroes: "Saul has slain his thousands, and David his ten thousands" (1 Sam. 18). But Israel did not glorify death in war. There are no cenotaphs in the Old Testament. Strangely absent are also the hero stories that fill the Homeric epics, or the tendentious accounts of succesful campaigns that fill the monuments of Egyptian and Assyrian monarchs. Lamech's song of bravery (Gen. 4:23, 24) becomes a vehicle to convey the fallen state of humanity. The warrior who defeated the enemy and brought peace and security was praised and valued, but if he died in battle he was mourned and pitied, rather than glorified, for the meaning of war lay not in bravery and self-sacrifice, but in the peace to be enjoyed thereafter.[23]

Holy War

A greater problem for Christians than the Old Testament wars generally have been those wars of which the Old Testament clearly states that God himself commanded them. 1 Samuel 15:1-3 may serve as an example:

> And Samuel said to Saul, "The Lord sent me to anoint you king over his people Israel; now therefore hearken to the words of the Lord. Thus says the Lord of hosts, 'I will punish what Amalek did to Israel in opposing them on the way, when they came up out of Egypt. Now go and smite Amalek, and utterly destroy all that they have; do not spare them, but kill both man and woman, infant and suckling, ox and sheep, camel and ass.' "

Such wars are reported especially for the period of Israel's conquest of the land of Canaan and the subsequent period of the judges, but they are also in evidence later, and as a type of war they affect the whole theology of the Old Testament. Modern scholars have given them the designation *Holy War* and have studied them as to their theory and their features. [24]

Their special character arises from the fact that Israel saw them as being God's wars, and that not only in the general way in which everything that happens in God's world must somehow be related to God's will, but in the special sense that God commanded them to Israel, or better, that God waged them, using Israel as his sword. God gave Israel the command to fight such a war. God was present in Israel's military camp so that the soldiers were to purify themselves ritually, just as if they were to partake in a worship ritual. God filled a leader with his spirit to take up the command, and sent his terror among the enemies, so that Israel could get the victory even with small numbers and without tactical advantages over the enemy. Thus it was God himself who had won the battle, using Israel as his instrument. The spoils belonged to God and were to be "devoted" to God, that is, killed or burned, as a great sacrifice.

In spite of their direct association with the will of God, Holy Wars share with other wars their roots in humanity's sin. Holy War is God's instrument to punish those powers that oppose his economy of history, that are of hardened heart (Exod. 7:3-5; Josh. 11:20; 1 Sam. 15:1-3); those who are guilty (Deut. 9:4, 5). When the prophets proclaim the reversal of Holy War against Israel herself, [25] it is Israel's hardness of heart, her covenant-breaking rebelliousness, that lies at the root. Great acts of God though they be, when seen as means to bring to pass the divine purposes, they are emergency measures when viewed within the economy of sin and salvation.

From the standpoint of the history of religion, it is true that the origins of the Holy War ideology may be found in humanity's search for divine sanction of its wars; as the earthly armies move on, the heavenly hosts are moving along invisibly and give victory. In the Ancient Near East such an understanding blends into the view that the microcosmos reflects the macrocosmos.[26] Translated into modern terms, every Hitler sees himself as the special instrument of Providence.

In Israel's Holy War doctrine, however, a significant shift has taken place. The heavenly hosts and Israel's armies no longer advance at the same pace; the former take over while the latter stand back. Strategic advantages and military strength must be discounted; Israel's collaboration becomes symbolic (that is, Judg. 7:2-8). God does not fight so much *with* Israel as *for* Israel. In the prophetic revival of Holy War ideology Israel's role becomes increasingly more passive, leaving the direction of history in God's hand: "In returning and rest you shall be saved; in quietness and in trust shall be your strength" (Isa. 30:15).[27]

This doctrine of Holy War represents a real challenge to the legitimacy of common war. Is the latter authorized by God also, but in a less specific way? Is it peculiar to segments of Israel's history with which God does not concern himself, that are neutral enclaves in the history of salvation, enclaves governed by the demands of expediency? Or is it a "wildcat" undertaking based on the arrogation of an autonomous authority properly reserved for God?[28]

The Coming Reign of Peace

We have seen that the Old Testament expresses peace ideals here and there for its own time. Its use of military images for God must be understood as intending to express God's sovereign power to achieve justice, and not misread as a glorification of warfare. The Holy Wars are emergency measures evoked by human sin, and the Holy War doctrine itself circumscribes the legitimacy of war as such. Nevertheless, the Old Testament sees war as an expected part of human existence and as such accepts it, albeit not unquestioned, for its own time.

The Old Testament's affirmation of peace, sporadic for its own time, becomes full and unrestrained for God's future, however. When God sets straight the disorientations of this world, when God's kingdom comes and God's will is done, when the powers of evil are divested of their hold on the world, then peace will reign, for the full and uninhabited will of God is a will for peace and not war. The Messiah will be the Prince of Peace (Isa. 9:6, 7). The Lord's kingdom will be a reign of peace, as we read in Isaiah 1:3, 4 (cf. Mic. 4:2, 3):

> For out of Zion shall go forth the law, and the word of the Lord from Jerusalem. He shall judge between the nations, and shall decide for many peoples; and they shall beat their swords into plowshares, and their spears into pruning hooks; nation shall not lift up sword against nation, neither shall they learn war any more. [29]

It is at this point that the New Testament's peace teaching has its primary point of contact: The Messiah *has* come, [30] and with his coming God's reign of peace has begun. The angels heralded him as bringer of peace: "Glory to God in the highest, and on earth peace . . ." (Luke 1:14). Jesus began his ministry with the proclamation. "The time is fulfilled, and the kingdom of God is at hand" (Mark 1:15). In his life God's will came to an expression so full and unhindered that it became a glimpse of how it is when God rules, when the powers of evil lose control. To that state belong the healing of sickness, the setting right of social relationships, such as the oppression of the poor (Matt. 11:4, 5), and to it belongs also peace. This proleptic manifestation of the kingdom within history illumines the direction and goal of history and, beyond that, establishes a foothold of God's future in the present.

The Church, Christ's body, is to be a continuation and extension of the presence of the coming reign of God in the world; it has sign-character, pointing to the day when it will be said of redeemed humankind:

> They shall hunger no more, neither
> thirst any more;
> the sun shall not strike them, nor any
> scorching heat.
> For the Lamb in the midst of the throne
> will be their shepherd,
> and he will guide them to springs
> of living water;
> and God will wipe away every tear
> from their eyes.   (Rev. 7:16)

But that fulfillment has not come even for the Christian. We still live in a world of warfare, the warfare which is to culminate in a great final conflict between God and the powers of evil. This warfare is a continuation of the Holy Wars of the Old Testament. [31] The

Christian, as the Israelite of old, believes that God fights "holy wars" and enlists believers in them. The weapons of this warfare, however, are now not swords or guns, for the warfare is directed against the principalities and powers, a warfare the weapons of which are spiritual.

Notes

[1] P. Miller, "God the Warrior," *Interpretation,* XIX (1965), 40.

[2] W. Klassen, "Old Testament," *Mennonite Encyclopedia*, IV, pp. 49-52. It would be desirable to trace this assertion in detail, especially for the more recent period.

[3] In some areas, such as the affirmation of monotheism, the New Testament does not advance significantly beyond the Old Testament. In others, as for example the insistence on monogamy, the New Testament continues a trend well under way in the Old Testament. As to war, the advent of the Messiah, proclaimed in the New Testament, creates a radically new orientation, as we shall try to show.

[4] G. von Rad, *Der heilige Krieg im alten Israel* (Zurich, 1951). References in this paper are to the third edition (Göttingen, 1958).

[5] W. Eichrodt comments on war, among other features of Israelite life, under "Weaknesses in the Validity of Moral Norms," *Theology of the Old Testament,* II (Philadelphia, 1967), 322f. First German ed., 1935. L. Koehler makes brief reference to war under "Gottestypen 3. Der Kriegsgott" and "Gott der Herr," *Theologie des Alten Testaments,* 3rd rev. ed.; (Tübingen, 1953), pp. 7f., 14f.; first published 1935. Th. C. Vriezen limits himself to a few remarks on Holy War under "God as the Creator, Saviour, and Maintainer," *An Outline of Old Testament Theology* (Newton, Mass., 1960), pp. 188f, first Dutch ed., 1949. P. Heinisch, like Eichrodt, discusses certain features of war under "Critique of Old Testament Morality," *Theology of the Old Testament* (Collegeville, Minn., 1955), pp. 212ff. First German ed., 1952. I can find no treatment of war, apart from the mandatory explanation of the epithet "Yahweh Sabaoth," by E. Jacob, *Theology of the Old Testament* (New York, 1958). First French ed., 1955.

G. von Rad, *Old Testament Theology* (2 vols.; New York, 1962 and 1965; first German edition 1957 and 1960), intensely aware always of the significance of the Holy War doctrine throughout Israel's history, conveys the impression that the theological significance of the Old Testament's concern with the subject of war is coextensive with the development of that doctrine. The Heidelberg dissertation of Chr. Grüneisen, "Der Krieg im Alten Testament," announced as being in progress in *Zeitschrift für die alttestamentliche Wissenschaft,* LXXXI (1960), p. 435, has not been available to me.

Separate attention to war has been given by M. Burrows, under "International Relations: the Use of Force," *An Outline of Biblical Theology* (Philadelphia, 1946), pp. 316-22, and by G. Ernest Wright, under "God the Warrior," *The Old Testament and Theology* (New York, 1969), pp. 121-50. Burrows surveys helpfully a variety of aspects of our subject, without attempting to gain a synoptic perspective. Wright, on the other hand, develops the theme of the Divine Warrior fully within a comprehensive understanding of Old Testament theology as determined by the metaphorical understanding of the universe as cosmic government. We might also mention the article by L. E. Toombs, "War, Ideas of," *The Interpreter's Dictionary of the Bible.*

[6] J. Pedersen, *Israel: Its Life and Culture* (London and Copenhagen), III-IV (1940), pp. 1-32. R. deVaux, *Ancient Israel* (New York, first McGraw-Hill Paperback edition, 1965), III, pp. 213-67, "Military Institutions." First French ed., 1958. Y. Yadin, *The Art of Warfare in Biblical Lands,* 2 vols. (New York, 1963),

originally in Hebrew.

[7] Of course, warfare in the Ancient Near East varied greatly from people to people, and from period to period, both in theory and in practice. (See the articles devoted to warfare, in *Iraq,* XXV (1963), pp. 110-90, for example.) The understanding of Holy War, or Yahweh's War, appears to have received its distinctive Old Testament formulation in connection with the faith of Israel, even though some evidence of Holy War outside of Israel, especially in Mari, has been found. P. Miller, "Holy War and Cosmic War in Early Israel" (unpublished dissertation, Harvard Divinity School, 1963); A. E. Glock, "Warfare in Mari and Early Israel" (unpublished dissertation, University of Michigan, 1968).

[8] For a generation now the methodology in Old Testament theology has been governed by the tension between the strongly divergent approaches of W. Eichrodt and G. von Rad (see bibliographical references above, note 5). The aspect which concerns us here is the question as to whether the Old Testament has something like a center, a theological core (Eichrodt), making an Old Testament theology possible, or whether each of its books and segments must be studied for its own peculiar theological kerygma (von Rad), so that the end result becomes a chain of theologies, as it were. No consensus has emerged from this lively debate. See E. Jacob, *Grundfragen alttestamentlicher Theologie* (Stuttgart, 1970); and R. Smend, *Die Mitte des Alten Testaments* (Zurich, 1970).

[9] See above, note 5.

[10] Granted that the categories "history" and "nature" are modern, they are helpful, nevertheless. In the Old Testament "natural" phenomena are drawn into the history of humanity; by contrast, the nature religions surrounding Israel tried to integrate human existence into the rhythms of nature.

[11] Burrows, p. 316.

[12] Our synoptic approach to the subject must of necessity employ comprehensive formulations, such as "sovereignty of God." A more extensive and longitudinal treatment would have to trace the stages of monotheism in Israel from its early and implicit assumption to its full and explicit formulation.

[13] The New Testament and the Christian Church speak of Satan as the one responsible for evil. The Old Testament makes mention of Satan only in a few places, and even there not in quite the same sense as we have come to think of him later. Christian theologians have, further, introduced such concepts as God's "permissive will" and God's "strange work." These are ways of emphasizing that we cannot ascribe everything that happens to the will and intention of God in the same way, even though we are not ready to say that there is anything which, in the last analysis, lies outside the sovereignty and control of God. To use such terms, then, is to give form and expression to a certain tension in Christian theology between the sovereignty of God on the one hand and the character of God as love on the other. These terms merely express this tension, however; they do not explain or resolve it.

[14] Again our synoptic treatment lacks differentiation here. While awareness of the story of the Fall (Gen. 3) cannot be presupposed everywhere in the Old Testament, and much less that comprehensive doctrinal significance with which later theologizing has invested it, an awareness of disharmony between divine intent and human condition cannot be denied. In this sense it is justified to speak of war as belonging to the fallen order.

[15] While the Hebrew verb translated as "kill" in this connection is almost coextensive with our "to murder," its definition could be given as "illegal, impermissible violence," as defined by the community. It would, therefore, include aspects of our "manslaughter" also. See J. J. Stamm and M. E. Andrew, *The Ten Commandments in Recent Research* (Naperville, IL, 1967), pp. 98f.

[16] This word, and similar Isaianic exhortations, must be understood against the background of Holy War, where Israel was to rely on God, rather than its own

military prowess, for victory; see G. von Rad, *Der heilige Krieg,* pp. 50-68, especially p. 57. It is less expressive, therefore, of a "peace mentality" than of noninterference in "divine strategy." But then, the peaceful disposition of Abraham toward Lot was rooted, no doubt, in his trust in God's leading also, so that no sharp distinction can be drawn between abstention from alliances and warfare in the Holy War context and the other instances expressing a high valuation of peace.

[17] Thus Eichrodt, II, pp. 322f.; and Heinisch, pp. 213f.

[18] Note especially the following treatments: F. M. Cross, "The Divine Warrior in Israel's Early Cult," *Biblical Motifs* (Cambridge, Mass., 1966), pp. 11-30; P. Miller, "God the Warrior," XIX, pp. 39-46; G. E. Wright, pp. 121-50.

[19] F. M. Cross, "Yahweh and the God of the Patriarchs," *Harvard Theological Review,* LV (1962), p. 256.

[20] See F. M. Cross, "The Divine Warrior."

[21] "To judge and to wage war and to procure justice is the same thing, if God does it . . . The wars of Yahweh are God's ways of bringing justice. Here it becomes evident that that which we called the warrior-God type (par. 4) is not an independent entity, but a special aspect of the fact that God is Lord, though an aspect which follows of necessity." (Koehler, p. 15; author's translation.) Similarly Eichrodt, I, par. 7. G. E. Wright (*op. cit.,* p. 126) comments upon the events in Joshua: "The Bible's most advanced interpretations in later ages saw there nothing but a most dramatic illustration of the power, grace, and justice of God." Cf. also P. Miller, "God the Warrior," p. 44; and A. Gelston, "The Wars of Israel," *Scottish Journal of Theology,* XVII (1964), pp. 325-31. Gelston's article, however, may serve as a particularly clear example of the general tendency to dwell upon an understanding of God's warrior activity as expressive of his sovereignty, stopping short of the theological dimensions of that sovereignty. The lordship of Yahweh in the Old Testament looks forward to the Day of Yahweh (which is roughly the equivalent of the kingdom of God in the New Testament), when God will defeat his enemies and establish in fulness his reign of justice and peace. The ultimate goal of God's assertion of his sovereignty over his enemies is that reign of justice and peace which lies beyond the assertion of sovereignty expressed in the language of war and victory.

[22] A good account of kingship in Israel can be found in J. L. McKenzie, *The Two-Edged Sword* (London, 1956), pp. 132-49, "King and Prophet." Over against the royal inscriptions of Egypt and Assyria which highlight the victories and braveries of their monarchs, the Old Testament presents a very sober story. "Not, indeed, that Hebrew story was indifferent to external glories, for the Hebrew storytellers were human; but the prevailing tone of the story of the kings is one and the same. It is the story of the failure of the Hebrew kings to realize the will of the Lord" (*ibid.,* p. 148). For kingship outside of Israel, see H. Frankfort, *Kingship and the Gods* (Chicago, 1948), as well as the vivid popular account of W. von Soden, *Herrscher im Alten Orient* (Berlin, 1954).

[23] David's lament over Saul and Jonathan (2 Sam. 1:19-27) is a typical funerary lament, filled with mournful, melancholy sadness; no heroism transforms this sadness of death into immortal glory. Mighty men of war, and some of their feats, are recounted in 2 Samuel 23:8-39. While the popular admiration of such heroes shines through this account, it has its place in the story of David now as a description of his incipient officialdom, and those named in it are still among the living followers of David; it is not a cenotaph of war heroes. Even more indicative of the disinterest in exalting the heroic is its treatment of the kings (see above, note 22). Some of the politically and militarily successful rulers, like Omri and Jeroboam II, receive next to no attention. Others, like Saul and Ahab, figure as exhibits of failure in their relationship to God, while their political and military accomplishments go almost unnoticed. For the contrast between this situation and the hero cult in the

epics and dramas of Greek antiquity, see M. Hadas and M. Smith, *Heroes and Gods* (New York, 1965), pp. 10-16, "The Hero and His Cult."

[24] See above, note 4. Also R. Smend, *Jahwekrieg und Stämmebund* (Göttingen, 1963). Smend prefers the designation "Jahwekrieg" ("war of Yahweh"). For a concise summary of its features, see G. von Rad, *Studies in Deuteronomy* (London, 1953; first German ed., 1948), pp. 47-49.

[25] J. A. Soggin, "Der prophetische Gedanke über den heiligen Krieg, als Gericht gegen Israel," *Vetus Testamentum*, X (1960), pp. 79-83. Also G. von Rad, *Theology*, II, p. 124.

[26] P. Miller, "Holy War."

[27] "The way in which, for Isaiah, Yahweh's activity [in Holy War] altogether excludes every human-military participation shows clearly, however, that Isaiah is not really renewing the [Holy War] conception of the ancient period, for after all, as we saw, that period did not yet know that opposition between divine and human activity [in Holy Warfare]." G. von Rad, *Der heilige Krieg*, p. 58 (author's translation). Cf. also page 66.

[28] Such seems to be the interpretation of the sin of Saul (1 Sam. 13 and 15), of the campaign of Ahab (1 Kings 22), as well as the treatment of Ben-hadad (1 Kings 20), and of the political and military activity of the kings of Judah in Isaiah's time (Isa. 7 and 30, 31). But even episodes of breach of Holy War (e.g., Josh. 7) may be mentioned here. I want to acknowledge, in this connection, a helpful discussion with Professor J. J. Enz of Elkhart, Indiana, who drew my attention to the dialectical or, perhaps, dialogical relationship between Holy War and common war.

[29] Other passages pointing toward God's ultimate reign of peace are Isaiah 52:7-12, Ezekiel 37:26 (cf. Ezek. 34:25-31), though this theme cannot be limited to such explicit statements, for it permeates all of the Old Testament's messianic expectations, as well as its more general pronouncements concerning God's future. Cf. also G. E. Wright, *The Old Testament and Theology*, pp. 138-44.

[30] Even when comparing the early church with the intense, eschatological expectations of the Essene community of Qumran, F. M. Cross can say: "The Essene and the Christian live in the Old Age, yet by anticipation in the new . . . For the member of the early Church, however, the time is 'later.' He stands on a new ground. The Messiah has come. The resurrection is not merely an anticipatory event. It shows that the New Age has come." *The Ancient Library of Qumran* (rev. ed., New York, 1961), p. 240.

[31] O. Betz, "Jesu Heiliger Krieg," *Novum Testamentum*, II (1958), pp. 116-37.

16
God as Warrior and Lord

I

There is scarcely a heresy which our late teacher, G. Ernest Wright, abhorred as deeply and combated as passionately as the reduction of Christian theology to the private realm of spiritual experience, of an idealistically conceived Christomonism which would abandon the political metaphors for God in the Old Testament and thereby become irrelevant to the socio-historical realities of our own time. We learned from him not only that God is the One who acted in history, but also that God is the One who acts in the socio-political realm today.

> The conscious rejection of political language as appropriate to an interpretation of my existence leaves me without a firm anchor to what appears to be my central problem as a human being. [1]

It is not surprising, then, that Professor Wright devoted two of the seven chapters of the work that may be called his theological legacy, *The Old Testament and Theology,* to a systematic presentation of two central political metaphors for God, namely "God the Lord" and "God the Warrior." In the first of these, Professor Wright depicts the cosmos as structured and ordered in analogy to a world government, with God in the image of the transcendent suzerain who grants Israel vassal status as "people of God" by means of a covenant patterned after the international suzerainty treaties of the second millennium B.C. The accent does not lie on an abstract monotheism, but on a "political monocracy." The point at issue—and the point jealously to be guarded—is expressed succinctly and brilliantly by the author:

> The purpose of the suzerainty language is to depict why creative, positive, righteous goals have an ultimate support in our world, why life is given for service for which one is accountable, and why, despite the suffering and injustice in the world, life in the service of the Ultimate understood as Suzerain is possible and triumphant. [2]

While the overt references to the Mosaic covenant recede in the New Testament, due to particular intertestamental developments, God's cosmic government forms the parameters for the mission of Jesus, no less than for that of Israel.

In his chapter on "God the Warrior," Professor Wright comes to terms with the reality of power in a sinful world, both for redemptive and for judgmental ends. In the face of ultimate power, experienced in history both as positive (creative and redemptive) and as negative (destructive and judgmental), it is possible to rest one's faith "in the creative end as the context of the whole" only if the Divine Monarch is also the Divine Warrior. It is the Divine Monarch or Lord who, out of concern for cosmic order, becomes the Warrior who ultimately exerts power and achieves victory in a sinful and disordered universe, using human agents with or without their own knowledge, "without in any way sanctifying the participants." [3] And again Professor Wright crystallizes the theological concern:

> God the Warrior is the theme that furnishes hope in time. What is, cannot be sanctified for the future because a vast tension exists between the will of the Suzerain and that of his vassals . . . Yet the strong, active power given language in the Warrior-Lord means that there is a force in the universe set against the forces of evil and perversity. Life, then, is a battleground, but the Divine Warrior will not be defeated . . . God the Warrior is simply the reverse side of God the Lover or of God the Redeemer. [4]

It is particularly significant to trace the Warrior theme, with Professor Wright, from its prominence in Israel's Conquest-theology (Joshua), where the Divine Warrior graciously conquers and gives the Promised Land to a weak and undeserving people; through the Royal (or Davidic) Theology of the Jerusalem circles, where stability and permanence are the concerns safeguarded by the Divine Warrior who subdues the enemies; to the prophetic reinterpretation of the Day of the Lord [5] as a day of darkness, in which God will wage holy war against Israel; and finally to the postexilic period which "Saw the re-emphasis on the Day as the time of victory in holy war and the time when the Divine Warrior in holy procession assumed the throne as Suzerain of the whole earth."[6] In apocalyptic literature this battle and victory takes on cosmic dimensions, and as such it eventually constitutes the metaphysical backdrop for the whole New Testament, concluding with the image of the New Jerusalem where God and Christ are enthroned and reign in peace, after evil has been subdued.

II

Dominant as this great synthesis of biblical faith under the umbrella of two political metaphors[7] loomed in his thinking, Professor Wright was acutely aware—at least during the dozen years of my acquaintance with him—of that challenge to his theology constituted by the existence of Christian pacifism. In part, he perhaps considered the latter to be the most palpable evidence of present-day idealistic misreading both of the Bible and of the realities of the human situation. He himself—so he told me, not without a little benevolent condescension, during my first year at Harvard—had at one time been carried away by the sweep of liberal idealism and signed a pacifist pledge. Thereupon he proceeded to expound the Old Testament's holy war theme to me, finding himself a little puzzled when I replied that it was just that doctrine which had helped me to ground my (Mennonite) peace church theology biblically.[8]

This awareness of Christian pacifism surfaces again when Professor Wright concludes the summary of the chapter "God the Warrior" with an unexpected, and editorially perhaps a little extraneous, account of a dialogue with "Mr. X," a respected theologian and a member of one of the historic peace churches.[9] In this friend and conversation partner Professor Wright does not find the telltale marks of an idealistic misreading or neglect of the Old Testament; on the contrary, he details the many biblical themes which he and Mr. X accept in the same manner. In fact, Mr. X also claims the need for the image of God the Lord and Suzerain, but because "only the ruling power of God actively at work in history can assure the ultimate success of the nonviolent imperative."[10] Thus Professor Wright places the crucial issue, as he sees it, before his partner: "Can it not be said that when the absolutes of the Kingdom-ethic are translated into absolutes for the present age, trouble always ensues?"[11]

Different ethical positions with respect to war and violence are in evidence here,[12] and it may be well to ask, with Professor Wright, what difference in images of the world might underlie a Christian pacifist position.[13] While I cannot speak for Mr. X, I have become aware of certain differences between my own understanding of the Cosmic Government and Divine Warrior metaphors and that of my respected teacher whose views concerning the Old Testament I share to a large degree. These differences make my pacifist position consonant, as far as I can see, not merely with a biblicist literalism concerning certain words of Jesus, but also with the political metaphors of the Old Testament.

My disagreement with Professor Wright can be presented in a brief thesis: his subordination of the metaphor of the Divine Warrior to that of the Cosmic Government of the Divine Lord as *one* feature of the latter telescopes into one what should be seen as two successive aspects of divine activity.

The order of the chapters under discussion ("God the Lord," followed by "God the Warrior"), an order deliberately chosen, already introduces an accent which is sustained in the presentation itself; when the order of God's cosmic realm is threatened by human rebellion, the Divine Suzerain goes into (punitive and/or redemptive) action as Divine Warrior. In other words, order and sovereignty are the starting point. Divine warfare serves a restorative purpose, a cosmic policing function, as it were. It represents a subordinate (and occasional?) aspect of the ongoing divine rule. In Professor Wright's own words, "a major [but only one!] function of the Suzerain will be understood to be his work as Warrior."[14]

However, the classical Divine Warrior passages of the Old Testament picture the Warrior as one who comes, conquers, and only then establishes his throne and dominion.[15] God's coming is, for Israel, not the awaited arrival of the expected authorities in charge of order, but the surprising appearance of an unknown or unexpected *gō'ēl,* who then demonstrates punitive and redemptive power and will, establishes government, and is worshiped as Lord.[16] Cosmic government is assumed as the final stage of the Warrior's coming; it does not form the conceptual umbrella under which the Warrior-function finds its subordinate niche.

It is this sequence which defines the kingdom in the New Testament, as Professor Wright also implies in his summarizing question to Mr. X.[17] Within it, and from my own particular pacifist frame of reference, I would answer: I understand the historical present not so much under the image of a Cosmic Government, as under that of bondage and exile, that is of the apparent domination of oppressive powers. God's power is also in evidence, but by way of vanguard operations of the Divine Warrior's host. These give promise of victory, and of the establishment of cosmic order, or God's kingdom, but my own proper stance toward them is the "quietness and rest" (Isa. 30:15) which allows the Divine Warrior to win the victory and establish Cosmic Government. The stance of "quietness" is the basis of my pacifism, and the incipient victory, my hope for universal peace. [18]

An outlook such as this perceives the present historical situation as less positively related to ultimate reality than Professor Wright would have it. [19] It senses a greater tension between our present and God's expected future. By way of contrast, Professor Wright is seeking a high degree of integration of present historical reality into God's ultimate reality. This greater optimism is undoubtedly related in good measure to his Presbyterian background, "which has generally been more a part of the establishment in this country than its critic." [20] It reflects also that close association of promised land, kingdom, and body politic which pervades the American ethos, bringing forth the most admirable human resources, and also the tragic national involvements of the past decade.

Notes

[1] G. Ernest Wright, *The Old Testament and Theology* (New York: Harper & Row, 1969) p. 145.

[2] *Ibid.,* p. 110.

[3] *Ibid.,* p. 130.

[4] *Ibid.,* p. 130.

[5] Understood as day of victory in holy war; cf. Gerhard von Rad, "The Origin of the Concept of the Day of Yahweh," *Journal of Semitic Studies,* 4 (1959), pp. 97-108.

[6] Wright, *The Old Testament and Theology,* p. 140.

[7] It should be pointed out that the two chapters under discussion are preceded, in Professor Wright's book, by a chapter on "God the Creator," and that the three together constitute the book's core content, set into a context of methodologically oriented chapters.

[8] A fuller exposition of my views on the subject can be found in my article, "War in the Old Testament," *Mennonite Quarterly Review* 46 (1972) pp. 155-66, reprinted in this volume, pp. 173-86.

[9] Wright, *The Old Testament and Theology,* pp. 148-50.

[10] *Ibid.,* p. 149.

[11] *Ibid.,* p. 149.

[12] Professor Wright is certainly not an advocate of war (cf. *ibid.,* p. 134), but he does see positive possibilities for the use of force (*ibid.,* p. 148), and he holds a rather high view of the American "establishment" (*ibid.,* p. 148) and its "civil religion" (*ibid.,* p. 113).

[13] Professor Wright's own presupposition prompts this query: "Yet if a group of people possesses, with minor variations, roughly identical images of the world, then the individuals in the group must possess approximately similar value systems"

(*ibid.*, pp. 152-53).

[14] *Ibid.*, p. 11.

[15] For a synthesis of the cultic, and eventually eschatological, motifs of conquest and kingship, in that order, as highlighted by the History-of-Redemption-school and the Myth-and-Ritual-school respectively, see F. M. Cross, "The Divine Warrior in Israel's Early Cult," in *Biblical Motifs: Origins and Transformations,* ed. A. Altmann. Philip W. Lown Institute for Advanced Judaic Studies, Brandeis University, Studies and Texts 3. (Cambridge, Mass.: Harvard, 1966), pp. 11-30; now embedded in F. M. Cross, "The Cultus of the Israelite League," Section II, *Canaanite Myth and Hebrew Epic. Essays in the History of the Religion of Israel* (Cambridge, Mass.: Harvard, 1973), pp. 77-111.

[16] We must remember in this connection that we are dealing with metaphorical language. It is not proper to subject such language to rational and prosaic interrogation, asking questions such as: "From where did the Divine Warrior come? Was he not God of the whole cosmos before?" etc. The fact is that Israel, at various junctures in her history, expressed the powerful coming of One who had not been expected in the face of her oppressive reality. This is true of the language complex under discussion, even though there may be other passages that affirm the ongoing rule of God. A smooth integration of images must not be forced here.

[17] Wright, *The Old Testament and Theology*, p. 149, quoted above.

[18] This is no different from language used by Professor Wright at points (cf. *ibid.,* pp. 140-43). Again, the points of difference are, first, a lesser sense, on my part, of the Cosmic Government as an appropriate metaphor for understanding present reality, and secondly, a sequential view of Divine Warrior and Cosmic Government, rather than one which telescopes the two together.

[19] See his statement quoted above, note 2.

[20] Wright, *The Old Testament and Theology,* p. 148.

17
Christian Perspectives on War and Peace in the Old Testament

The wars reported in the Old Testament have always been, and continue to be, a problem for Christians.[1] The data that generally constitute the basis for the Christian's uneasiness are the following:[2]

1. A considerable amount of space in the Old Testament is devoted to war.

2. God is called a warrior and reveals himself repeatedly in the context of war.

3. God commanded Israel to wage wars, some of them aimed at the annihilation of their enemies.

4. Israel took possession of the land of Canaan by way of conquest.

5. Prominent religious leaders in Israel were often also prominent leaders in war, or more generally, the military and the religious dimensions of life are intertwined in the Old Testament.

A fuller consideration of the data for our subject, however, must also include a list of peace emphases:

1. There are praises of peace in the Old Testament, as well as condemnations of war.

2. There are instances of peace making.

3. There are calls to pacific behavior and renunciation of self-defense.

4. Certain common features of warfare are rare or restrained, such as mutilation of enemies and glorifications of the war hero.

5. The (messianic/eschatological) images of God's coming reign picture ultimate peace as God's goal.

These are the basic data, though it would not be right to say that there is unanimity with respect to them. Israel's conquest of Canaan, in particular, has been the subject of controversy. While the Old Testament presents it as a great military conquest, the German Old Testament school of A. Alt and M. Noth has argued that in actual fact the Israelite tribes infiltrated the land in a much more peaceful way, claiming that the grand panorama of the conquest was a later theological formulation highlighting God's power and leading.[3] While this gives some comfort to a Christian pacifist like Roland Bainton,[4] it still leaves one with the fact that Israel believed in a God whose character was compatible with such conquest. On the whole, however, the points as presented form the building materials with which a Christian theologian must begin in order to gain perspective on war in the Old Testament.

If we pursue a little further the analogy of erecting a building, we could think of certain theological theses as the instruments which theologians bring to the task. These are mainly the following:

1. God is sovereign, and what God does is right.
2. Humanity is sinful, and all human actions are tainted by sin.
3. God accommodates to humanity's sinful state.
4. God sees human instruments to punish sin and generally to accomplish goals.
5. God intends to lead humanity back to its original calling.
6. The peaceful way of Jesus expresses God's intention most perfectly.
7. Not all parts of the biblical canon are equally authoritative.

I believe that all of these theological theses, except perhaps the last, are generally accepted by Christians. Furthermore, all those who ponder the question of war in the Old Testament draw on several, if not all, of them in their quest. If these theses could be arranged in a generally recognized order of priority, it would be possible to develop a theology of Old Testament warfare acceptable to all Christians. But it is precisely at this point where diversity sets in, governed by the relative weight which different theologians attach to each of these theses.

This can be illustrated simply with reference to thesis (7): "Not all parts of the biblical canon are equally authoritative." Someone adopting this thesis radically can dispose of the problem of war in the Old Testament in short order by excluding the Old Testament from the Christian canon, as the second-century Gnostic Marcion did.

Luther's well-known principle, namely that the Old Testament should be read for that which promotes Christ (*was da Christum dringet*), leans heavily on thesis (7) also. However, his even greater insistence that humanity is sinful, and that even the Christian is simultaneously righteous and sinful (*simul justus et peccator*), that is, on our thesis (2), made it necessary for him to relate the higher way of Christ, our thesis (6), to this fact. He did so in his famous doctrine of the two kingdoms, leaning on Augustine's two cities, of course. [5]

These are only two illustrations to show how the relative weighting of the theological theses stated will result in different perspectives on the Old Testament wars. The number of possible nuances seems almost infinite. In what follows, however, I want to sketch three major approaches, based in each case on a particular way of arranging the theses discussed. Having done that, I shall outline in the last part of this paper my own theological priorities and the synthesis to which they lead me.

If we leave aside the allegorizing interpretation of the Old Testament during the Middle Ages and those historicist approaches [6] of more recent times which remove the problem from the theological realm, there appear to be three major hermeneutical groupings among those attempting to cope with the wars in the Old Testament from a Christian perspective. Using the theme of the rule of God as our focal concern, we can formulate their positions as follows: The Old Testament story may appear (1) as the account of God's victorious rule, or (2) as the history of the preparation of God's coming rule, or (3) as the history of failure of one form of God's rule.

The Old Testament Story as the Account of God's Victorious Rule

In this perspective, the sovereignty of God ranks high (Thesis 1). It is inconceivable that whatever happened should have deviated significantly from God's actual will and the exercise of God's authority. If the wars carried out by Israel under God's command appear to conflict with the nature of God revealed elsewhere in the two Testaments, humanity's sinfulness (Thesis 2) and God's accommodation to it must account for this (Theses 3-4). As the sinfulness of humanity generally has not changed essentially, similar uses of military power to uphold a legitimate state and to subdue evil and punish sin must still be exercised today, so that Old Testament Israel becomes somewhat of a paradigm for modern statehood. The more perfect way of Jesus (Thesis 6) is applicable to the private life of the believer. Through one's actions as a citizen it will filter into public policy as an ameliorating influence, but not in such a way as to change the basic character of its power structure. Such a change is not to be expected until God will bring about a new eschatological era. Finally, this perspective involves a very uniform view of the biblical canon, considering both Testaments, and all parts of each, to be the word of God which expresses God's sovereign rule (vs. Thesis 7).

I believe that this sketches in a general way the approach of Calvin[7] and of much of the Reformed tradition, including North American right-wing conservatism, but not only it. As a prominent contemporary representative, I wish to cite my teacher, G. Ernest Wright. Wright was certainly not a right-wing conservative, but he was a staunch Presbyterian. Having moved through a stage of post-World War I idealistic pacifism, he reverted to a theology consonant with his tradition. As a sensitive theologian, however, he was keenly aware of the challenge to his position represented by Christian pacifism, a challenge which he tried to meet in the work which represents his theological legacy, *The Old Testament and Theology* (1969).[8]

Two of the central chapters of this work are entitled "God the Lord" and "God the Warrior," respectively, and in that order.[9] At the risk of great oversimplification, one could sketch his thought as follows: The universe is to be seen under the metaphor of a "political monocracy" under God as the cosmic suzerain, to whom the people of God, in both Testaments, are related in a covenant modeled after a suzerainty treaty. In Wright's own words:

> The purpose of the suzerainty language is to depict why creative, positive, righteous goals have an ultimate support in our world, why life is given for service for which one is accountable, and why, despite the suffering and injustice in the world, life in the service of the Ultimate understood as Suzerain is possible and triumphant.[10]

This sovereign Lord reaches into the universe, as a vassal state, to exert power, a power that can be felt to be punitive and destructive, or creative and redemptive, depending on one's circumstances. Using an image not employed by Wright himself, one could say that God's universe, according to Wright, is a well-governed and, where necessary, well-policed state. For these purposes God the Warrior also engages human beings as instruments, without thereby justifying their actions. Wright himself understands his theology as an affirmation of trust in God's governance, of the possibility of positive life (*shālôm*) and as a source of hope for the future. In his own words:

> God the Warrior is the theme that furnishes hope in time. What

is cannot be sanctified for the future because a vast tension exists between the will of the Suzerain and that of his vassals . . . Yet the strong, active power given language in the Warrior-Lord means that there is a force in the universe set against the forces of evil and perversity. Life, then, is a battleground, but the Divine Warrior will not be defeated. . . . God the Warrior is simply the reverse side of God the Lover or God the Redeemer. [11]

I am devoting so much attention to Wright because I believe that his position is an impressive contemporary statement of the type of serious Christian theologizing with which pacifist perspectives on the Old Testament, or better, the Bible, have to come to terms. Elsewhere I have stated my objections to Wright's theology in greater detail. [12] Here I merely want to note that its major weakness seems to lie in an inadequate eschatology. In spite of some passages to the contrary, Wright's cosmic state seems static, and his theology attempts to integrate the believer's life into what is, rather than to stretch forward with sufficient urgency and hope toward what is not yet, but is expected to come.

The Old Testament Story as the Account of the Preparation of God's Coming Rule

From the time of Lessing and Hegel on, there exists a multitude of developmental models that want us to see the Old Testament, including its wars, as appropriate for its time, but eventually superseded, also appropriately, by the New Testament, and, in the case of Hegel, by subsequent Christian culture. Some of these models are basically secular developmental and evolutionary schemes applied to the Bible. Where they become explicit theological, they tend to highlight the thesis that God accommodates to humanity's state or readiness (Thesis 3), even at the risk of allowing his sovereign will to be obscured. God's sovereign rule is, in fact, at work all the time, but often in ways hidden or partially hidden through the limitations of the human condition. There is revelation of God's rule or kingdom.

This approach has attracted thinkers of most diverse stripe. Lessing's brief but impressive picture of God the Great Educator belongs here (*Von der Erziehung des Menschengeschlechts*), [13] as one model of coping with otherwise unacceptable Old Testament data. So does Hegel's idealistic conception of history. [14] On a less grand scheme, some contemporary Old Testament theologians will observe certain data in the biblical story which give evidence of ethical refinement as that story proceeds, though few would advocate a consistent and optimistic evolutionary development. [15]

Pacifist theologians have felt attracted to this camp also. Jacob Enz, for example, expresses his theology succinctly in the subtitle of his book, *The Christian and Warfare: The Roots of Pacifism in the Old Testament.* [16] Far from attempting to "convert" the Old Testament as such retroactively to a pacifist position, he nevertheless finds there an amazing array of "roots" for the peace teachings of Jesus: The power of the word as a deed; the covenant (peace treaty) mode of relating God and humankind as well as person and person to each other; the concern for the foreigner; the limitations imposed on absolute kingship; the authority of the prophetic word over kings; the abdication of reliance on military supremacy in favor of trust in God, in the holy war context; specific calls to refrain from armament and self-defense (Isaiah, Jeremiah); specific instances affirming peaceful solutions to conflict; the theology of incarnation of God, first in a people, then in Christ. It is worth noting some of his most potent formulations. Thus he condemns "the heresy of Testamental Christianity" [17] and claims that the New Testament writers "knew that they had the highest even of the Old Testament on their side." [18] His position is summarized in the following quotation:

> The victory of implicit theological pacifism in the Old Testament prepares for incontrovertibly explicit pacifism in the New Testament. [19]

Millard Lind, colleague of Enz at the Associated Mennonite Biblical Seminaries at Elkhart, can also be placed into our second group, though only in part. [20] For Lind, the God-intended form of Israel's existence was that of a peaceful theocracy. Yahweh himself led and protected the people, fighting for them by means of miracle, and without their effective participation in battle. In Lind's own words:

> Basic to all that follows is . . . the testimony that Yahweh the warrior fought by means of miracle, not through the armies of his people; "it was not by your sword or by your bow" (Josh. 24:12). By miracle we mean an act of deliverance that was outside of Israel's control, beyond the manipulation of any human agency. This conviction was so emphatic that Israel's fighting, while at times a sequel to the act of Yahweh, was regarded as ineffective; faith meant that Israel should rely upon Yahweh's miracle for her defense, rather than upon soldiers and weapons. The human agent in the work of Yahweh was not so much the warrior as the prophet. [21]

This understanding of the respective roles of Yahweh and Israel emerges most clearly, according to Lind, in the central saving event of Israel's story, the exodus from Egypt. As he interprets Exodus 1 to 15 he considers it "obvious that the exodus and wilderness period is the time of holy war 'par excellence' ": [22]

> We note that Yahweh is first called warrior [Exod. 15:3] . . . in a situation where he exercises his judgment by a nature miracle, where Israel does not fight at all. This is especially decisive since the Reed Sea deliverance forms the paradigm for Israel's future salvation. [23]

This insight persisted, if not always lived out fully, from the exodus from Egypt on and through the period of the Judges. Then Israel suffered a "Constantinian Fall" with the coming of the monarchy, and specifically with David. Throughout the period of the monarchy, Israel's story was a story of failure, which made it necessary for the prophets, unsuccessful as they were in stemming the tide in their own time, to proclaim that God would restore the intended condition for his people in time to come. Thus Lind's approach places him partly in the camp of those who see the Old Testament as a story of failure. We note also that he is forced to highlight the nonviolent dimensions of Israel's early existence in a way that puts some strain on the data. Further, his judgment on the monarch can be maintained only by relying on a canon within the canon, even as far as the Old Testament is concerned, for David and the monarchy fare much better, of course, if the whole Old Testament is allowed to speak.

John Howard Yoder, though he devotes only limited attention to the Old Testament in his *The Politics of Jesus,* [24] assigns it a preparatory role towards the unfolding of the nonviolent way of Jesus. While Yoder's association of the preaching of Jesus with the proclamation of the Old Testament's Jubilee Year must remain tentative, he captures an extremely important interpretive insight when he treats Israel's wars of conquest as reported in Joshua and Judges. These materials, as indeed all literary texts, must be read for what their authors meant and what their first readers or hearers heard them say. While we who would like to see a peaceful people of God are bothered by the wars reported in them, the first readers or hearers must have been impressed by the many instances where Israel was victorious, by God's help, either without military action or against all military probability. Thus these apparently so warlike pages usually constitute a call toward reliance on God, over against reliance on military might. [25] Yoder then proceeds to trace this theme elsewhere in the Old Testament, and to show how Jesus and his disciples were nourished on it by way of reading the Old Testament.

In this survey of perspectives on Old Testament wars as held by prominent Mennonite pacifists, I ought to mention Guy F. Hershberger in this second group of theologians. [26] In view of the scope of his book, Hershberger could give only limited attention to the Old Testament. Somewhat like Lind, and of course long before him, Hershberger viewed the Old Testament story as one of departure from an original ideal. God's perfect will for Israel was a peaceful existence, just as it is for the New Testament people. Hershberger believes that "the entire Scriptures correctly interpreted will show the Old and the New Testaments to agree that the way of peace is God's way for his people at all times." [27]

Again somewhat like Lind, Hershberger stresses God's original intention to lead Israel out of Egypt and into the promised land in a peaceful way, by means of miracle (Exod. 23:20-33). The deliverance at the Red Sea highlighted this. However, Israel lacked trust and relied on her own efforts. Warfare resulted, as God by way of his "permissive will" allowed Israel to experience the cause-and-effect chain initiated by her sinful self-reliance.

> The various Old Testament commands of God requiring killing, such as the command to slay the Amalekites, to hew Agag to pieces, and to kill the giant Goliath, were permissive commands given to a sinful, lean-souled people who had chosen to live on the lower, "sub-Christian" level. [28]

God, however, kept prodding Israel toward peace in various ways and situations. We see this, for example, in the command to love one's neighbor, in the commandment "Thou shalt not kill," and in events such as Elisha's conciliatory attitude toward the defeated Syrians. The prophets called Israel to repentance and peace, and Jesus finally reinstated God's perfect will.

For the purpose of our study we note, then, that Hershberger sees a basic continuity between the Old Testament's peace ideal and the gospel of peace proclaimed by Jesus. On the other hand, Israel's lack of trust and compliance often makes much of the Old Testament into an obstacle path to peace, rather than a preparation of God's peaceful rule. To this extent Hershberger, like Lind, belongs at least partially to the company of those who regard the Old Testament as an account of failure. To these we must now turn our attention.

The Old Testament Story as the Account
of the Failure of One Form of God's Rule

A clear separation of the Testaments, together with a rejection of the Old as authoritative for the Christian, goes back as far as Marcion, the Gnostic heretic of the second century A.D. In the twentieth century a total rejection of the Old Testament has been advocated by the prominent liberal church historian Adolf von Harnack. These have been lone voices on the fringes of Christian theology. Of much greater consequence for Christian thought and life has been the emotional rejection of the Old Testament by countless Christians, a rejection based mainly on the inability to reconcile the wars of the Old Testament with the life and teachings of Jesus Christ. [29]

There are also, however, some articulate Christian theologians who have seen the Old Testament as a story of failure. Rudolf Bultmann stands out as a twentieth century proponent of this hermeneutic. [30] He traces three themes of failure through the Old Testament, with the aim of demonstrating how each reaches a point of no return, so that a totally new beginning becomes necessary, a new beginning effected by Jesus Christ. They are the themes of covenant, of divine kingship, and of the people of God, understood as possibilities to be realized within history. As a demonstration of ways that lead to failure, Bultmann is ready to grant the Old Testament pedagogical relevance and authority, however, instead of pleading for its deletion from the canon. [31]

Bultmann's negative valuation of the Old Testament is not rooted specifically in the problems created by the wars. Others, however, have declared it a story of failure with specific reference to the issues of war and peace. Among these is the famous church historian and Quaker pacifist, Roland Bainton. In his work, *Christian Attitudes Toward War and Peace* (1960), [32] Bainton traces pacifism to the New Testament and the early church, the just war theory to classical antiquity, and the origin of the crusading idea to the Old Testament. Having defined a crusade as "God's war," he makes the amazing claim: "As such it could scarcely have originated in antiquity save among the Jews." [33] Since Bainton accepts Alt's and Noth's theory of a peaceful infiltration of Canaan by Israel, rather than a violent conquest, he doubts that a real crusade actually took place in Israel before the time of the Maccabees. However, such doubt is based on his skepticism regarding the historicity of the conquest under Joshua, and not on any reservations concerning the crusading mentality of the Old Testament. In sharp contrast to Millard Lind,

Bainton sees a certain amelioration of the warlike spirit of Israel effected by the monarchy which led Israel from a crusading phase to a just-war phase in her history. Nevertheless, it was precisely during this more tempered phase when, in the reconstruction accepted by Bainton, the "Deuteronomists" constructed the account of the conquest and, in the Books of Numbers, Joshua, and Judges, represented their (crusading) ideal as having been actualized in the taking of the land. These developments toned down the peaceful characteristics associated earlier with Yahweh as the giver of *shālôm*. When attempts of living out these new holy war ideals under Hezekiah and Josiah had failed, the prophets helped Israel to accept defeat from God's hand. In the Babylonian exile and later, however, the seeds of nationalism and the crusading spirit incubated again, first in apocalyptic expectations, and eventually to break loose with full force in the Maccabean revolt.

What alternative remains, thus, for Bainton, a peace-loving man, than to reject the Old Testament? But further, how can he justify his rejection of it if the (pacifist) early church obviously accepted it as its Bible? Bainton answers this with an astounding combination of offended pacifism and literary-critical reconstruction:

> The Christian Church for centuries was unaware of the stages in the historical development of the rise, fall, and revival of the crusading ideal [in the Old Testament], and the early Fathers never so much as suspected that the wars of conquest of Canaan might have been only the romancing of reformers whose program was never attained. The books of Deuteronomy, Numbers, Joshua, Judges, and Maccabees were taken over into the Christian canon of Scripture. Thereafter the wars of Yahweh might be allegorized but they could not be omitted; not until the rise of modern biblical criticism did anyone suggest that they had never occurred. The architects of the Christian crusade, therefore, drew their warrant from the books of conquest and of the Maccabean revolt. [34]

Such a position highlights what G. Ernest Wright would have called "Christomonism" and results in serious tampering with the biblical canon.

Jean Lasserre, French Reformed pacifist and author of *War and the Gospel,* [35] rejects the Old Testament in matters of war and peace almost as vehemently as Bainton does. He logically begins his discussion with the canon:

> Calvin's fundamental error over the problem of war seems to lie precisely in the fact that he founds his ethic indifferently on the

two Testaments, giving the same authority to both. [36]
Lasserre is not about to delete the Old Testament from the Christian canon, however. He warns explicitly against both the Marcionite and the Constantinian heresy. In a somewhat lonely concession he even admits that "the Old Testament already contains the Gospel in embryo." [37]

On the whole, though, Lasserre views the Old Testament in bleakest terms. It is for him a story of brutality and massacre, of disregard for human life, of bloodshed, and of scandalous (in the literal sense of the word) declarations regarding wars of extermination commanded by God. "There is a striking contrast here between the two parts of the Bible." [38] The decisive question for Lasserre, then, is: "Where does the nonviolent gentleness of the Gospel come from?" [39] Certainly not from the Old Testament, but neither from the nations and religions of Greece, Rome, or the Ancient Near East. He concludes:

> I can see only one satisfying answer: the systematic refusal of violence was a personal contribution by Jesus of Nazareth, his original discovery. [40]

Jesus had to assert it against the contrary messianic expectations of his contemporaries, and to brace himself against his own temptations. Eventually he died for it on the cross. Lasserre demonstrates the dilemma of many a Christian: asserting a Christomonism that would tear the Bible in two, he nevertheless feels constrained to retain the Old Testament for reasons that are not too clear while denouncing it in harshest terms.

Peter Craigie, author of a recent monograph, *The Problem of War in the Old Testament* (1978), [41] approaches this topic as a sensitive Christian as well as an Old Testament specialist. The chief value of this book lies in its breadth of approach to the subject and in its application of several important principles of interpretation. Craigie reminds us, for example, that we need to be conscious of the intent and the limitations of religious language. Instead of a flat literalism in understanding references to God as warrior, we ought to ask what such language intends to say. It is the language of incarnation. God participates in human history for both punishment and salvation, accommodating to the sinful human condition (our Theses 2-6). [42] In another helpful reminder, Craigie points out that the message of the Old Testament is distorted if the wars of conquest are highlighted and the accounts of defeat are ignored. God participates in a history marked by both victory and defeat. In the end, it is the defeat of the kingdoms of the Old Testament which provides the total message: the manifestation of the kingdom of God in a political state was a failure, but this failure was necessary to demonstrate "that redemption was not to be found in the human institution of the state."[43] In this sense, "the kingdom of Israel prepared the way for the kingdom of God as inaugurated in the person and teaching of Jesus."[44]

This aspect justifies my inclusion of Craigie in this third category, which views the Old Testament as an account of failure. Craigie's work, reviewed here in excerpt only, shows other dimensions, however. With Wright and others, he sees the sinful human condition as continuing unchanged from Old Testament times. The state is still, by definition, incapable of being transformed into the kingdom. Christ's call to nonviolence, which Craigie takes seriously, is applicable essentially to the private realm, only indirectly affecting the state. All of this leads Craigie to an acceptance of what is essentially Luther's two-kingdom theology, the Christian being a citizen of each, suspended somewhere between pacifism and acceptance of just war, though unable to affirm either fully.[45] The contrast to Wright lies more in Craigie's mood than in his theological position.

My Own Position

Finally, I must outline my own position. I propose to do this in two steps. First, I want to look at the data again and ask to what extent war is actually a problem inherent in the Old Testament, and to what extent it is a problem of Old Testament interpretation, or rather, misinterpretation. In a second step, then, I will try to explain how I, as a pacifist Christian, come to terms with the Old Testament's war data as I see them.

Before attacking these tasks, however, I must raise a preliminary consideration. War is one aspect of evil in the world. Monotheism is inherently plagued by the problem of evil. How can evil be present in a world created and ruled by a God who is totally in control and who wants the good of creation? This problem must not be dumped onto the Old Testament and its wars. The problem of war in the Old Testament is the problem of apparently greater and more directly God-related evil there than elsewhere in human history.

1. With this consideration in mind, we turn to the data of the Old Testament. Was Israel particularly warlike and bloodthirsty? She was not pacifist, that is clear. Millard Lind goes too far in portraying

Israel's passivity in the holy wars of her early history, although he is right in his claim that God's action for Israel, rather than Israel's military activity, was God's intention in that context. On the other hand, Bainton's claim that the accounts of the conquest of Canaan—even though he considers them historical fiction—were the origins of the idea of the crusade, is not only historically inaccurate, but preposterous, when one compares them to the wars of the gods waged by Egypt, Assyria, and others throughout the ancient world. Historically, Israel's wars of conquest of Canaan represent a minor military event in the Ancient Near East. A small and strategically disadvantaged people was able to conquer more numerous and technologically more advanced enemies due to exceptionally favorable circumstances which secular historians might term good fortune, while faith ascribed them to the intervention of God.

In her history subsequent to the conquest of the land, Israel waged small-scale warfare with neighboring states, achieving larger territorial dimensions only during David's reign. Her wars would merit only marginal mention in a military history of the Ancient Near East. In addition to the smallness of the Old Testament states, which itself necessarily limits a people's military exploits, there were restraining forces at work that were rooted in Israel's faith, such as the limitation of the kings' national ambitions by law as well as by the prophets. All in all, the military history of the Old Testament people might be compared to that of the Netherlands, or Poland, or Greece in our era, but in no way to that of the great military powers of today.

While we look at the interpretation of this history on the pages of the Old Testament—and I agree with Bainton that raw fact and interpretation are not identical, though they should also not be torn apart—certain aspects of Irael's wars are highlighted. What are they? What would ancient readers of the Books of Joshua and Judges, for example, have found remarkable? J. H. Yoder points out correctly that such readers would have been struck by the de-emphasizing of Israel's military achievements in favor of her passivity and her trust in God. The so-called holy war doctrine *limits* military initiative and national glorification, rather than firing them on. Instead of exploitation her actual military victories during the conquest to construct a national epic of heroism and glory, as even small and avowedly peaceful modern states like Switzerland do, Israel—under the impact of her faith—highlighted her weakness and signed away her military achievements to God. Nor was this

God a projection of the national superego, whose glory would then have expressed Israel's glory. God was the God of the whole world to whom Israel's defeats were ascribed just as readily as her victories. Craigie's reminder is most pertinent when he emphasizes that we must hear the message of Israel's whole story, a story containing both victory and defeat, instead of isolating the wars of conquest for our attention.

What about God in this picture? Did God not command Israel to wage certain wars and exterminate certain enemies? That is true. Does that not mean, then, that the Old Testament proclaims a warrior God, cruel and bloodthirsty, who cannot be reconciled with the Father of Jesus Christ? In response to this, we must first of all heed Craigie's reminder concerning religious language. The references to God as warrior and king are intended to highlight, metaphorically, God's sovereign authority and power to establish justice rather than God's violence. But that still leaves God's expressed will for Israel to conquer the land of Canaan and to destroy its inhabitants. Here interpreters necessarily divide along the lines of their real (if not always their professed) view of inspiration. Strict supernaturalists will see these commands as unique and exceptional decisions by the Creator, Maintainer, and Taker of all life that the lives of particular people at that time were to be ended in a particular way, involving Israel as the agent. No precedent was set, and no definition of war under God was given. Those less literal and supernaturalist in their understanding of inspiration might operate with the concept of God's permissive will here. Israel might have misunderstood God's full intention, acting rashly in those wars, but God accommodated to Israel's hardness of hearing, and was still able to achieve the same goals.

The Old Testament itself treats those wars as exceptional and does not make them the model for further conquests. The prophets who, in a sense, revive the holy war doctrine (Isaiah, Jeremiah, and others) do so with emphasis on Israel's passivity, rather than her active pursuit of military exploits in the hope of divine support. In their end-time prophecies (the Day of Yahweh) they announce God's ultimate victory, but without Israel's agency, to usher in the era of ultimate, God-intended peace. These peace projections are more than the peace utopias of antiquity. For Israel believed in a historical movement toward a God-set goal, while the cyclical nature religions of antiquity saw life as moving in cycles of ever-repeated sameness. Therefore, images of ultimate justice and peace, as drawn by the prophets, could act as goals for historical movement, while such images in the nature religions had to remain utopian dreams not affecting present realities.

2. So much for the Old Testament's war content. How can I, as a pacifist Christian, live with it? As I said already, coming to terms with the wars of the Old Testament does not resolve the problem of evil in the world. But the presence of evil, in a world ruled by God, is assumed in the New Testament, and also in our world, just as much as in the Old Testament. Jesus never denies, but rather assumes, that the one sovereign God rules the whole world and is thus, in the last analysis, responsible in some sense for the wars and violence of the Roman Empire, including his own crucifixion.

It is the role of the believers in God's governing of the world that is different in the two Testaments. According to the Old Testament, as I have argued, Israel participated in the general warfare of the Ancient Near East in a modest way, partaking in both victory and defeat. In the New Testament, the believers are taught to refrain from war and violence.

I, for my part, prefer to join the second group of interpreters, as discussed above, that is, the company of those who see the Old Testament story as an account of God's preparation of his coming rule. With Jacob Enz, I see the roots of pacifism, though not pacifism, in the Old Testament. To my mind, the Old Testament makes it perfectly clear, in the various ways listed already, that warfare is not an expression of God's full will for humankind, but rather a concession to humanity's sinful condition.

How does the believer relate to this sinful condition? G. E. Wright, representing the Calvinist tradition, accepts it as characteristic of the present world and submits to God's governing and policing of that world both as the object and as a participant. Luther sees God's redemptive love in operation as God's "strange work" through the state and as God's "proper work" through the nonviolent ways of the individual believer. Some pacifists, while recognizing the state as God's agent, see the believer as withdrawing from participation in it, or at least in its exercise of violence.

To me, the believer's pacifism is best described as a proleptic sign of the eschatological reign/kingdom of God.[46] The human condition is less static and more open than Wright and others would see.[47] The Old Testament expressed in many ways that God's ultimate will is peace. Its eschatological passages see this peace as a goal and future reality of God's coming rule. The New Testament claims that this eschatological rule or kingdom has begun in a new and real way in Jesus Christ. Within a sinful world Jesus announces and demonstrates a life ruled fully by God. The church, as his body, is to live out signs of the kingdom in his wake, one of them being the sign of peace.

The aim and purpose of such pacifism is not so much the gradual quantitative "conquest" of the world, although its effectiveness in peacemaking should not be underestimated. Rather, it is the establishment of samples of life under God's rule. Such islands of God's eschatological rule will challenge the reign of violence, leading sometimes to the reduction of violence—and we should not underestimate the impact of such witness—and sometimes to incite a violent world to direct its violence against those upholding the way of peace. [48] In either case, however, it will keep alive a prodding force toward peace in the world. Ultimate peace, however, is hardly to be expected from an evolution of a peaceful society through the impact of such a witness; it must wait for a special act of God, a Day of the Lord.

Notes

[1] For a recent analysis of the nature of this problem see Peter C. Craigie, *The Problem of War in the Old Testament* (Grand Rapids: Eerdmans, 1978), especially chapter 1.

[2] For a fuller presentation of these data see my article "War in the Old Testament," *The Mennonite Quarterly Review* 46 (1972): pp. 155-66, reprinted in this volume, pp. 173-86 and Craigie, *The Problem of War.*

[3] Martin Noth, *The History of Israel,* revised trans. by Peter Ackroyd, second edition (New York: Harper & Row, 1960), pp. 68-84. A summary of this position, together with a penetrating critique, can be found in John Bright, *Ancient Israel in Recent History Writing* (Studies in Biblical Theology 19, Chicago: Alec. R. Allenson, Inc., 1956).

[4] Roland H. Bainton, *Christian Attitudes Toward War and Peace: A Historical Survey and Critical Re-evaluation* (New York: Abingdon, 1960), pp. 45-49.

[5] For a brief but authoritative discussion see Heinrich Bornkamm, *Luther's Doctrine of the Two Kingdoms,* trans. by Karl H. Hertz (Facet Books, Social Ethics Series 14, Philadelphia: Fortress, 1966).

[6] I have reference here to the historico-critical approach symbolized by the name of Julius Wellhausen, which aimed at the reconstruction of the historical development of the religion of Israel, being little interested in discussing the Old Testament's current theological relevance.

[7] Most relevant to our topic is Calvin's discussion of war in *The Institutes of the Christian Religion,* Book 4, chapter 20. A helpful collection of excerpts on war from various of his writings is provided by William Kyle Smith, *Calvin's Ethics of War* (Annapolis, Maryland: Academic Fellowship, 1972). Cf. also Craigie, *The Problem of War,* p. 27. It should be added that Calvin, though holding a very high view of Scripture, was also governed strongly by the dictates of practical reason and common sense.

[8] G. Ernest Wright, *The Old Testament and Theology* (New York: Harper & Row, 1969).

[9] For a summary and critique of these chapters see my article "God as Warrior and Lord: A Conversation with G. E. Wright," *Bulletin of the American Schools of*

Oriental Research (G. E. Wright Memorial Volumes) 220 (December, 1975), pp. 73-75, reprinted in this volume, pp. 187-92.

[10] Wright, *Theology*, p. 110.

[11] *Ibid.*, p. 130.

[12] See above, pp. 187-92.

[13] Gotthold Ephraim Lessing, *The Education of the Human Race*, trans. F. W. Robertson, fourth edition; (London: 1883).

[14] Emil L. Fackenheim, *The Religious Dimension in Hegel's Thought* (Bloomington, Indiana: Indiana University Press, 1967).

[15] W. Eichrodt, *Theology of the Old Testament*, II trans. J. A. Backer (Philadelphia: Westminster Press, 1967) pp. 322 f. P. Heinisch, *Theology of the Old Testament* (Collegeville, Minn.: Liturgical Press, 1955), pp. 212 ff.

[16] Scottdale, Pa.: Herald Press, 1972.

[17] *Ibid.*, p. 59.

[18] *Ibid.*, p. 80.

[19] *Ibid.*, p. 89.

[20] Millard C. Lind, *Yahweh Is a Warrior: The Theology of Warfare in Ancient Israel* (Scottdale, Pennsylvania: Herald Press, 1980).

[21] *Ibid.*, p. 23.

[22] *Ibid.*, p. 46. See also Lind's earlier article "Paradigm of Holy War in the Old Testament," *Biblical Research*, XVI (1971), pp. 16-31.

[23] Lind, *Yahweh Is a Warrior*, p. 49.

[24] Grand Rapids: Eerdmans, 1972.

[25] This mode of warfare, with its total reliance on God to win the battle and vanquish the enemy, has been called "holy war" by Old Testament scholars. Its classical description is found in Gerhard von Rad, *Der heilige Krieg im alten Israel* (Zurich, 1951; Third edition; Goettingen: Vandenhoeck and Ruprecht, 1958). In keeping with his assumption of a peaceful infiltration (*Landnahme*) of the Israelites into Canaan, von Rad limits the practice of holy war to the wars of self-defense waged by Israel during the period of the judges. Others, rejecting the hypothesis of a peaceful infiltration, apply holy war theology to the conquest of Canaan; cf. Frank Moor Cross, *Canaanite Myth and Hebrew Epic: Essays in the History of the Religion of Israel* (Cambridge, Massachusetts: Harvard University Press, 1973), pp. 99-111; and John Bright, *A History of Israel*, second edition (Philadelphia: Westminster Press, 1972), pp. 137-39. Millard Lind has made a good case for the paradigmatic holy war character of the exodus from Egypt; see his "Paradigm of Holy War in the Old Testament." *Biblical Research* XVI (1971), pp. 16-31, and *Yahweh Is a Warrior*, ch. III.

It must be emphasized that "holy war" here is a limited phenomenon in Israelite practice, though its theological reverberations permeate the Old Testament as well as the New; see von Rad, *Der heilige Krieg*, pp. 50-84, and my article "War in the Old Testament." Such holy war is emphatically not the Muslim *jihād* to expand the faith, as that term is generally understood in the Western world. Craigie points out that the Muslim understanding of it is very complex, and that there are strong trends in present-day Muslim thought to emphasize the more peaceful aspects of the *jihād*-tradition. (Craigie, *The Problem of War*, pp. 22-26.) Having dissociated the Old Testament's "holy wars" from the Muslim wars of conquest and missionary expansion, we must grant, however, that the latter were often understood by their proponents as an extension of the former (Craigie, *ibid.*).

[26] Guy F. Hershberger, *War, Peace and Nonresistance*, revised edition (Scottdale, Pennsylvania: Herald Press, 1953), pp. 15-41.

[27] *Ibid.*, p. 14.

[28] *Ibid.*, p. 31.

[29] There is irony in the fact that many who reject the Old Testament on this basis

do not adopt the peace teachings of Jesus for themselves. The scandal for them lies in the association of an otherworldly Jesus and his supposedly serene and impenetrable religious sphere with a God at work in the midst of a cruel and sinful world, a world in which they themselves participate as a matter of fact, but from which they wish to exempt their saintly Jesus.

[30] Rudolf Bultmann, "Weissagung und Erfullung," *Probleme alttestamentlicher Hermeneutik,* ed. Claus Westermann (München: Chr. Kaiser Verlag, 1963), pp. 28-53.

[31] *Ibid.,* p. 52 f., with reference to Paul in Galatians 3:24.

[32] See above, note 4.

[33] Bainton, *Christian Attitudes,* p. 44. At one point (p. 44f.) Bainton rightly distinguishes between *holy war* and *crusade:* "The crusade went beyond the holy war in the respect that it was fought not so much with God's help as on God's behalf." However, he considers the crusade to be a logical and historical outgrowth of Israel's holy wars. I would argue, instead, that crusades, understood as "wars of the gods," in which humans fought in the service of, or on behalf of, their god(s) can be found throughout the Ancient Near East from the earliest times on. Earliest Egyptian art shows Pharaoh, a god in Egyptian theology (cf. the emblem of the Horus-falcon on the Narmer Palette) defeat the enemies single-handedly. That his armies did the actual fighting seemed inconsequential; the god gained the victory. The Assyrians understood their campaigns of conquest and expansion as a service to their gods Asshur and Ishtar. The holy wars of Israel were different in accenting the very limited nature of human participation, and it was this aspect that was developed in later theology, prompting Isaiah to call king and people to "be still" and refrain from reliance on arms and diplomacy; Jeremiah to call for surrendering Jerusalem to the Babylonians; and eventually Jesus to proclaim a kingdom of peace. The Old Testament phase of this development is described in Walther Zimmerli, *Old Testament Theology in Outline,* trans. D. E. Green (Atlanta: John Knox Press, 1978), pp. 59-64. Thus a direct line of development leads from the early holy wars, not to the crusade, but to the peace teachings of Jesus. The revolt of the Maccabees, the Muslim *jihād,* the medieval crusades, and Communism's revolutionary thrust to conquer the world are essentially different phenomena, even if the model of Joshua's wars has often been appropriated by such movements.

[34] *Ibid.,* p. 51f. While Bainton highlights the Old Testament's supposed contribution to the rise of the crusade, he groups its expectations of universal peace with the general hopes of antiquity for a return of a peaceful golden age, thus robbing them of any distinctive character, in spite of his insightful sentence: "Among the Gentiles the picture of the golden age could convey less comfort to these who held a cyclical view of history [than it could to Israel with her teleological view of history], for though peace might come again, so also would war." (*Ibid.,* p. 21).

[35] Jean Lasserre, *War and the Gospel,* trans. Oliver Coburn (Scottdale: Herald Press, 1962).

[36] *Ibid.,* p. 59.

[37] *Ibid.,* p. 62.

[38] *Ibid.,* p. 59.

[39] *Ibid.,* p. 62.

[40] *Ibid.*

[41] See above, note 1.

[42] Craigie, *The Problem of War,* p. 39f.

[43] *Ibid.,* p. 99.

[44] *Ibid.,* cf. Bultmann.

[45] Craigie, pp. 102, 107-111. It should be pointed out that Craigie does not refer to

Luther explicitly, and that his understanding of the Christian's dual citizenship owes much to Jacques Ellul.

[46] For further discussion of the biblical meaning of "sign" see my "Sign and Belief" in *Call to Faithfulness* ed. H. Poettcker and R. Regehr (Winnipeg: Canadian Mennonite Bible College, 1972), pp. 33-44, reprinted in this volume, pp. 15-26.

[47] See above, p. 196f., and my article "God as Warrior and Lord."

[48] In these respects, though not throughout, I find myself in agreement with Jacques Ellul, *Violence: Reflection from a Christian Perspective,* trans. C. Kings (New York: Seabury, 1969).

Index

Index of Subjects and Names